REFORM AND INSURRECTION
IN RUSSIAN POLAND, 1856–1865

This volume is published with the help of a
grant from the late Miss Isobel Thornley's
Bequest to the University of London

Reform and Insurrection in Russian Poland 1856-1865

BY

R. F. LESLIE

GREENWOOD PRESS, PUBLISHERS
WESTPORT, CONNECTICUT

PREFACE

IN this work I have tried to give a short account of the Polish insurrection of 1863 and its antecedents. This revolt is the subject of a vast literature and in consequence I have been faced with the problem of which aspects and episodes to exclude rather than which to include. The Poles rose in revolt against foreign occupation in 1794, 1830, 1846 and 1863. Poland was the country of classic insurrections just as France was the country of model revolutions. The Polish revolts were brought about by the lower ranks of society and in each case the upper classes, fearing radical control of the national movement, sought to keep leadership in their own hands. I have already attempted to analyze one stage of the Polish national struggle in my *Polish Politics and the Revolution of November 1830* (Athlone Press, 1956). The distinction between 1830 and 1863 is that in the latter insurrection the social question had emerged before and not after the revolt had broken out. It is this social question, the problem of how Poland was to achieve her passage from one form of social organization to another, which has interested me. This meant in fact the political and economic emancipation of the Polish peasantry and their admission to civil rights. The insurrection of 1863 has a modernity which other Polish revolts lacked. Imperial Russia was faced with a problem which has troubled and is still perplexing at the present time European states governing colonial territories in which the native population seeks to rid itself of foreign domination. Liberation has never meant merely freedom from external control. Before the moment of insurrection the insurgents must debate the principles upon which the social reconstruction of their country shall be carried out after the foreigner has been expelled. The occupying power, therefore, is presented with an opportunity of prolonging its tenure by entering into that debate and appealing to the self-interest of the more moderate of the contending groups within the country. It has been said that revolutions are made in spite of the revolutionaries in the sense that the coincidence of economic and political crises produces the mass discontents and the uprising of the workers at the seat of power, which the revolutionary class, though surprised, exploits. Revolutions, however, are produced by internal pressures. Insurrections on the other hand are caused by external pressures which place the occupied society in a state of permanent provocation. Insurrections are necessarily acts of free will, decisions to take up arms made by the insurgents themselves, who make rather than are overtaken by events, but I try to show in this work that free will is not evenly distributed within the insurgent class. Free will is exercised most liberally by the younger and least experienced insurgents, who terrify the propertied classes. For this reason there appears what I will term the paradox of insurrection, the appearance of the counter-revolution before the insurrection and the revolution implied by it have occurred. I have no doubt that the factors which appeared in Poland before and during 1863 have been seen in other countries with a tradition of insurrection. Certainly in the nineteenth century there are parallels in Hungary, Italy and Ireland, while the twentieth century, pre-eminently the century of insurrection because of the decline of the imperial powers, provides many examples of features apparent in this Polish insurrection. The January Insurrection of 1863 was the last of the great Polish revolts, fought in terms of the past, but in a wider sense it was one of the first of the modern insurrections.

I must acknowledge with gratitude a grant towards the publication of this book from the late Miss Isobel Thornley's Bequest. I must thank also the government of the Polish Republic and especially its Ministry of Higher Education for the provision of a grant to enable me to study in Poland. Foreigners in Poland are certain of a warm welcome. I am most grateful to Professor Tadeusz Manteuffel, director of the Instytut Historii (Polish Academy of Sciences) and to my friend, Professor Stefan Kieniewicz, for assisting me during my stay in Warsaw. The Marie Curie Skłodowska University in Lublin kindly enabled me to visit Lublin and examine papers in the Provincial State Archives. Similarly Dr. Marian Tyrowicz entertained me in Cracow, where I was able to see documents in the Museum of the Czartoryski Princes, the Polska Akademia Umiejętności and the Provincial State Archives in the Wawel Palace. For reasons of economy I have not been able to include in this book all the materials I collected during my last visit to Poland. I must add that the views I express in this work are my own and not necessarily those of the Polish scholars who have so gladly helped me.

Queen Mary College   R. F. L.
November 1961

CONTENTS

ERRATA

p. 21: The President of the Senate of the Free City of Cracow was Wodzicki, not Schindler.

p. 23: The King of Prussia in 1823 was Frederick William III, not Frederick III.

p. 40: Niegolewski's Christian name was Wladyslaw, not Walery.

p. 82: (five lines up from bottom) Jasniewski should read Jankowski.

p. 130: Count Lambert was not dismissed, but resigned.

pp. 212-213: Recent research has shown the Bobrowski-Gabrowski episode in a different light (see Kwartalnik History,4, 1963).

CHAPTER I

The Polish Revolutionary Movement, 1832–48

IN 1833 the international influence of imperial Russia reached its highest point with the treaty of Unkiar Skelessi and the convention of Münchengrätz. The Straits Convention of 1841, though it replaced a unilateral Russian guarantee to Turkey, in effect only strengthened Russia's position in the south by securing the concert of Europe's recognition for the closure of the Black Sea to vessels of war. From the Arctic Ocean to the Caspian everything which arms and diplomacy might have done to ensure the security of Russia's great land frontier had been achieved under Alexander I and Nicholas I. Germany was divided and Austria was friendly. Russia had established treaty rights in the Principalities and Serbia. Turkey and Persia scarcely constituted a threat. The Swedish nobles in Finland and the Germans in the Baltic provinces had been bought with charters of liberties. The Polish revolt of November 1830 in the Kingdom of Poland had been suppressed. The foundations of Russian strength, however, were weak. The Russian population might grow from 35·5 million in 1800 to 68·5 million in 1850, but Russian industrial production was falling behind that of the western European states. In 1851 there were only 1,004 kilometres of railway line in the Empire and in spite of the urgency of the Crimean War only 1,170 in 1857. The real power of Russia was declining throughout the 1830's and 1840's, though her treaties with the other European powers multiplied. Even the validity of her treaties was open to question in an epoch in which the *régimes* with which they had been concluded might be overthrown by revolutionary movements.

Apparent preoccupation with the affairs of the Ottoman

Empire never meant that Russian statesmen lost sight of the Polish question. Three great crises had threatened modern Russia with dissolution and each had come from Poland: the Polish capture of the Kremlin in 1610, the expedition of Charles XII of 1709, and Napoleon's invasion in 1812. The Polish insurrection of 1830–1 offered a conventional military challenge which Russia knew well how to repel. The disbanding of the Kingdom of Poland's regular army in 1831 brought about a change in the struggle. The Polish revolt against Russia in 1863 was to use the weapons of revolutionary ideas. Polish conspiracies could not overthrow the government of Nicholas I in the height of his power, but after 1856, when Russia had been defeated in war and the dynasty exposed to criticism, there was a possibility that a Polish insurrection might not only expel Russia from Poland, but also set in motion events within Russia proper to bring down the whole structure of Tsarist autocracy.

The development of revolutionary thought among the Poles after 1832 was indeed slow. The passage of Polish refugees across Germany in the autumn of 1831 was met with sympathy and understanding. Most of the *émigrés* settled in France as their predecessors had after Kościuszko's revolt of 1794. In France a community of about 5,000 Poles established itself, growing in strength as fresh recruits joined them from the homeland.[1] The emigration was an impressive body. The arts were represented by the poets Mickiewicz, Słowacki, Krasiński and Norwid. Chopin, who had left Poland before 1830, chose to remain in exile. The first of the eminent modern historians of Poland, Lelewel, settled first in Paris and later in Brussels. The concentration of talent abroad undoubtedly gave the *émigrés* an optical illusion of their own importance. The Poles at home were circumscribed by the rigours of censorship and could not express themselves freely. Abroad the *émigrés* were at liberty to conduct the great debate on the causes of failure in 1831 and plan the tactics of the future. They were never to control the risings of

---

[1] *Kronika emigracji polskiej*, ii (1835), p. 307, put the total emigration at 5,050, of whom 4,500 were resident in France. *Kalendarz pielgrzymstwa polskiego na rok 1838* (Paris, 1838), p. 53, gave the total number as 7,000 in 1837, of whom 4,982 were in France.

the future, because the leaders at home were deeply suspicious of direction from abroad, but they were to create a climate of opinion in Poland which had an important effect upon the course of the struggle against Russia.

Discords had appeared during the war in 1831 which were not resolved in emigration. The common factor in Polish thinking was the conviction that they ought to work for the independence of Poland within the frontiers which had existed before the partition of 1772. To insist upon anything less would have been to desert the insurgents of 1831 in western Russia, who, unlike the citizens of Congress Poland, had not been offered an amnesty. The fact that the Poles within the Russian Empire and in the eastern half of Austrian Galicia were in a minority did not enter into their considerations. The Ruthenians of Galicia had given little evidence of hostility to the Poles and scarcely presented a moral problem. The native Lithuanians of Samogitia were Catholics who preferred a connection with Poland to the dominion of Orthdox Russia. The White Russians were almost entirely without national consciousness. The Polish *émigrés*, uncritical of their own national claims, were concerned not with ends, but with means.

The means adopted by the conservative elements among them were those that came naturally to their leader, Prince Adam Czartoryski, the president of the National Government until disturbances in Warsaw on the night of 15/16 August 1831 had forced him to flee. Czartoryski had been the foreign minister of Alexander I and could conceive only diplomatic solutions. He wished the Poles abroad to remain united in their aims and purposes and wait for a general European war, when the western powers in their own interest might restore Poland as a buffer against Russia. Realizing that the promotion of a general attack upon all three partitioning powers would bring them only closer together, Czartoryski was ready to accept in the first instance a territorial settlement which fell short of the 1772 ideal. Czartoryski and the group he assembled at the Hotel Lambert in Paris showed a strong preference for reconstructing Poland with Austrian aid. Austria was likely to quarrel with Russia in south-eastern Europe, where she would almost certainly receive the support of Britain and France. In the event of a successful war Poland might be re-created by a union of Galicia, the Kingdom and the western *gubernii* of Russia. The Hotel Lambert set up a network of contacts in south-eastern Europe to keep itself informed of possible political movements; conservative at home, the Czartoryski group may have played an important, though minor, role in the process of national liberation in the Balkans. Seeking to obtain the support of established governments, the Czartoryski faction was compelled to offer respectable political solutions. The new British constitution of 1832 or the Orleanist system in France was the ideal. A programme of strong monarchical government required a king. Realizing that a Habsburg candidate for the throne of the new Poland might meet with opposition from powers fearing lest Austria become too strong in central Europe, Czartoryski's supporters at one time put forward a plan for making Czartoryski himself king. He was represented as the 'king *de facto*' and an almost regal court ceremonial was introduced into the Hotel Lambert, with Czartoryski and his wife playing monarchical parts and their eldest son, Witold, adding a touch of reality by engaging in scrapes of which many an heir apparent has been guilty. Czartoryski's nephew, Władysław Zamoyski, filled the role of mayor of the palace with equal enthusiasm, often adopting policies which were entirely his own. There was a certain solemn absurdity in the Czartoryski faction's antics, but it could never be ignored. Born into the eighteenth-century salon society, Czartoryski and his clan could gain the ear of courts and cabinets. In an age of mass movements, however, when industrialization was transforming mankind, the aged Czartoryski was an anachronism. He was never to influence Polish politics in a decisive manner. Even the great Polish aristocrats, Sapiehas, Sanguszkos, Zamoyskis and Radziwiłłs, succumbing to a traditional suspicion of one of their own caste who seemed to claim pre-eminence, were cautious of accepting his leadership. Czartoryski was still less admired by the extreme left wing of the Polish emigration, which regarded him as being out of tune with the times.[1]

[1] Marceli Handelsman's *Adam Czartoryski*, 3 vols. (Warsaw, 1948–50), is compiled from the author's posthumous notes; M. Kukiel, *Czartoryski and European Unity, 1770–1861* (Princeton, 1955), holds Czartoryski in high esteem.

The Polish left wing looked not to governments but to peoples, of whose support their own warm reception in Germany made them certain. In France there was traditional attachment to the Polish cause. Far from thinking themselves to be the remnants of a defeated army, the left-wing Poles believed themselves to be on the crest of a revolutionary wave, which would sweep triumphantly across Europe, delivering humanity from despotism. Their exile would be of short duration and within a few years they would be back in Poland, taking the battle to the frontier of 1772. They had small regard for Czartoryski's plan of creating an army in exile on the pattern of Dąbrowski's legions in Italy during the revolutionary wars. As legionaries they would be silenced by military discipline. The Polish legions, moreover, would be stationed on the periphery of Europe, in Portugal, Spain, Algeria, Egypt and Turkey, far from the centre of the coming struggle in which the peoples of Europe would launch themselves against monarchical reaction. The unpopularity of Czartoryski was shown by the left-wing declaration of July 1834, signed by 2,840 exiles, that he was the enemy of the emigration.[1] The left wing turned instead to the inspiration of the western European revolutionary movement.

Paris was the centre of an international revolutionary movement, ready to receive the Poles with their military experience as valuable allies. The concept of the Carbonarist organization in Paris, *La Haute Vente Universelle*, was that the world revolution should be directed centrally by an international committee. The Poles were encouraged to throw in their lot with the movement. Lelewel, the radical, though ineffectual member of the Polish National Government of 1831, found himself under strong pressure to give a lead. The non-party 'Temporary Committee of the Emigration' established in November 1831 was too closely connected with the moderate constitutionalists of 1830–1 who were disliked by members of the radical Warsaw Patriotic Society. Lelewel therefore set up his own 'Polish National Committee' in December 1831 in order to declare Polish solidarity with the struggling peoples of Europe. Manifestoes were drawn

[1] Cf. *Akt z roku 1834 przeciw Adamowi Czartoryskiemu wyobrazicielowi systemu polskiej aristokracyi* (Poitiers, 1839).

up, appealing to every likely source of support, the British House of Commons, the French Chamber of Deputies, Casimir Périer, the Hungarians, the Italians, the Jews and the Russian people.[1]

The French government had good reason to fear Polish activity, for the Polish emigration was a powerful accretion of strength to the French revolutionary movement. Under a law of April 1832 political exiles were obliged to take up residence where the government ordered, if they wished to remain in France and draw the dole which public opinion forced the authorities to provide. In this way the more dangerous *émigrés* were broken up into small groups and scattered throughout France, where they could be kept under the watchful eyes of the prefects. Lelewel's address to the Russian people brought down upon him the diplomatic intervention of the Russian ambassador, who induced the French government to dissolve the National Committee and expel Lelewel from France.

The National Committee of Lelewel had little influence. As early as March 1832 a small group had broken away to form its own 'Polish Democratic Society' in order to bring Polish exiles into closer contact with the European revolutionary movement. It announced its intention of reorganizing Poland on democratic principles and carrying enlightenment to eastern Europe. Though it consisted at the beginning of only about a hundred members scattered among the French departments, the Democratic Society exerted a considerable influence upon Polish thought in emigration. Its first appeals, like Lelewel's, were addressed to the problem of international solidarity. J. N. Janowski pointed the way to salvation by seeking friendship with the Germans:

The German people, whose blessings changed after the fall of Poland into a cry of despair, who greeted her defenders fleeing before the vengeance of the bloodthirsty Tsar with shouts of joy and hope, as if they were its own victorious troops, has a clear conception of Freedom and will certainly rouse itself from its long lethargy, if only the cock of the Gauls shall not fall asleep.[2]

[1] These addresses are printed in J. Lelewel, *Polska, dzieje i rzeczy jej*, xx (Poznań, 1864).

[2] 'Spomnienia przeszłości—widoki na przyszłości', in a collection of tracts, *Towarzystwo Demokratyczne Polskie—Do Polaków, 1832–3*, pp. 13–14.

Friendship for other peoples automatically meant that the Poles should devote their efforts to the cause of humanity at large:

When the future of Poland depends upon the progress of humanity, then he who does not uphold the continuous progress of humanity does not sincerely wish the happiness of Poland.[1]

In the pursuit of justice Janowski adopted the catch-phrases of French radicalism. In future the qualification for public office was to be ability and not noble birth:

There will be no barons, no counts, no honourables, nor even esquires, but only people and men.[2]

In a society governed by *Liberté, égalité, fraternité* the people were to be sovereign:

A good government ought simply to be a machine for carrying out the will of the sovereign people and officials the motive power of that machine.[3]

The people of Poland, however, were predominantly peasants. It was inevitable that thought should be directed to the agrarian question. Here Lelewel lent the authority of his historical knowledge, asserting that the peasants of old had owned the soil, but had been robbed of their rights by the *szlachta*; there was no historical record to prove that the peasants had ever surrendered their title to the land, from which he drew the conclusion that they could still be considered the owners of it.[4] He went as far as to praise the agrarian legislation of Joseph II and Frederick II in the Polish territories. For him conversion of labour services into money rents would be another form of exploitation.[5] The majority of the *émigrés* persisted in the old Polish notion that the term *party* was synonymous with *faction*, a view which accounts for the persistent attempts of General Dwernicki to set up an organization which embraced all political points of view, but the movement of the extreme left

---

[1] *Ibid.*, p. 15.

[2] J. N. Janowski, *Prawa człowieka i obywatela, oraz Katechizm polityczny* (Anjou, 1834), p. 11.

[3] *Ibid.*, p. 15.

[4] Cf. 'Treść Kubrakiewicza uwag nad konstitucją 3 maja, co do prawa własności gruntu (5 July 1833)', in J. Lelewel, *Lotniki—piśmiennictwa tułaczki polskiej* (Brussels, 1859), p. 35.

[5] 'Myśli skreślone z powodu pisma Kubrakiewicza', *ibid.*, pp. 55–6.

towards some form of vague populism began to have its effect. Even the Czartoryski group felt it necessary to pay lip-service to doctrines of social justice, establishing an 'Association of Polish Unity' with a programme of equality before the law, personal freedom, freedom of religion and speech, security of property, strong government, and, significantly, the grant of freeholds to the peasants, with safeguards for the rights of third parties, which in effect meant the emancipation of the peasants with payment of compensation to the landlords.

The impetus towards a closer definition of the left-wing programme arose from the disappointments of political action. The Carbonarists, thinking in terms of a revolutionary wave, refused priority to the Polish question and the Poles were at first inclined to play their part in the general European revolution. The largest Polish Carbonarist branch in France at Besançon undertook to assist the attempted *coup d'état* at Frankfurt in 1833, but marching by way of Switzerland they heard that the revolution had to be called off and that the French authorities had closed the frontier against their return. The presence of 500 Polish revolutionaries in Switzerland alarmed the three partitioning powers and diplomatic intervention forced all except 100, who remained in the canton of Berne, to leave the country in December 1833, but they were enough to provide seventy-five men to Mazzini for his attack upon Savoy on 31 January/1 February 1834. This comic-opera affair met with inevitable failure in the hands of Mazzini and the military commander, Ramorino, who was already hated by the Poles for his decision as a Polish Corps commander to lead his men over the Galician frontier in September 1831.[1] In April 1834 it was evident from the French government's suppression of disturbances in Lyons and Paris that the revolutionary impulse in France had ceased and that the world revolution was improbable in the foreseeable future.

There had always been Poles in exile who had rejected the policy of submission to the demands of the general revolution. Józef Zaliwski, one of the leading conspirators in the Warsaw

---

[1] Cf. E. E. Y. Hales, *Mazzini and the Secret Societies* (London, 1956), pp. 111–35. W. Prechner, 'Wyprawa do Sabaudji w r. 1834', *Przegląd Historyczny*, xxiv (1924), deals more fully with the part played by the Poles.

rising of 1830, from 1832 planned his own invasion of Russia with the purpose of paralyzing the Russian government by a widespread guerrilla campaign. Maurycy Mochnacki, the foremost literary critic abroad, had condemned the practice of joining any and every insurrection, which he considered as foolish as relying upon the aid of foreign governments. He urged his compatriots instead to think only of their task in Poland, writing in his celebrated 'Circular from Auxerre in 1834': 'Let us believe in nothing but ourselves alone.'[1] Lelewel likewise came to the conclusion that 'it is my belief the Polish nation cannot resurrect itself except at home and by its own forces . . . not counting upon help'.[2] In December 1832 he had supported Zaliwski's projected expedition, 'The Vengeance of the People'. In May 1834, attracted by Mazzini's doctrine that every nation had a mission to fulfil, which it would be apostasy to refuse, Lelewel and his followers entered into the filial branch of Young Europe, 'Young Poland', founded with the object of transferring the struggle to the homeland. The cosmopolitan revolution was rejected and Polish revolutionaries returned to the national egocentricity which had always better suited their instincts.

The internal forces open to the appeal of the revolutionaries were as weak as the international movement. Congress Poland and western Russia were exhausted by the struggle of 1831. Poznania was for the moment still occupied with the completion of agrarian reform initiated by the Prussian decree of 1823. Galicia, on the other hand, for the first time since it had passed into Austrian possession in 1772, seemed to offer a field for revolutionary activity. Apart from Poniatowski's expedition to Lvov in 1809, there had been little response to the national cause until 1831 when refugees from Congress Poland and Russia brought home to the Galician Poles the need to share in the struggle for independence.[3] The same may be said of the

[1] 'Pismo okólne officerów, podofficerów i żołnierzy z zakładu Auxerre', M. Mochnacki, *Pisma Rozmaite* (Paris, 1836), p. 466. Cf. also 'O charakterze polskiej emigracji' (1 July 1832), *ibid.*, p. 115.

[2] *Listy emigracyjne*, edited by H. Więckowska (Cracow, 1948), 1 (1831–5), p. 240 (a letter of *c.* 27 January 1834).

[3] A. Józefczyk, *Wspomnienie z ubiegłych lat* (Cracow, 1881), p. 11, wrote that only in 1830 did he cease to consider himself an Austrian and begin to think of himself as a Pole.

tiny Free City of Cracow, where the rule of the senatorial oligarchy, bolstered by the foreign Residents, was becoming intolerable. Conspiratorial groups arose in 1831, but it was only in March 1833 when Zaliwski arrived to prepare for the invasion of Congress Poland that revolutionary activity became at all serious. Zaliwski brought with him men of all shades of opinion, some of whom aired their views on the agrarian question to the alarm of the Galician landlords, who had no objection to supporting the national movement, but had not fully realized that independence might be accompanied by a measure of social and economic justice for the peasants. So bad an impression did they obtain that Zaliwski was obliged, shortly after his return from Congress Poland and before his arrest by the Austrian police in August 1833, to protest that, though he himself favoured the grant of freeholds to the peasants, he had never suggested that this should be done without compensation being paid to the landlords.[1] Upon the peasants of Galicia Zaliwski made no impression at all. Karol Borkowski recalled that on his capture he was placed in the custody of two Polish-speaking soldiers, who in response to his argument that they too were Poles replied: 'Oh no, we are all subjects of His Majesty the Emperor.'[2]

The Galician conspiratorial movement lost the support of the landlords almost from the outset, except in the circles of Tarnów and Rzeszów, where the attitude of the local Austrian bureaucrats was regarded by the smaller gentry as being intolerable. It was mainly the petty intelligentsia and estate officials who were attracted to the conspiracies. The Carbonarist 'Union of Friends of the People', formed from among Zaliwski's supporters, was broken up by the Austrian police in the middle of 1834. The leadership of the movement fell into the hands of the Lvov intelligentsia, led by Franciszek Smolka, who entertained the curious notion that he could not join the conspiracy until he had first resigned his post in the public service, on the grounds that he must not take a conspiratorial oath while he was bound by an official one.[3] Radical attitudes could not be expected of

---

[1] K. Borkowski, 'Pamiętnik historyczny o wyprawie partyzanckiej do Polski w roku 1833', *Biblioteka Pisarzy Polskich*, VII (Leipzig, 1862), pp. 28–33.

[2] *Ibid.*, p. 49.

[3] K. Widmann, *Franciszek Smolka—jego życie i zawód publiczny* (Lvov, 1891), p. 21.

men like Smolka. Even the determined emissary of Young Poland, Szymon Konarski, who in the summer of 1835 managed to set up in Cracow the 'Association of the Polish People', before he moved on into Lithuania, where he met his death on the gallows, evidently could not produce a programme which pronounced clearly upon the all-important peasant question.[1]

The students of Cracow, however, were less deterred by consideration of landlords' rights. Within the territories of the Free City a scheme of voluntary liquidation was already in progress and the students could therefore move further to the left without being considered to threaten property rights. It was the radical student, Gustaw Ehrenberg, alleged to be a bastard of Alexander I, who composed the song, *Cześć Wam Panowie Magnaci*, the most bitter of Polish revolutionary hymns, condemning the upper classes for their half-measures in 1831 and promising the *szlachta* the gallows in the next rising. The Cracow conspirators defeated their own ends in January 1836 when they put into operation their 'Penal Statute', a set of revolutionary rules which included the death sentence. A Russian agent, Behrens-Pawłowski, was murdered and the tutelary powers used the incident as an excuse to occupy the Free City to restore order, the Austrians remaining until 1841. The leadership of the national movement in Galicia thus passed back into the hands of the timid Smolka and his friends at Lvov. A radical 'General Confederation of the Polish People' at Bochnia, founded in June 1837, attempted to make contact with the peasants, but the *starosta*, Breinl, soon found traces of its activities. Smolka in June 1837 was so alarmed by the growth of radical feeling that he actually dissolved all subsidiary branches of the Association of the Polish People and suspended the activity of the central committee, though not without some ineffectual protest from a group of young conspirators who from September 1837 took the name of 'Young Sarmatia'. Young Sarmatia was soon discovered by the police. During 1840–1 almost all the Galician conspirators, including Smolka, were arrested. When Smolka emerged, chastened, from prison in 1845 he was convinced that legal activity offered the best course for

[1] Cf. the oath taken by the 'Association', N. V. Berg, *Pamiętniki o polskich spiskach i powstaniach, 1831–1862* (Cracow, 1880), pp. 424–6.

the Polish nation. Ten years of conspiracy in Galicia yielded nothing. So depressing was the experience that the poet, Seweryn Goszczyński, in December 1838 warned the Democratic Society that it must avoid hasty action and above all not alienate the landed proprietors.[1]

On 4 December 1836 the Polish Democratic Society's central committee in France, the *Centralizacja*, had taken the step of synthesizing opinions current in left-wing *émigré* circles and publishing them in the form of the *Manifesto of the Polish Democratic Society*.[2] Like many other Polish political writings of this period it was verbose and even poetic, but it was nevertheless the most influential document in the history of Poland in the nineteenth century. In its preamble it made the usual assertion that Poland, long the bulwark of Europe in the east, had fallen upon hard times because the democratic principle had degenerated into caste privilege, depriving the masses of their just place in the constitution. The Polish authorities of 1830–1 were criticized for their narrow exclusiveness; if they had appealed to the masses:

the people would have risen as one man, have braced the gauntlet of war on their vigorous arm, and crushed the invaders without foreign aid; and Poland, from the Oder and the Carpathian mountains to the Borysthenes and the Dwina—from the Baltic to the Black Sea, would have founded her independence upon the general happiness of her sons.[3]

It therefore recommended that the first step in the next rising should be an appeal to the people at large:

If our next revolution is not to be a sad repetition of the past, the first battle-cry must be the emancipation of the people, their restoration unconditionally to the ownership of the soil, of which they have been plundered, the restitution of their rights, the admission of all, without distinction of birth or creed, to the enjoyment of the blessings of independence.[4]

The Democratic Society thus pronounced unequivocally in

---

[1] Z. Wasilewski, *Z życia poety romantycznego—Seweryn Goszczyński w Galicji* (Lvov, 1910), pp. 110–39.

[2] An English translation was published by the London branch in the spring of 1837.

[3] *Manifesto*, p. 16.   [4] *Ibid.*, p. 13.

favour of peasant emancipation without compensation being paid by the peasants, but it should be observed that there was even here an attempt to achieve a compromise. It was proposed to abolish the dues of peasants and grant them their freeholds upon the criterion of present possession. There was to be no redistribution of land to meet the claims of the landless. The remarks appended to the Manifesto by the central committee in the Polish edition reveals that the Society would have nothing to do with communal property, which was part of the programme of a small group of peasant soldiers who had settled in Portsmouth and Jersey and set up 'Communes of the Polish People'.[1] Wiktor Heltman, the chief theorist of the Society, saw history as the struggle between individualism and collectivism, the former tending towards anarchy and the latter towards despotism. The aim of the Society was to find the golden mean between these two extremes. In Poland individualism was to be tempered by the spirit of fraternity. The Society painted a charming picture of the people it did not know:

The suffering people with us resemble not the suffering people of western Europe; ours have not been contaminated by the corruption and selfishness of the privileged classes; they possess still all the simplicity of their ancient virtues, integrity, devotedness, religious feelings, manners benign and pure. Upon a soil so fresh and untainted, and tilled by the honest arm of fraternity and liberty, the old national tree of equality will easily shoot up and flourish anew.[2]

The romantic concept of the people as the repository of the national virtues in their purest form had not been put to the test, nor yet had a means been found of informing the people that the first act of the revolution would be their liberation. The advice given by Seweryn Goszczyński with regard to Galicia was discouraging, but it contained a germ of truth. It was safer first to win over the landed gentry and establish revolutionary cadres than to attract police attention by active propaganda among the peasants. As late as 1843 Tomasz Malinowski, the leader in the Central Committee who had been appointed to organize Poznania, was still insisting upon the need for extreme caution: 'We will state boldly that it is better to do nothing

[1] Cf. 'Uwagi Centralizacyi przy dyskussyi nad Manifestem', *Manifest Towarzystwa Demokratycznego Polskiego* (Poitiers, 1836), p. 67.
[2] *Manifesto*, p. 14.

than to do it badly.'[1] Thus what promised to be a popular movement to free the peasants began like all other Polish conspiracies as an association of intellectuals seeking the support of the *szlachta*, from whom they proposed to liberate the people.

At the beginning of the 1840's the attention of the Polish Democratic Society turned to Prussian Poland where conditions were different from those in Galicia. In 1823 the Prussian government had produced a decree for agrarian reform in the Grand Duchy of Posen, which had initially given the Polish gentry some misgivings, but by the 1830's and 1840's this scheme, which secured the separation of the village from the manor by the surrender of peasant land in return for freedom from labour dues, was working smoothly and not without profit to the gentry themselves. The Poznanian *szlachta* therefore had little to fear from the Democratic Society's agrarian policy which was hardly applicable in the local conditions. The accession of Frederick William IV in 1840, moreover, indirectly encouraged the growth of Polish radicalism. The restrictions imposed after 1831 under the campaign of germanization associated with the governor, Edward Flotwell, were relaxed and the attack upon the Catholic Church called off. The Polish language was once more permitted in the schools. Poznania therefore became attractive to the Poles in the other parts of Poland, and in the years 1842–4, when the extradition convention with Russia was allowed to lapse, about 3,000 young men crossed into Prussia from the Congress Kingdom to avoid conscription into the Russian army. They quickly turned Poznania into a hotbed of intrigue.[2]

A group of fiery young landlords, which went by the name of the 'Fronde', was assembled by Władysław Kosiński. On the left the Poznań bookseller, Stefański, formed his own 'Association of Plebeians', which, as the name suggests, sought support among the lower classes. The *émigrés* from the Congress Kingdom everywhere clamoured for action and loudly condemned the policy of delay adopted by the Democratic Society.

---

[1] T. Malinowski, *Kilka rad ku oswobodzeniu Polski* (Paris, 1843), pp. 71–2.

[2] Cf. J. Moraczewski, *Wypadki poznańskie z roku 1848* (Poznań, 1850), pp. 7–8. A. Guttry, *Pamiętniki . . . z lat 1845, 1846, 1847* (Poznań, 1891), I, 11–13, and H. Kamieński, *Pamiętniki i wizerunki* (Wrocław, 1951), p. 24.

Henryk Kamieński in the Congress Kingdom wrote a long textbook on the guerrilla tactics to be adopted when the insurrection was called.[1] His cousin, Edward Dembowski, son of the senator, Leon Dembowski, was active everywhere in Poznania, Cracow and Galicia, enlisting support for a fresh revolt. His contacts with literary circles in Warsaw enabled him to extend his influence to the Kingdom of Poland, whence he had been forced to flee in 1843. He had a link likewise with the smaller landed proprietors in the western regions of Galicia, especially in the circle of Tarnów. Here a landlord, Franciszek Wiesiołowski, had built up a small conspiracy which was willing to join forces with the Poznanians.[2] Though Dembowski threatened him with death, Franciszek Smolka on his return from prison in 1845 refused to associate with the new conspiratorial movement, for which reason it made little progress in the eastern regions of Galicia.[3] The growth of activity in western Galicia, Cracow and Poznania, however, was strong enough to create a minor crisis in the Central Committee of the Democratic Society. It had become plain that the Democratic Society would no longer command respect if it did not fall in with the mood prevailing at home. Malinowski, the agent in Poznania, continued to urge delay when discussions were held at Versailles in the winter of 1843–4, but it was always difficult for Poles to stand aside from a political eruption, even when they were certain there was small chance of success. Wiktor Heltman insisted that the Democratic Soicety must join with the movement at home or forfeit all claim to their countrymen's respect. Malinowski persisted in his opposition, but Heltman carried the Central Committee which capitulated to pressure at home and agreed to prepare for an insurrection upon the principles of its Manifesto of 1836.[4]

[1] *O prawdach żywotnych narodu polskiego* (Brussels, 1844) was published with the aid of the Democratic Society which omitted passages critical of itself.

[2] The Austrian authorities subsequently found it difficult to believe that Wiesiołowski could collect only 75 crowns from the whole of the province in 1845, cf. F. Wiesiołowski, *Pamiętnik* (Lvov, 1868), pp. 40–1.

[3] K. Widmann, *Franciszek Smolka*, pp. 103–4.

[4] W. Heltman, *Emigracja polska od 1831 do 1863* (Leipzig, 1865), and J. Alcyato, 'Wypadki w 1846 roku, *Wizerunki polityczne dziejów państwa polskiego-Polska w kraju i za granicą od 1831 do 1848 r.*', in *Biblioteka Pisarzy Polskich*. XXIX (Leipzig, 1864), pp. 160–2.

The Polish propertied classes had long known that the younger generation was planning an insurrection, which would in all probability bring down upon Poland fresh repressions if it failed, while, if it succeeded and the Polish Democratic Society's programme of agrarian reform were put into effect, it would demand material sacrifices of themselves. A mixture of concern for their country and regard for their own interests led the upper classes to seek means of circumventing revolution and neutralizing revolutionary feeling. In Poznania the Polish philanthropist, Dr. Marcinkowski, led a movement 'for the founding of the Poznań Bazaar in 1838, a chamber of commerce where the local *szlachta* and the townspeople could meet for business and cultural gatherings. He was likewise active in promoting the 'Society for Academic Assistance', which aided young Poles to obtain higher education and found them posts on the completion of their studies. In the Kingdom of Poland Count Andrzej Zamoyski began a movement for the improvement of agricultural techniques by holding annual displays at his property of Klemensów, near Lublin. Zamoyski, enamoured of the English landlord and tenant system, believed that conversion of labour services into rents would remove a cause of tension between the village and the manor and thus render revolutionary propaganda innocuous.[1]

In Galicia Prince Leon Sapieha, brother-in-law of Prince Adam Czartoryski and Andrzej Zamoyski, laboured hard to create the institutions necessary to a modern society, savings banks, credit banks, schools and railways. In common with men of property in other countries threatened with left-wing revolutions the Polish enthusiasts for the so-called 'organic work' argued that they were laying the foundations of future independence, which could only be postponed by premature revolutions. By strengthening the economic position of the country the Poles, they pleaded, would be able to speak with a greater degree of authority to the occupying powers. This was not a policy which had much appeal to the military-minded Polish youth in the growing political tension of the 1840's, nor did it find acceptance with the extremists of the right wing who could see no virtues in the change of the social order.

[1] For Zamoyski's activity see Chapter II, pp. 64-5.

The landlords of Galicia in particular found themselves in a position of acute difficulty. On the one hand the revolutionaries were proposing an immediate insurrection, while on the other hand the peasants, hit hard by crop failures, threatened to break the bonds of social discipline. In Vienna the central government appeared to be paralyzed and to have no policy to meet the growing crisis. Within the Galician Estates, a purely deliberative body without executive powers, the conservatives led by Prince Władysław Sanguszko were at loggerheads with the moderates under Prince Leon Sapieha, who urged a scheme of limited agrarian reform in order to meet the challenge of the revolutionary agents offering the peasants unconditional freeholds, and the Austrian bureaucracy which represented the Emperor as the only true friend of the people. In March 1842 discussion on the agrarian question led only to disagreements which were not resolved until the Galician Estates met in the autumn of 1845. At last the procrastination of the conservative opposition had disappeared. In 1845 there were rumours of revolution and fear of imminent peasant revolt. Even the conservatives were willing to submit to the proposal of Maurycy Kraiński that the Estates must there and then consider the abolition of labour services. The real problem before the gentry was to induce the Austrian government, which they had never really pressed in the matter, to acquire a similar sense of urgency, but it was not easy to influence the Galician chancellor in Vienna, Inzaghi, a bureaucrat immersed in the routine of office and unable to exert influence in the circumstances of paralysis produced by the rivalry of Kolowrat and Metternich. The Galician viceroy, the Archduke Ferdinand, took little interest in the government of the province and was himself opposed to reform. The real initiative rested with Baron Krieg, the provincial president, who, often thought of as the enemy of the Poles, was at this stage pressing them to take decisive action.[1] As head of the provincial administration he received all resolutions of the Estates for transmission to higher authority. In 1843 he had watered down a motion of Tadeusz Wasilewski. In 1844 he made no textual alterations, but in 1845 he altered the Polish resolution in a more radical sense, deleting 'the conver-

[1] L. Sapieha, *Wspomnienia* (Lvov, 1912), pp. 338–9.

C

sion or redemption of the above-mentioned duties' and sub-
stituting 'the conversion of serf duties into rents in corn or rents
in money, or the complete redemption of them'.[1] To this he
added a fresh clause which touched upon a subject, which the
Polish gentry had not discussed, and proposed the division of
the common lands and the abolition of common pasture rights,
which might have made possible the complete separation of
noble and peasant lands. The Archduke Ferdinand wished the
Polish motion to stand in its original form, but Krieg ignored
him and transmitted the amended text to Vienna. His view was
that a crisis was approaching and that a measure of reform
must be introduced to satisfy the peasants. The views of the
szlachta were immaterial because the peasants and not the
nobility were the allies of Austria. It was however too late for
the lethargic administration in Vienna to reach a decision to
ward off the crisis.

During the winter of 1845–6 the Poznanian conspirators prepared their rising. The Polish Democratic Society despatched
to Poznania its own military expert, Ludwik Mierosławski,
a non-commissioned officer in 1831, who aspired to lead vast
armies against Russia. Throughout his career Mierosławski
had a strong preference for the largest possible military units,
fighting pitched battles and settling the whole Polish question
at one stroke. To the Poznanians he expounded his plan of the
rapid formation of three armies, of which two were to secure
the neutrality of Austria and Prussia and a third to march
against Russia and drive her back to the limits of historic
Poland.[2] This Napoleonic plan at first enchanted the conspirators, but it soon produced second thoughts. Fantasy was attractive only if it were not the basis of action. The Poznanian rising
was betrayed by a half-hearted conspirator before the date set
for its outbreak, 21/22 February 1846. Mierosławski and almost
all the Poznanian leaders, except Heltman, who had come forward from France, were arrested. In Congress Poland a feeble
outbreak at Siedlce was suppressed by the peasants who were

---

[1] Cf. S. Kieniewicz, 'Sprawa włościańska w galicyjskim sejmie stanowym',
Sobótka, ɪɪɪ (1948), pp. 182–3.

[2] Cf. the Prussian prosecutor's quotation of his plans, 'Sprawa więźniów poznań-
skich 1846–1848 roku', *Biblioteka Pisarzy Polskich*, xxɪx, 212–13.

to be freed when the insurrection began.[1] Only in Cracow and Galicia did the Polish insurgents take up arms.

In Galicia the penalty was paid for not having enlightened the peasants of the insurgents' intentions towards them. The whole of southern Poland had been severely affected by the elemental disasters of the 1840's and the murmurings of the peasants had been enough to induce a change of attitude in the Galician Estates. The Polish situation had much in common with the state of affairs which prevailed among the French peasants during the *Grande Peur* of 1789. There were stories that the gentry intended to slaughter the peasants and they, uncertain of the Austrian government's power to protect them, formed themselves into bands. When the gentry of western Galicia rose in revolt, the peasants in the circles of Tarnów, Rzeszów, Wadowice, Nowy Sącz and Sanok turned savagely against their landlords, murdering some and handing others over to the authorities, but there was in their behaviour something more than a primitive desire for revenge. Jakób Szela, the peasant leader in the circle of Tarnów, often represented in Polish martyrology as a bloodthirsty villain, was evidently a man of considerable moral authority among the rural population, respected for a long legal struggle he had waged against the Bogusz family in a land dispute. The peasants directed their action almost entirely against the landlords and their agents. Only a few women were killed, usually accidentally, and none were raped. Everywhere the peasants represented themselves as acting on behalf of the Emperor. This was no doubt a carefully considered policy which had the aim of preventing reprisals from being taken against them when Austrian control was restored.

The local Austrian officials found themselves enveloped by what might easily have become a social revolution. In the circle of Tarnów the *starosta*, Breinl, was terrified lest the peasant movement turn against the government and sought to conciliate them by promises of rewards for their assistance against the *szlachta*. In the circle of Bochnia the *starosta*, Bernd, acted in the same manner. Elsewhere local officials were able to show neutrality in the struggle between the peasants and the gentry and

[1] Cf. the newpaper account reprinted in *Rewolucja Polska 1846 roku*, edited by S. Kieniewicz (Wrocław, 1949), pp. 91–2.

even to maintain order.[1] The Austrian government was fortunate in the fact that the peasant rising was confined almost entirely to the ethnically Polish, or Mazur, districts of the province; in only one Ruthenian district was there an outbreak of disorder, at Horożana in the circle of Sambor.[2] The Polish insurgents for their part found support only among the peasants in the upland regions where labour services and exploitation by landlords scarcely constituted a problem; in Chochołów the mountaineers prepared to rise against the Austrians, but the peasants in the lowlands had already settled the fate of the insurrection.[3] How many Poles died in the course of the short-lived rising will never be known exactly. A reasonable guess is that there were about 1,100 victims of the peasants' action.[4] Three thousand persons were arrested and 430 manors were plundered. The peasant rising was almost certainly not instigated by the provincial administration in Lvov. The conservatively inclined Archduke Ferdinand in fact sent the official, Lażański, and Colonel Benedek to do what they could to restrain the peasants, but it was already too late to prevent the massacre.

In 1846 the city of Cracow found itself perilously poised between the miserable failure in Poznania and the appalling events in Galicia. Cracow might easily have stood aside, but instead there occurred a rising which exhibited in miniature all the features of a typical Polish insurrection.[5] The conspiratorial committee headed by Jan Alcyato, representing the Democratic Society, and two local leaders, Jan Tyssowski and Ludwik Gorzkowski, had little confidence in their chances, but the Residents representing the tutelary powers were not certain of their ability to maintain order, especially when in reply to their inquiry of 17 February the Senate declared that it would be powerless in the event of disturbances. On the morning of 18 February the Austrian general, Collin, was sent into the city

---

[1] Cf. S. Kieniewicz, *Ruch chłopski w Galicji w 1846 roku* (Wrocław, 1951), pp. 238–254.

[2] Cf. W. Czaplicki, *Powieść o Horożanie* (Lvov, 1862).

[3] Cf. the memoir of Jan Andrusikiewicz in S. E. Radzikowski, *Powstanie chochołowskie w roku 1846* (Lvov, 1904).

[4] S. Kieniewicz, *Ruch chłopski*, pp. 256–60.

[5] The most modern account is M. Żychowski, *Rok 1846 w Rzeczypospolitej Krakowskiej i Galicji* (Warsaw, 1956), pp. 235 ff.

with 1,281 men, but with the arrival of alarming news from Galicia withdrew in accordance with contemporary military practice in order not to be shut up in a medieval city, in which regular troops would enjoy little military advantage over the insurgents; with Collin went the local militia, the gendarmerie and the president of the Senate, Father Schindler. The city was thus left wide open for the insurgents to seize. The Cracow conservatives were beside themselves with anxiety and a meeting was held in the house of Count Józef Wodzicki to arrange for the organization of a local security system. The leading conspirators would gladly have called off a rising, but the wife of the secretary-designate, Rogawski, soundly upbraided the menfolk for their lack of courage. Alcyato bitterly denounced a revolt as folly and departed to Paris, but on the morning of 22 February Tyssowski, Gorzkowski and a certain Alexander Gregorzewski presented themselves to the security committee formed by the Wodzicki family and declared themselves to be the 'National Government of the Polish Republic'.[1] About thirty to forty men of the more prosperous class, stewards, manor clerks and estate officials, entered the city to sustain the insurrection.[2] The insurgents called all former soldiers to the colours and appointed an ex-officer, Edward Skarzyński, commander-in-chief. Disputes arose immediately and on 24 February Jan Tyssowski declared himself dictator.[3] The propertied classes had no intention of permitting the unknown Tyssowski to issue manifestoes in the name of the Polish nation. More frightening still was the arrival of the radical Edward Dembowski, the personification of the social revolution, from the salt mines at Wieliczka where he had confiscated 100,000 *złp*. On the night of 24/25 February a plot was hatched in the house of a former rector of the university, Adam Krzyżanowski, who induced a popular professor of Polish literature, Michał Wiszniewski, to take command of the revolution and himself become dictator.[4] Edward Dembowski,

[1] Cf. H. Barycz, 'W przededniu ruchu rewolucyjnego w Krakowie w r. 1846 (Relacja K. Rogawskiego o wypadkach w dniach 8 do 18 lutego 1846)', *Przegląd Historyczny*, XXXVI (1946), pp. 124–34.

[2] Cf. A. Grabowski, *Wspomnienia* (Cracow, 1909), I, 155.

[3] For details of Tyssowski see M. Tyrowicz, *Jan Tyssowski, Dyktator Krakowski r. 1846* (Warsaw, 1930).

[4] M. Polaczkówna, 'Michał Wiszniewski, 1830–1848', *Rocznik Krakowski*, XII (1909), pp. 59–163.

however, arrived to threaten him with revolutionary justice, whereupon he fled the city. Dembowski, as co-secretary of the revolutionary government, now forced the dictator Tyssowski, who on 24 February had threatened the people with severe punishments if they attacked the *szlachta*, to change his tune. Labour services were to be abolished and the revolutionary decrees promulgated. An end of titles was proclaimed and the workers of the city promised double wages.[1] Dembowski then decided that the revolution must go out to the people of the countryside to explain its aims. To win over the peasants he organized a procession of forty priests and 500 other persons to advance to Gdów beyond Podgorze, the suburb on the right bank of the Vistula, but as the column advanced in solemn step Colonel Benedek arrived with a few regular troops and a swarm of peasant auxiliaries who fell upon the procession. Dembowski was killed and his followers dispersed. The inevitable capitulation followed, but not before the conservatives in Cracow were certain that the Russian army was near enough to the city to protect them from the Austrians. So disgusted were the burgesses of Cracow with the conduct of Austria that they looked upon the Russians as their saviours from rapine and indiscriminate slaughter.[2]

Thus the great Polish insurrection planned by the Polish Democratic Society came to an end. The least of Poland's troubles was that the Free City of Cracow was incorporated into the Austrian Empire. Of far greater importance was the feeling of disappointment and disillusionment experienced by the Polish educated class. The insurrection had been based upon the assumption that there would be a spontaneous uprising of the people throughout the provinces of the former Polish Republic, impressed by the self-sacrifice of the gentry in granting them freeholds, but instead of rallying to the national cause the peasants had turned against it. The Polish nation appeared

---

[1] For the decrees and announcements of the Cracow government see S. Wachholz, 'Akty prawne rewolucji krakowskiej z roku 1846', *Czasopisma Prawno-Historyczne*, VIII (1956), z.1, pp. 311–47.

[2] There is an extensive contemporary literature on the Cracow revolution. Eyewitness accounts are J. Wawel-Louis, *Kronika Rewolucyi Krakowskiej w roku 1846* (Cracow, 1898); W. Kopff, *Wspomnienia z ostatnich lat Rzeczypospolitej Krakowskiej* (Cracow, 1906); and F. Hechel, *Człowiek Nauki taki, jakim był* (Cracow, 1949).

not a score of millions strong, but only as an educated minority powerless to defeat Austria, Prussia and Russia. The feeling of disillusionment was summed up by Bronisław Trentowski:

Hitherto we have counted with certainty upon the people, and today we see that the nation is still only the *szlachta*. Confidence in our strength has been extinguished, leaving behind only a silent and painful feeling of shame. . . . Not long ago everyone believed, everyone was certain, that the Fatherland would by itself throw off its yoke, and that soon, perhaps tomorrow or the next day. Now we may not think of an independent Poland. Before we may work again for this most holy of political objects, we must see to the end of the long social war that has flared up between the peasantry and the noble order. There are those who say that there will be a Poland. But when? After a hundred, two hundred, three hundred years![1]

Sentimental love of the people gave way to fear. The revolutionaries threatened to take away the estates of the gentry and the people their lives. The lesson of 1846 for most Poles in Galicia and Poznania was that insurrection brought no profit. The only course left was the peaceful accumulation of Polish resources proposed by the moderate conservatives.

The renunciation of revolt meant collaboration with the partitioning powers and the acceptance of the division of Poland, the so-called 'tri-loyalism' by which Poles accepted political assimilation with the Austrian, Prussian and Russian communities. Thus in Poznania there was an appeal for collaboration. Eugeniusz Breza could describe Frederick III as 'le meilleur Polonais après Casimir-le-Grand' for having initiated agrarian reform in Poznania in 1823 and thus forestalled a peasant uprising.[2] Breza was anxious to combat the view that after 1846 Poles and Germans could never find common ground and that the Poles ought to throw in their lot with the Russians, who were at least Slavs. The influential Count Tytus Działynski had actually appealed to Russia through the ambassador in Berlin, though from the Russian side there was no inclination to respond to his pleas.[3] No one cared openly to praise

[1] B. Trentowski, *Wizerunki duszy narodowej s końca ostatniego szesnastolecia* (Paris, 1847), pp. 2–3.

[2] E. Breza, *De la Russomanie dans le Grand Duché de Posen* (Berlin, 1846), p. 9.

[3] Cf. Peter von Meyendorff, *Politischer und privater Briefswechsel, 1826–1863* (Berlin-Leipzig, 1923), I, 345–8. *Lettres et papiers du chancelier Comte de Nesselrode (1760–1856)* (Paris, 1904–12), VIII, 337.

the Austrian government after the Galician massacres, but the idea was taken up in conservative circles that the Poles might find a compromise with Austria. The Polish dramatist, Count Alexander Fredro, attempted to prove that a contented Galicia might make a contribution to the stability of the Austrian Empire, for it would show that Slavonic nations could live in peace under the Habsburgs.[1] Count Agenor Gołuchowski, who had taken employment in the Austrian bureacracy in Galicia, was in these years working for the establishment of mutual trust between the Poles and Vienna, hoping that the Polish aristocracy might survive the crisis, if it could obtain by a constitutional compromise control over the local administration of the province.[2] In the Congress Kingdom the Marquis Alexander Wielopolski launched his celebrated attack upon Metternich and appealed for collaboration with Russia. In his pamphlet *Lettre d'un gentilhomme polonais sur les massacres de Gallicie adressée au Prince de Metternich*, published in 1846, he wrote:

Comme vous [i.e. Austria] et avec vous, les Russes ont détrôné notre roi, nos institutions, nos libertés; ils laissent intact l'ordre social; la vindicte publique, ils la font exercer d'une main de fer par les organes de leur lois, et ils n'ont jamais aliéné à des assassins la souveraineté de leur czar.[3]

Wielopolski's argument was that the Poles should identify themselves with the young and vigorous Slavonic civilization of Russia and turn their backs upon the decrepit west. In this manner the Polish conservatives in Prussia, Austria and the Kingdom sought to combat the revolution from which they had as much to lose as the partitioning powers.

The Polish Democratic Society did its best to save its reputation. Mierosławski, who had broken down under interrogation, tried to redeem himself at his trial in Berlin, which he sought to turn into a political demonstration, pleading that the Poles intended to make war, not upon Germany, but upon

---

[1] For the text of Fredro's memorandum see S. Schnür-Peplowski, *Z papierów po Fredrze—Przyczynek do Biografii Poety* (Cracow, 1899), pp. 71–91. Cf. also W. Wyka, *Teka Stańczyka na tle historii Galicji w latach 1849–1869* (Wrocław, 1951), p. 8.

[2] Cf. B. Łoziński, *Agenor hr. Gołuchowski w pierwszym okresie rządów swoich* (Lvov, 1901).

[3] p. 39.

Russia, the real enemy of German unification. Avoiding discussion of the part played by the citizens of Poznania in the rising, he claimed sole responsibility for the Polish Democratic Society, thus enhancing its importance and prestige abroad when at home it had reached the nadir of its influence. Mierosławski refuted the accusation made by the prosecutor that the Society was designed to spread 'communism', which he condemned as a smear:

Indeed, everything that is revolution or militant democracy and cannot be regimented, but they want to hold in the bonds of restraint, the public prosecutor calls communism. What is this communism according to our enemies? In these days it is just the same as sorcery and alchemy were in the middle ages.[1]

In Paris the Democratic Society, instead of falling in with the mood of despair prevailing in Poland, decided that it must make a direct appeal to the people by publishing pamphlets with a strongly religious, but unmistakably revolutionary tone.[2] In this way the Democratic Society sought to save its reputation and preserve its policy, but it did little more than convince moderate Poles at home that it had lost touch with reality.[3]

The Democratic Society's policy of linking a national insurrection with agrarian reform found one convert at least in the Austrian government. It at first seemed likely that the Austrian government would pass over the events of 1846 with a mere commendation of the peasants for their loyalty,[4] but a letter of the peasant leader, Szela, of 1 April to the provincial government proposed that labour services should be limited to one day per morg and that the remainder should be converted into money rents; it was bluntly stated that the peasants had no intention of returning to their former obligations.[5] Though it was not proposed that labour services should be abolished

[1] For Mierosławski's speeches of 3 and 5 August 1847 see *Biblioteka Pisarzy Polskich*, XXIX, 248–77.

[2] Cf. *Boże słowa do ludu polskiego* (1847), and *Słowa prawdy dla ludu polskiego* (1848).

[3] Strong objections were raised to its claim to have played the leading role in the events of 1846. Cf. W. Kosiński, *Sprawa polska z roku 1846 przed sądem opinii publicznej wytoczona* (Poznań, 1850), pp. 10–11, 16–17, 23.

[4] Cf. the imperial circular of 12 March 1848, M. Sala, *Geschichte des polnischen Aufstandes vom Jahre 1846* (Vienna, 1867), pp. 295–7.

[5] S. Kieniewicz, *Ruch chłopski*, pp. 336–7.

absolutely, the letter revealed that the Democratic Society's programme was very close to the peasants' aspirations. The Archduke Ferdinand would have preferred to meet the situation with a pacification, but he was recalled to Vienna before he could carry out his intention. After discussion in Vienna it was at length decided to combine the minimum of concession with the maximum of coercion. On 13 April 1846 an imperial patent was signed, abolishing all long-distance carting services, additional days of labour and compulsory hired labour, and granting to the peasants the right to make direct appeal to the court of the circle. A promise was held out that labour services might in future be converted into rents under government supervision. In the meantime labour services were to be restored. In the second half of April 50,000 troops were concentrated in Galicia and the peasants compelled to fulfil their obligations to the manor, whippings and beatings being administered upon a liberal scale where resistance was met. Szela was eventually deported to Bukovina where he was given a new farm and kept out of harm's way. As far as Galicia was concerned nothing was solved. The province remained in a disturbed and dangerous state, stricken with famine and typhus. There were even reports of cannibalism.[1] Traditionally the manors aided the peasants in times of distress, but after 1846 the gentry were not ready to offer relief. Nevertheless, no one doubted that if a fresh emergency arose more concessions would be required to meet the peasants' demands. On the Russian side of the frontier Nicholas I decided to meet the emergency before it arose. In the Kingdom of Poland the ukaz of 7 June 1846 granted security of tenure to peasants holding more than three morgs of land, a security which the *Code Napoléon* had denied them, while instructions were given for the acceleration of the official survey and definition of peasant obligations in western Russia.[2]

The history of eastern Europe might have been different if the Galician and Poznanian Poles had not been shaken in 1846. When the revolutions swept Europe in 1848 and paralyzed governments both in Berlin and Vienna the initiative had passed

---

[1] J. Szewczuk, *Kronika Klęsk elementarnych w Galicji w latach 1772–1848* (Lvov, 1939), pp. 183–4, 189.
[2] See below, Chapter II.

out of Polish hands. Instead, the Poles looked to Germany for salvation. The German liberals knew that it was Russian policy to uphold the rule of the petty princes in Germany and prevent unification. Many believed that the first step of the German revolution ought to be war against Russia. Nicholas I had no illusions concerning the dangers of the German situation. The agreements of 1833, by which Austria, Russia and Prussia had undertaken to maintain a common policy of vigilance in the Polish territories, extraditing Poles who committed political offences in one part of Poland and took refuge in another, had been dropped by Frederick William IV on his accession. The Prussian royal patent of 3 February 1847, summoning a united diet of the eight constituent portions of the Kingdom, showed that the king was ready to meet his own liberal opposition half-way. The breakdown of monarchical solidarity called for energetic measures on the part of Russia when revolution broke out in Vienna on 13–15 March and in Berlin on 19–20 March 1848. A partial mobilization was carried out in Russia in order to concentrate 350,000 troops in Congress Poland, while another 100–150,000 men were called to the colours to provide a reserve to reinforce the forward army. On 27 March Nicholas I issued his manifesto, declaring his determination to uphold the *status quo*. These were steps calculated to put heart into the Prussian conservatives who controlled the administration and the army; the experience of 1813 had taught them to look upon Russia as an ally. The German liberals, who favoured war against Russia to drive her back beyond the Niemen, not only realized that they would meet with a determined resistance from the Russian army, but suspected also that they could not rely upon the Prussian army to act as the instrument of a forward policy. Sentimental love of the Poles, moreover, soon gave way to a more realistic appraisal of the Polish question. An independent Poland erected to defend Germany against Russia would in its turn grasp at West Prussia and parts of East Prussia and Silesia. For the German liberals the object of the revolution was to strengthen Germany, not to call into question the validity of the eastern frontier. For that reason the Germans looked with some tolerance upon the acts of the royal Prussian bureaucracy and army in Poznania.

Already on 18 March a second decree had been issued summoning the combined diets to Berlin, and the Poles were able even before the revolution broke out to take the first steps towards forming a National Committee. When it was discovered that the revolutionaries had triumphed in Berlin an extraordinary meeting of the Poznań town council was called to appoint a security guard to prevent the military from taking control of the city. So powerless was the government that it was forced to rescind the state of siege which had existed since 1846. Mierosławski and his fellow prisoners were released from the Moabite prison in Berlin and formed their own 'Revolutionary Committee', but Mierosławski's assumption that he would take control of an insurrection in the whole country was little to the taste of the Poznanian leaders. When a deputation of the Poznanian National Committee arrived in Berlin on 21/22 March the conservative elements had already decided that Polish demands must be modified. The original Polish manifesto had stated: 'We, as Poles, having our own history and being a completely different and separate national element, do not wish to be and cannot be embodied in the German Reich.'[1] Instead the deputation was prepared to ask only for local administrative autonomy. The real state of opinion among the Poznanian leaders was revealed in the manifesto of 25 March 1848.[2] It confirmed the peasants in possession of their freeholds, lest otherwise they obtain the impression that a Polish government would repeal Prussian legislation; a promise was made that taxes would be reduced, and assurances given that in other parts of Poland labour services would cease and freeholds be granted when independence had been won. Special care would be taken of the landless peasants and the town workers. Rewards would be given to landless peasants who fought for their country's independence. What was missing from the manifesto was an immediate summons to arms. The Polish leaders were waiting for the German revolution to make war upon Russia. For the moment, the government gave its verbal assent to the appointment of Polish officials, the enlistment of a national guard and Polish control over the schools. A promise was even

[1] S. Karwowski, *Historia Wielkiego Księstwa Poznańskiego* (Poznań, 1918), I, 362–3.
[2] *Rok 1848 w Polsce*, edited by S. Kieniewicz (Wrocław, 1948), pp. 41–3.

made to withdraw the regular army from Poznania. The local German population soon discovered that as Polish self-confidence grew they were being pushed into the background. On 29 March 1848 the Polish National Committee chose to lecture the Germans for their lack of fraternity, pointing to Polish respect for other nationalities as an example for them to emulate.[1] Confidence was expressed that the new Germany would find a solution of the German-Polish question in Poznania.

In fact the new Germany was not to decide the issue. When the revolution broke out in Prussia the court was divided into two parties, the pro-Poles like General von Willisen and the anti-Poles, strongly entrenched in the administration. On 29 March the ministry was changed and the Rhenish liberals, Campenhausen and Hansemann, who favoured the Polish cause, brought in. Orders were given for the formation of a Polish army corps and in general it appeared that the Prussian government would do its best to promote Polish independence. Czartoryski and his followers, believing that at last a diplomatic solution was possible, moved forward to Berlin. In Poznania the National Committee set up its own 'War Department' to organize a levy of the entire male population between the ages of 17 and 50. On 28 March orders were given for the concentration of the Polish levies on the eastern frontier. On 3-4 April Ludwik Mierosławski was able to concentrate 7,000 badly armed men in the towns of Września, Ksiąz and Pleszew. The Prussian cabinet toyed with one policy, the Prussian military implemented another. The local commander, von Colomb, secured reinforcements and at the head of 30,000 men made himself the real arbiter of the situation. On 3 April Poznań was occupied and a state of siege proclaimed. On 30 March, however, the government in Berlin had decided to send General von Willisen to Poznań to secure a definitive agreement with the Poles. The King for his part had ordered von Colomb to suppress the Polish movement by force if necessary. Thus Willisen found himself in the position not of a negotiator, but rather of an arbiter between the army and the Poles. When he arrived in Poznań on 5 April he found that von Colomb was making preparations to attack the Polish levies. His first step was to appeal

[1] K. Rakowski, *Powstanie poznańskie w 1848 roku* (Lvov, 1900), (notes) pp. 17-19.

for a general disarmament of the Poles,[1] but the Poles were convinced that by a show of resistance they could obtain their own national military organization. The government in Berlin, however, declined to accept a separate Polish army in Poznania and ordered Willisen to inform the Poles that they must accept its decisions by 11 April. Von Colomb, for his part, was ordered by the royal cabinet to disperse the Poles by force if Willisen failed to obtain their submission. The Polish National Committee decided in principle that it must submit. For Mierosławski in the Polish camp the situation was critical. His own authority was barely recognized and the forces nominally under his command, though now risen to 9,000, scarcely capable of resisting regular Prussian troops. There was no alternative but to submit to Willisen's terms. Conversations were held with Willisen at the farm of Jarosławiec, near Środa, on 11 April and the bases of agreement reached.[2] Persons unfit for service were to return to their homes and members of the *landwehr* to join their headquarters, but it was conceded that persons who had volunteered were to remain in Września, Książ, Pleszew and Miłosław, provided that not more than 500–600 and 120 horses were concentrated in each place; pending their embodiment in a Poznanian division they were to remain under the supervision of a Prussian officer and be maintained at the expense of the Polish gentry. Equally limited were the subsequent proposals for the reorganization of Poznania. The Grand Duchy was to be divided into German and Polish districts, the German to be incorporated in the German state.

The Polish levies in the camps became restive. They disliked Mierosławski and would have preferred General Kruszewski, who was serving in the Belgian army, but unable to obtain his release. Upon Mierosławski they heaped their criticism of the Jarosławiec agreement. Polish officers who had served in relatively high ranks during the war of 1831 resented being commanded by Mierosławski, who had been only a sergeant. The radical elements clamoured for action against the Prussian army which was preventing supplies reaching the Polish forces. Von

---

[1] S. Karwowski, *Historia Księstwa Poznańskiego*, I, 399–401.

[2] S. Kieniewicz, *Społeczeństwo polskie w powstaniu poznańskiem 1848 r.* (Warsaw, 1935), pp. 167–70.

Colomb ignored Willisen and on 20 April refused to allow him to enter Poznań. On 21 April all Polish institutions were dissolved. Mierosławski knew that if he fought the Prussian army he would be defeated and that, if he refused to fight, he would for ever be a laughing-stock. The Polish National Committee in Poznań confessed its bankruptcy and dissolved itself on 30 April, protesting in eloquent terms against the wrongs they had suffered at the hands of the Germans.[1] When the Prussian army moved forward to disarm the Polish levies, it met with resistance. The Poles enjoyed a few fleeting successes, but there was no response to their appeal for a general rising. On 9 May, their ammunition exhausted, the Polish forces capitulated. Thus came to an end the shadowy autonomy of 1848 in Poznania. When on 24 July the Polish question came up for discussion at the Frankfurt parliament the Poles were to find that they obtained as little sympathy from the German liberals as they had received from the Prussian military. If it had not been for demoralization of 1846 they would surely have given a different account of themselves.

The reaction to the news of disturbances in Germany and Austria was even more timid in Cracow. The middle-class attitude is illustrated by the entry of Hechel in his diary: 'Let us wait quietly for the further development of this mighty European renaissance.'[2] Under pressure from a delegation led by Count Adam Potocki the local imperial commissioner, Deym, consented to release political prisoners and to the enlistment of a national guard, but the propertied classes did not press him for more. At Tarnów the magnate, Władysław Sanguszko, fearing another massacre, urged the *starosta* to concede just enough to satisfy local feeling. At Lvov conservatives and radicals combined to work out a programme, not of revolution, but of common action to obtain concessions. The result of their labours was the address to the Emperor of 19 March.[3] Thirteen demands were made, which included the classic points of western European liberalism, together with specific require-

---

[1] *Rok 1848 w Polsce*, edited by S. Kieniewicz, pp. 107–11.

[2] F. Hechel, *Kraków i ziemia krakowska w okresie wiosny ludów—Pamiętniki* (Wrocław, 1950), p. 89.

[3] Reproduced in *Rok 1848 w Polsce*, edited by S. Kieniewicz, pp. 199–202.

ments for Galicia: the safeguarding of Polish nationality, the appointment of Poles to the administration, the creation of Polish military units and, above all,

the complete abolition of labour services and all serf obligations, which the Galician landed proprietors wish to resign in favour of their existing serfs. Likewise, the complete abolition of the serf status and of mutual rights which have existed up to this time between the proprietor and the serf, and, simultaneously with it, the regulation of landed properties.

The economic aspects of the address did not please the landlords, but they felt obliged to make this gesture in view of the excitement in the streets of Lvov. On 21 March a National Guard was formed to ensure that order be maintained, but the governor, Franz von Stadion, was not prepared to tolerate the exercise of authority by the Poles and ordered it to dissolve. On 26 March, therefore, the local leaders decided to appeal over his head by sending a deputation to Vienna, headed by Prince Jerzy Lubomirski and including men of the moderate and constitutionally-minded left like Florian Ziemiałkowski and Leszek Dunin-Borkowski. Stadion was not sorry to see Lvov denuded of its political talent, but when the deputation arrived in Cracow, the railway terminus, it obtained a clearer picture of the extent of political disorder in Europe and decided that the address to the Emperor must be given a sharper form.

On 6 April the Lvov delegation together with representatives from Cracow drafted a fresh address.[1] Once more there was not the slightest suggestion that the Poles in Galicia wished to break with the Habsburg monarchy. It is true that a national army was demanded, but it was represented that Galicia was unprotected:

For this reason, lest we become prey to your enemies and ours, we need your care; we wish to be in alliance with Austria and all her constituent peoples. This alliance can exist only upon the basis of sincerity and friendship, upon the basis of common freedoms which accord with the times, as indeed already they exist in Hungary and especially in the Duchy of Poznań.

[1] *Ibid.*, pp. 224-31.

It appeared that the Poles demanded regional autonomy and the new address was stronger in a political sense than the original address drawn up in Lvov, but Point 12 watered down the proposals made to settle the agrarian question:

The liberation of those who up to now have been serfs from labour services and servile duties. The granting to them of property rights to serf lands is a vital question and even a historic fact, confirmed on the one side by the will and ardent desire of those who up to now have been the owners of labour services and on the other by the general demand of those who up to now have been serfs. A provisional committee will announce the cessation of labour services and the grant to the peasants of property rights over the non-noble lands in the whole country, while the diet, which is to be called, will make pronouncement only on the subject of peasants' pasture rights, the demesnes, the urbarial tax [i.e. a levy upon estate owners in the Austrian Empire upon the value of labour services and other peasant duties], the regulation of property and, in general, on the conditions under which exemption from labour services and dues shall be changed into a law binding all parties.

The implication of the change of wording was that the Galician landlords, though they recognized that they dare not prevent the peasants from obtaining their freeholds, wished to retain in their own hands control over the woods and pastures without which the peasant economy would collapse. In this way the supremacy of the gentry could be maintained, while demands for the traditional liberal freedoms would satisfy all except the most radical of the left wing. When the address was presented the head of the administration in Vienna, Pillersdorf, merely advised the Emperor to give the address careful consideration, which signified, in view of the Emperor's personal incapacity, that Pillersdorf was playing for time. The success or failure of the national delegation to Vienna depended upon what happened in Cracow and Lvov.

In Lvov Stadion was left without direction from the central government and interpreted silence to mean that he had a free hand to extricate himself from his local difficulties. His hand was forced by the appearance of a representative of the Polish Democratic Society in Cracow, Zienkowicz, a Cracow man himself, and able to rally left-wing support in the city. On 7

April a newly created national committee issued an 'Address to the Landlords of Western Galicia', which called for a voluntary resignation of labour services on Good Friday. The arrival of Wiktor Heltman in Lvov seemed to point to a similar development of radical activity in the eastern regions of the province. Zienkowicz could not hope to call an insurrection, but his action at least showed that the left wing hoped to establish a claim upon the loyalties of the rural population.[1] Stadion attempted to wriggle out of this situation by calling for 26 April a session of the provincial estates, which, being elected under the old narrow franchise, would provide a platform for the Galician conservatives, who could act as a counter-weight to the left wing, but the left in Lvov set up its own organization, the National Council, on 15 April and fell into line with the appeal from Cracow to make a voluntary resignation of labour services. Stadion, therefore, fell back upon another device. Since 1830 it had become increasingly obvious that the Ruthenian population of eastern Galicia would not for ever tolerate a Polish hegemony. The canons of the Uniate cathedral of St. George at Lvov and the obscure, but politically conscious intelligentsia of Ruthenian speech combined on 19 April at Stadion's suggestion to submit a petition to the Emperor on the lines of the Polish address, but emphasizing their own national rights. The other element to which Stadion could appeal was the peasantry. He could not allow the Poles to carry out a voluntary surrender of labour services, lest it appear that the Austrian government was no longer seriously concerned with the welfare of the common people. On 22 April, therefore, acting on his own authority, he issued a decree proclaiming that on the order of the Emperor labour services were to cease with effect from 15 May and that the landlords would obtain compensation from the state.[2] The administration in Vienna was compelled to supply him with an imperial patent back-dated to 17 April, which seemed to prove that the magnanimity of the Emperor owed nothing to Polish pressure. At one stroke Stadion

---

[1] For the text of the Cracow circular see 'Demokracya polska na emigracyi', *Biblioteka Pisarzy Polskich*, xxxv, 165–6.

[2] A Russian version of the decree may be found in N. Milyutin, *Izsledovaniya*, ii, fascicule K, pp. 1–3.

had shown the Poles that initiative was retained by the government, which could appeal both to the Ruthenians and to the peasants, whether Ruthenian or Polish.

Difficulties remained but the issue was never in doubt. At Cracow the Poles received shorter shrift. Demonstrators demanded that an order forbidding the entry of *émigrés* be rescinded. The local military commander, General Castiglione, decided on 26 April to disarm the population, but when he met with resistance he withdrew to the Wawel castle and began a bombardment. At once the conservatives, headed by Count Adam Potocki and Prince Stanisław Jabłonowski, offered their submission. The *émigrés* were expelled, the National Committee dissolved, the National Guard suppressed and restrictions placed upon all public meetings.[1] No more trouble was experienced by the Austrians in Cracow. Only Lvov remained, a Polish city in a largely Ruthenian countryside. Stadion continued to play upon Polish differences, setting up on 27 April a *Beirat*, consisting of three Ruthenians, one Roman Catholic priest, two Jews, five officials of Polish nationality, including Agenor Gołuchowski, well known for his devotion to the Habsburg dynasty, and six Polish landlords, which was to serve in an advisory capacity, but the battle had already been won. Stadion was called to Vienna to take charge of affairs at the centre and the Poles were left to play their own game of politics undisturbed. The National Council at Lvov, unsupported by the leading Polish politicians who had gone to Vienna to take part in more exciting events, fell into the hands of second-rate leaders, attempting to counter the claims of the Ruthenian *Holovna Rada*, set up on 2 May by Bishop Jakhimovich, by establishing a pro-Polish *Sobor Rusky*. An effort was made to compose Polish and Ruthenian differences in Prague at the Slavonic Congress,[2] but events in Prague had little bearing upon the situation at home. Polish activity was ineffectual. A group of landlords formed their *Towarzyszenie Ziemiańskie*, to present their views. Leon Rzewuski, a

---

[1] The Cracow committee withdrew to Breslau where it drew up a protest against the action of Castiglione, cf. 'Protestacya komitetu narodowego krakowskiego z powodu bombardowania Krakowa', in L. Zienkowicz, *Wizerunki polityczne dziejów Państwa Polskiego, Biblioteka Pisarzy Polskich*, xxxi, 187–91.

[2] W. T. Wysłocki, 'Kongres słowiański w r. 1848 i sprawa polska', *Roczniki zakładu narodowego im. Ossolińskich*, i–ii (1927–8), pp. 517–731.

grandson of the Rzewuski who had been one of the authors of the Confederation of Targowica, placed before the public his own curious form of socialism in his paper, *Postęp* (Progress). In September Wiktor Heltman began to publish *Dziennik Stanislawowski* with the object of keeping alive the old ideal of a united Poland which seemed likely to be submerged in the prevailing provincialism. Altogether twenty different publications were issued in Galicia by various Polish organizations and groups in 1848. The extent of political disarray was revealed when elections to the Vienna parliament were held in June 1848. Galicia returned twenty-seven landlords, twenty-four professional men, fifteen priests of whom six were Roman Catholic and nine Uniate, two Jews and thirty-one peasants, of whom seventeen were Poles and fourteen Ruthenians.[1] The appointment of a Polish governor of Galicia, Wacław Zaleski, an official from the Galician chancery in Vienna, did nothing to aid the Polish cause; he arrived in Cracow on 18 August and unaccountably spent two months there dealing with matters of small importance. In Vienna the Polish deputies could not act as a united body, the landlords being unable to make common cause with the peasants. The absence of positive achievement discredited the Polish leaders in the eyes of the working class at Lvov. At the beginning of November the workers began to erect barricades in the streets. The Polish National Guard did what it could to restrain the populace, but the Austrian commander, General Hammerstein, at last had the excuse for which he had been waiting. On 2 November 1848 Hammerstein, following the example of Castiglione at Cracow, opened a bombardment of the town, killing fifty-five persons and wounding another seventy-five. A state of siege was proclaimed, which was later extended to the whole of Galicia. Thus Galicia was submerged by the same military coercion which had overwhelmed Bohemia and Austria. Zaleski was recalled to Vienna and replaced by the ultra-loyalist, Agenor Gołuchowski. There had scarcely been a revolution at all, but the Polish national movement had been strong enough to force the administration to make concessions to the people. As a result of Stadion's decree of 17 April,

---

[1] This is the analysis of S. Kieniewicz, 'Galicja w latach 1846–1848', *W stulecie wiosny ludów—Wiosna ludów na ziemiach polskich*, 1 (Warsaw, 1948), p. 328.

540,000 peasants obtained their freeholds. The landlords lost 16,800,000 days of manual labour and 14,400,000 days of labour with animals. As in 1846 only the common people were to emerge victorious.

The Polish national movement had been virtually defeated as early as April 1848. A conference of moderates and conservatives met in Breslau in May 1848 with the object of co-ordinating Polish efforts, but it was difficult to obtain recognition for a central body directing the affairs of all Poland. The two delegates from Lvov made it clear that they would not place the National Council in Galicia under the direction of any superior organization. August Cieszkowski, the philosopher, suggested an interregional organization on the pattern of the Anti-Corn Law League, but even this failed to meet with approval. Beyond the conference room the Polish democrats viewed with suspicion the deliberations of the right wing, but their fears were groundless. Even the conservatives could not find common ground.[1] Throughout Europe Poles fought for the revolution which would not bring their own country relief. The poet, Adam Mickiewicz, having broken in 1847 with his spiritual master, the half-saint, half-mountebank Andrzej Towiański, went to Rome in the hope that Pius IX would bless the revolutionary movement. Mickiewicz held that:

the appearance of the Christian spirit in politics, the building of a state for Christ, must take its beginning from Rome which is both a state and a church. This state was created on earth by the spirit.[2]

Pius IX, however, refused to grant Mickiewicz's standard a public blessing, which alone could have induced the Polish peasant soldiers in the Austrian army to join his legion. The King of Sardinia proved no more helpful than the Pope. Władysław Zamoyski, for good measure, added his own spiteful criticism of Mickiewicz's legion, but it fought on and is commemorated by a statue in Rome. Mickiewicz, however, returned to Paris where in March 1849 he founded his newspaper, *Le Tribune des Peuples*, only to see his naïve faith in the Bonapartes destroyed by Louis Napoleon's expedition to Rome to restore the temporal

[1] See M. Tyrowicz, *Polski kongres polityczny w Wrocławiu 1848 r.* (Cracow, 1946).
[2] S. Kieniewicz, *Legion Mickiewicza 1848–1849* (Warsaw, 1957), pp. 35–42, discusses the motives of Mickiewicz's conversion from mysticism to a policy of action.

power of a Pope who now had publicly declared against the revolution. No more fortunate was General Wojciech Chrzanowski, who in January 1849 took command of the Italian armies in the north and became the target of abuse for the Italians' poor performance at the battle of Novara. No more successful was Franciszek Sznajde who led the revolutionary forces in the Bavarian Palatinate. The only officer to enhance his reputation was Ludwik Mierosławski, commander-in-chief of the abortive rising in 1846, commander of the Poznanian levies in 1848, commander of the Sicilian army until he was forced to flee in May 1849, and finally the leader of the Baden rebels against a combined army of Prussian, Bavarian and Federal troops. Mierosławski won an international reputation as one of the leading revolutionary soldiers of the age, a name to cause a shudder of fear in the spines of Polish conservatives, a Polish Mazzini and Garibaldi in one person.

The largest single effort made by the Poles was in Hungary. Galicia had been flooded with refugees from the Kingdom of Poland and *émigrés* from France expecting action and ready to fight, but the National Council in Lvov would not step beyond the limits of legality and itself ceased to exist at the beginning of November 1848. Two leading Polish generals in emigration, Dembiński and Bem, threw in their lot with the Magyars, and likewise Józef Wysocki, a military expert of the Polish Democratic Society. A large number of Poles were induced to cross over into Hungary and form Polish units. The Magyars were not entirely certain of them, because the Poles as Slavs might have some reservations in fighting to secure a Magyar domination. There were moreover political differences among the Poles, the right quarrelling with the left. Nevertheless, the Polish legionaries in the service of Hungary fought well enough to be regarded as the nucleus of a Polish national army. Nicholas I had watched the German situation carefully, though as early as April 1848 Meyendorff in Berlin had advised him that there was no real threat to the western frontier.[1] By 1849 it was safe for Russia to adopt a forward policy, Germany being relatively quiescent and the Principalities under control. Intervention in Hungary had the double advantage of removing the

[1] *Briefswechsel*, II, 65.

dangerous Polish legion from the political scene and restoring the power of Austria, which could then be turned once more to the Germanic Confederation. The compact of Nicholas I and Francis Joseph of 21 May 1849 and the surrender of the Hungarian forces under Görgey at Világos to the Russian army under Paskevich on 13 August 1849 marked the end of all Polish hopes of salvation from the European revolution of 1848.

The experience of 1848 was to convince conservatives and moderates everywhere that the best course for Poland was to work within the confines of legality. The events of 1848 confirmed the feelings which followed the disaster of 1846 that 'organic work', the laying of the material foundations of future independence, would yield more than futile insurrections. In Poznania August Cieszkowski formed his Polish League on 25 June 1848 in accordance with the proposals he had made at Breslau, professing its policy to be the peaceful pursuit of Polish independence. Two hundred and forty-six local branches were established in Prussian Poland, but in March 1850 the government issued a decree forbidding all centralized associations. Without central direction the Polish League lost its sense of purpose.[1] The Prussian government kept up its administrative pressure to discipline the Poles. The provincial president in Poznań, Beuermann, began in February 1850 to issue a newsletter, 'Friend of the Peasants', to combat the League's own paper for peasants, 'The Greater Pole' (*Wielkopolanin*), and began to sow discontent in the countryside against the *szlachta*. On 1 July 1850 a Prussian decree suppressed the Polish opposition press, including not only *Wielkopolanin*, but also *Gazeta Poznańska* and *Przegląd Poznański*. In 1848 there had been some landed proprietors who had threatened to evict peasants renting portions of their estates if they stayed faithful to the King of Prussia: 'Go to your king and let him give you your keep if you are so faithful to him!'[2] By 1850 they were anxious for loans from the Poznanian credit institution, the *Landschaft*, but it was not until 1858 that limited credit facilities were again placed at

---

[1] For details see W. Jakóbczyk, 'Cieszkowski i Liga Polska', *Przegląd Historyczny*, XXXVIII (1948), pp. 137 ff.

[2] Cf. W. Jakóbczyk, 'Z dziejów pruskiej propagandy w Poznańskiem', *Roczniki Historyczne*, XIX (1950), p. 186n.

their disposal, with the consequence that between 1848 and 1860 489,000 morgs of land passed out of Polish hands into the possession of Germans. When Prince William, however, assumed the regency, he ordered a cessation of electoral pressure, with the result that by 1864 as many as twenty-six Polish members were returned to the Prussian parliament. Some intellectual freedom was allowed again in December 1858. The Poznań 'Association of the Friends of Learning' (Towarzystwo Przyjaciół Nauk) was founded by Count Tytus Działyński, while Hipolit Cegielski undertook the publication of *Dziennik Poznański*. The more liberal *régime* found the Poles less willing to risk political adventures. In 1858 two revolutionary addresses were published, but the Polish deputy, Walery Niegolewski, showed that they were the work of *agents provocateurs* and succeeded in proving that the police chief, Bärensprung, was involved in their production. There was even a revival of sentimental friendship for the Poles among the Germans. When in February 1863 Bismarck proposed to aid Russia in her task of suppressing rebellion in the Congress Kingdom, 246 out of 303 deputies to the Prussian parliament recorded their votes against this policy. There was little thought that the Poles presented a threat to Germanism in the east.

The situation was the same in Galicia, except for the complication of the agrarian question. Stadion's hasty decree of April 1848 and not the law for the rest of the Austrian dominions, which had passed through the parliament of 1848, provided the basis of the settlement in Galicia. The Polish landlords were anxious to secure compensation for themselves in a form which would do least harm to the agricultural economy. In April 1849 a delegation of four landed proprietors was invited by Bach to Vienna to discuss the terms of a final settlement,[1] but in the background lurked the Uniate priest, Litvinovich, representing the claims of the Ruthenians. The Poles would have liked the peasants themselves to be responsible for the payment of redemption dues, for that might have been a means of compelling them to continue to work on the demesnes and

---

[1] For the papers of the leading member, Kraiński, see S. Inglot, 'Maurycego Kraińskiego Regesty materiałów do historii zniesienia stosunku poddańczego w Galicji', *Archiwum Komisji Historycznej* (Serja 2-ga), IV (XVI) (Cracow, 1948).

even presented possibilities of evicting them, if ever they fell into arrears, but Litvinovich reminded them of the real state of affairs in the province. He declared that payments by the peasants to the landlords after the promise of the Emperor that they would be given complete freedom from the manor 'would lead to a bloody revolution, which the whole of the Austrian army would not be able to crush'. For all the Polish protests the decree of Stadion was allowed to stand and the peasants were confirmed in their rights.

Politically the Galician Poles were disorganized after 1848. In Cracow an aristocratic group favoured collaboration with a federal Austria, but the centralist Bach showed not the slightest interest in courting it and even imprisoned its leader, Adam Potocki, for eight months in 1851–2. In Lvov Prince Adam Sapieha rejected the policy of collaboration propounded through the Cracow newspaper, *Czas*, and recommended instead that the Poles should make themselves strong economically through the Savings Bank, the Land Credit Society, the Agricultural School and railway construction. The leaders of the Lvov bourgeoisie, Smolka and Ziemiałkowski, continued to put forward, though without much hope, the middle-class demands for equality and freedom. It mattered little what any Polish group said, because none was likely to obtain a hearing. In these circumstances an unusual degree of initiative was enjoyed by the new provincial governor, Agenor Gołuchowski, who had an opportunity to put into practice his view that only complete and absolute obedience to the government could serve the Polish cause. During the passage of the Russian army through Galicia in 1849 to enter Hungary he was largely responsible for the provision of supplies. Bach never trusted Gołuchowski completely, but Gołuchowski's conviction was that real power lay with the Emperor and that the ultimate goal was an alliance between the Galician Poles and the throne. Every effort was made to represent the Ruthenians as untrustworthy. When the Crimean War began it was easier for Austrian statesmen to think of the Ruthenians as potential allies of Russia and the Poles as friends. From this time onwards the vexed question of woods and pastures, left untouched by Stadion's decree, began to be resolved in favour of the landlords. In arbitration disputes no peasants were admitted to the courts and out of 30,000 suits only a few hundred were solved in their favour. In the course of time, though 70 per cent of the arable land passed into the possession of the peasants, only 0·7 per cent of the woods and pastures were given to them. There were in Galicia 500,000 small holdings absolutely dependent upon them. The Galician landlords were able to exert enough influence over the peasants by threatening to exclude them from the pastures to be certain of securing an endless supply of cheap labour.

In the crisis of 1859 the Bach centralist system itself was discredited and the dynasty presented with the alternatives, either of bringing the German middle class into the government, for they would have preserved centralism, or of forming an alliance with the regional aristocracies. It was the latter course which Francis Joseph at first preferred and Gołuchowski himself was called to Vienna as minister of state to devise a solution. The October Patent of 1860 proposed a central Reichsrath to deal with common affairs and local diets to advise the provincial administrations, but foreign affairs were reserved to the monarch. Some concession was made to Hungarian separatism by the establishment of a *Large Quorum* to deal with all affairs including those affecting Hungary, and of a *Small Quorum* for business which did not concern her. This system, however, broke down under the Magyars' demand for the constitution of 1848 and complete separation. In consequence Gołuchowski was dismissed and the October Patent replaced by Schmerling's February Patent of 1861, with its emphasis upon a two-chamber central parliament. Local diets, elected under a system of four curias, the landlords, the capitalists, the middle class and the peasants, were to deal with provincial affairs outside the cognizance of parliament. In general Schmerling favoured the interests of the landlords or the Germans, but in Galicia 50 per cent of the mandates were given to the peasants, who were regarded as Austrian loyalists opposed to complete local autonomy. Gołuchowski's deeply laid schemes had come to nothing. The Polish deputies in Vienna adhered to the autonomist point of view when the Reichsrath met in April 1861, but were isolated by the Hungarian refusal to attend. The Ruthenians, however, joined Schmerling's centralist majority and were rewarded with the appointment of a new viceroy, Mensdorff-Pouilly, who made a series of concessions to their national claims. In 1862 two chairs in the Ruthenian language were established in Lvov where there was no chair of Polish. An order was given that in the eastern districts of Galicia officials should make themselves acquainted with Ruthenian. The question of woods and pastures had gone so far that there was small likelihood of a reconciliation between landlords and peasants. So strained were relations that at the meeting of the Galician diet in April 1861 Count Adam Potocki actually proposed that a declaration be made that on no account would labour services be reintroduced. Galicia had too many problems of her own to consider the wider question of Polish independence.

Only in Congress Poland and western Russia did the spirit of resistance to partition survive. The defeatism which pervaded all the educated classes of the community in Poznania and Galicia was absent from Poland under the dominion of Russia. Instead there was a cowed submission under which lay a smouldering resentment. The disappointments of 1848 had been felt and the same lessons drawn as in Prussian and Austrian Poland, but the absence of personal experience of defeat and after 1856 the belief that Tsarist autocracy could be forced to release its hold upon Poland encouraged once more the growth of revolutionary feeling. It was in Congress Poland that the Poles were to offer their most resolute challenge to foreign occupation.

CHAPTER II

Poland under Russian Dominion: the Social Question

THE long weary years between 1832, when the Organic Statute for the Kingdom of Poland was promulgated, and the crisis of 1861, which brought the Marquis Alexander Wielopolski into the administration, seem at first sight to contain little of note. The Viceroy, Paskevich, ruled the Kingdom with an iron hand and scant regard for the wishes of the *szlachta*. The Polish political class was expected to give unquestioning obedience to the commands of the administration. The stagnation of these years, however, should not be taken for an absence of important developments within the Kingdom. It was a period when the old structure of Polish society began to break up. Expansion of trade and industry began to produce more modern conditions. The Jews were seeking to throw off the shackles of social inferiority. The Christian middle class was developing aspirations of its own. Above all, agriculture was beginning to rid itself of labour services. Polish society in the Kingdom and to the east in parts of Lithuania was undergoing the strains and stresses of transition from one form of social organization to another. It was against the background of these events that the crisis of 1861 arose and the insurrection of 1863 broke out. The Polish revolt of 1863 was not only a struggle against Russian occupation, but also a contest to determine the direction which future Polish political and economic development should take.

In 1831–2 began the process of whittling away all institutions which in any way gave the Kingdom of Poland a Polish character. The separate Polish army, the Alexander University in Warsaw and the constitution of 1815 were suppressed. In place of the constitution was promulgated the Organic Statute of 1832.[1] The Statute was never put into operation in its entirety, but its provisions were none the less important, because in future years appeal was to be made to them. At the top was the Council of State, through which must pass all projects of decrees. The general direction of the government was in the hands of the Administrative Council, of which the Viceroy was chairman. The three main departments of state were the Commissions of Finance, Justice and, most important, Internal Affairs, which controlled the police, the church and education. Laws were henceforth promulated in the form of Ukazy. It was laid down that the *szlachta* might from time to time be called to assemblies in individual provinces and districts, ostensibly to discuss matters which had formerly come before the central diet, but in practice these assemblies never met. This provision seems to have been inserted only to enable the Tsar to plead that he had not contravened the implications of the Final Act of the treaty of Vienna, which stipulated, though vaguely, that there should be some form of national representation in partitioned Poland. At first there was no attempt to bring about an assimilation with the Russian Empire, but gradually it was made plain that the Kingdom would cease to be an entirely independent administrative unit. In December 1839 the first step was taken in this direction. The educational system was placed under the administration of the Curator of the Warsaw Education Region, which in its turn was dependent upon St. Petersburg for its orders.[2] In December 1841 the Polish *złoty* was replaced by the Russian rouble, though Polish money continued to circulate. At the same time the Council of State was abolished and its place taken by the Ninth and Tenth Departments of the Russian Senate, which were given the task of framing laws for the Kingdom and controlling the Polish judiciary.[3] In 1842 the administrative system was reformed and in 1844 the eight provinces, or *województwa*, officially termed *gubernii* since March 1837, were reduced to five *gubernii*.[4] The one concession which

---

[1] For the text of both these documents see *British and Foreign State Papers*, 19 (1831-2).

[2] *Dziennik Praw Królestwa Polskiego*, XXIV, 232-53.

[3] *Ibid.*, XXVII, 330-45.   [4] *Ibid.*, XXXIV, 452-9.

Nicholas I made before his death was the appointment in 1851 of a marshal of the nobility for each of the *gubernii*, with the right to present petitions, but this was a privilege of which they did not avail themselves. Under this system the Kingdom enjoyed peace and tranquillity. There were many Russian officers, when later the Poles became vociferous, who looked back to the rule of Paskevich with regret and who argued that there was only one possible system of government in the Kingdom, military dictatorship. That policy, however, could no longer apply in the changed circumstances which followed the peace of Paris in 1856.

The defeat of Russia in the Crimean War altered the situation completely. The military monarchy had been judged by its own standards and found wanting. Though Alexander II bore a close resemblance to his father, Nicholas I, he could not continue to govern Russia under the old system. If Russia was to regain her international influence reform would have to be undertaken. Reform within Russia required a modification of the policy to be adopted towards the western frontier. The forward foreign policy of Alexander I and Nicholas I was clearly an impossibility after 1856. Russia did not cease to be interested in western and central Europe, but she could no longer dominate Germany. Her isolation required that she find an ally lest she be exposed once again to attack in the south. Prussia was a broken reed, but an understanding with the disreputable *régime* of Napoleon III seemed to offer a way out of Russia's difficulties for the time being at least. The desultory negotiations, culminating in the uneasy entente with France of 3 March 1859,[1] had some influence in their turn upon the Polish situation. The state of French opinion was such that the Russian government was compelled to show some deference to its exaggeratedly pro-Polish sentiments. The semi-tyrannical system of Nicholas I and Paskevich could no longer be maintained, if the entente with France were to be made a reality. At the same time a contented Poland was necessary for the smooth execution of reforms within Russia. The abolition of serfdom would undoubtedly cause grave misgivings among the Russian gentry and arouse intense

[1] See B. H. Sumner, 'The Secret Franco-Russian Treaty of 3 March 1859', *English Historical Review*, XLVIII (1933).

dissatisfaction among the peasants. Any reform of serf conditions would have to be favourable enough to the peasants to prevent a jacquerie, but at the same time sufficiently unfavourable to retain the political loyalties of the gentry. There was every likelihood that there would be widespread disturbances in the Empire when the decree of emancipation was promulgated. This emergency could be met only by the disciplined regiments of long-service soldiers, who had lost all contact with the soil. In these circumstances there could be no thought of a fresh conscription in the Empire, because conscription would create discontents in the countryside precisely at the moment when reform was in the air. Half-trained peasant levies were in any case not the best material with which to suppress agrarian disorders. It followed therefore that the First Army based upon Warsaw, formerly the spearhead of Russian intervention in central Europe, should, if it were required, be able to send units into the Empire to guard against disturbances, which in its turn meant that fewer men would be available to meet the dangers of a nationalist movement in the Kingdom.

It seemed logical in the light of Russia's general position that with the death of Paskevich in 1856 a milder system of government should be introduced in the Kingdom and Lithuania. In December 1855 Vladimir Nazimov had been appointed to the governor-generalcy of Vilna, with authority over the four *gubernii* of Vilna, Grodno, Kovno and Minsk and a general direction to pursue a conciliatory policy. Paskevich's successor in the Kingdom was Mikhail Dmitrievich Gorchakov, the defender of Sebastopol and cousin of Alexander Gorchakov, who succeeded Nesselrode at the Russian foreign office in April 1856. Mikhail Gorchakov's appointment augured well for the Poles, because he had the reputation of being an honest and fairminded man and was undoubtedly inclined to leniency, but Russia was, in spite of her weakness, not under pressure to hasten reform. Alexander had declared in favour of reform in his address to the Moscow nobility on 30 March 1856, but he offered his opinion that 'it is far better that it should come from above than below', which supposed that the government still had the initiative. The limit of Alexander II's readiness to make concessions in the Polish areas was at first the removal of useless irritants. The speech of the Tsar to the Marshals of the Polish nobility in the Kingdom on 23 May 1856, during his visit to Warsaw, was an indication that the Poles would discover that only practical solutions could find an acceptance in St. Petersburg. No encouragement was given to the idea that the Kingdom might be enlarged by the inclusion of western Russian provinces within its boundaries. There was no promise even of the restoration of the constitution of 1815. The Tsar demanded co-operation and warned the Marshals against daydreams: ' . . . C'est à Vous, Messieurs, de me faciliter ma tâche, mais je Vous le répète, point de rêveries, point de rêveries.'[1] Alexander's words no doubt gave some offence and were presented as an insult to the Polish nation, but the Polish nation in the past had suffered much more than a stern speech from a Tsar and could well afford to wait to see what might emerge. Alexander's speech to the Moscow nobility was a plea for co-operation between the upper classes and the dynasty in defence of the social order. His speech in Warsaw amounted, though in different circumstances, to an identical proposal. When Gorchakov assumed the duties of Viceroy and commander-in-chief of the First Army in March 1856, it was revealed that at last there was an administration in the Kingdom opened to persuasion at least from the upper classes. Gorchakov was willing to seek advice and serve the interests of the Polish landed gentry. Within a year considerable progress had been made towards a reconciliation with the upper classes. Evidently Gorchakov sought to associate Andrzej Zamoyski, the leading figure in the Kingdom, with the government of the country by referring to him difficult questions for his consideration and advice. Mansfield, the British consul-general, who was always carefully fed with information concerning political developments by the leading Polish landlords, reported that:

my friend Count André Zamoyski, in discovering the importance of such reference, said he could not take the responsibility of making recommendations involving the welfare of his countrymen without being allowed to consult some of them. To this proposition no exception was taken and the consequence is that no measure of any weight

[1] H. Lisicki, *Aleksander Wielopolski* (Cracow, 1878), II, 17.

is initiated by the government without being in the first instance discussed by a committee in Count Zamoyski's house.[1]

The Polish aristocracy came to occupy the privileged position of having access to the counsels of the Viceroy, but without having to bear the odium of being open collaborators. In this situation there was little reason to press for constitutional change. Any extension of the right to discuss important questions would mean the consultation of wider interests than their own. The way was open for the pursuit of the policy of 'organic work', the building up of Poland's economic and material resources for the future.

The relaxation of tension proceeded slowly. Alexander II marked his visit to Poland by the grant of an amnesty to political offenders both in the Kingdom and in the former eastern provinces of historic Poland. Poles were at last admitted to posts in the Imperial administration, which seemed to put an end to their ostracism in Russia. A long-standing grievance was remedied in November 1856 when Fijałkowski was appointed to the Archbishopric of Warsaw, which in spite of the concordat Nicholas I had chosen to leave vacant. A charter was issued for the establishment in the Kingdom of an 'Agricultural Society' in November 1857, the object of which was to provide an open forum of discussion for the improvement of farming techniques, though not initially to consider the economic aspects of tenurial reform or bring labour services to an end. The government went half-way towards restoring the intellectual life of Warsaw; the Alexander University was not revived, but in June 1857 a medical school was established to train physicians. The attitude of the Russian authorities, reflecting that of the Polish partisans of 'organic work', was that the Poles might with profit devote themselves to serving the material interests of their country, but there would be no concessions to forms of education or to institutions which tended to give them politically undesirable notions of their own distinct national character.

Indeed the Kingdom of Poland, the artificial creation of the Vienna Treaty, shut off from the sea, backward and in parts even primitive, was not a country in which all classes of

---

[1] F.O. 65/502, Mansfield to Clarendon, 26 July 1857.

the community lived in idyllic harmony. The social system inherited from the era of the Polish Republic was more complex than many Poles would have cared to admit. The statistics available for 1859 reveal an extreme diversity of race and religion. Out of a total population of 4,764,446 persons of both sexes, 3,648,261 were Slavs, 260,966 Germans, 249,947 native Lithuanians and 599,875 Jews; there were, besides, small communities of Dutchmen, Englishmen, Frenchmen, Italians, Greeks, Tartars and gipsies, but these cannot be considered a serious factor. From the point of view of religious denominations the Christian population was composed of 3,657,140 Catholics, 215,967 Uniates, 274,707 Lutherans, 4,189 Calvinists and 4,856 Orthodox, apart from a number of minor protestant sects. While in normal circumstances race and religion might have been a determining factor in political consciousness, the low level of education and widespread illiteracy offered a serious hindrance to the spread of interest in public affairs. There were 122,393 persons estimated to have received a higher education and 784,520 who could read and write, but 3,857,533 were completely illiterate. In the whole Kingdom there were 1,437 educational establishments of all kinds, at which 82,209 pupils were under instruction, of which 834 schools and 46,350 pupils fell within the *gubernia* of Warsaw, the most prosperous part of the Kingdom. Yet even within the city of Warsaw with its population of 161,361 there were 65,660 illiterates against 74,162 with an elementary and 21,539 with a higher education. In the countryside the peasant population was almost entirely illiterate. In fact, the old distinction between the Polish nation and the Polish people, for which there are two Polish words, *naród* and *lud*, the one politically conscious and the other indifferent to the national cause, still held good.

Polish feeling tended to show considerable emotional solidarity, but this could hardly be shared by the Jews, who formed so large a part of the urban population. There had been little progress towards merging the Jews with the Polish nation, which would greatly have strengthened the national movement. In 1859 1,164,487 persons were called townspeople, of whom 653,307 were Christians and 511,180 Jews. Out of 161,361 persons in Warsaw there were 42,639 Jews. In some provincial towns the proportion of Jews was much higher. Lublin had a population of 18,304, of whom 10,413 were Jews, while in Suwałki there were 7,525 Jews out of a total of 11,930. The importance of conciliating the Jews was considerable, because in the Kingdom, besides Warsaw, there were only six other towns with over 10,000 inhabitants which had substantial Christian populations; many persons classed as bourgeoisie were in fact peasants living in places traditionally described as towns, but long since decayed into villages. A section of the Jews was ready to extend the hand of friendship to the Poles.[1] There was always a certain willingness among the less fanatical Jews to seek some accommodation with the Christian community and in the 1850's a westernizing element in Warsaw, prominent in the city's commercial life, was attempting to induce Jews to abandon the conception of their own separateness. Unfortunately, anti-Jewish feeling was strong among the Poles and did not decline as the nineteenth century progressed and Christians entered into competition with Jewish traders. At one end of the social scale was the blank, fanatical catholicism of the illiterate working class, which could easily produce a pogrom. In 1857, when a comet was falsely predicted for 13 June, some priests gave out that the end of the world was at hand and troops had to be posted to guard the Jewish quarter of Warsaw, lest working men, anxious to ensure their passage into heaven, should seek to purchase it by a massacre of the Jews. No comet appeared and the crisis passed, but the British consul was not the less impressed by the anxiety which the rumour had caused: 'It is curious to observe in the 19th century a movement and its consequences which remind us forcibly of the dark period of the middle ages.'[2] In the little town of Turek near Kalisz the opposition of the Christian population to repair of the synagogue resulted in three days' rioting during August 1857, which had to be put down by a cossack hundred.[3]

The educated classes, however, were not free from petty anti-Jewish prejudices. The newspaper, *Gazeta Warszawska*, which

[1] For a discussion of intellectual trends in the Polish Jewish community see M. Bałaban, ' Żydzi w powstaniu 1863 r.', *Przegląd Historyczny*, xxxiv (1937–8), pp. 564–99.

[2] F.O. 65/502, Mansfield to Clarendon, 14 June 1857.

[3] W. Przyborowski, *Historya dwóch lat*, i, 234–5.

was read by the *szlachta* of the Kingdom, took a strongly anti-
Jewish line and in January 1859 made some criticism in bad
taste of the Jews, who retaliated by getting articles published
in the Continental press defending their position, including one
in *L'Observateur Belge* in March 1859 under the title of 'The per-
secution of the Jews in Poland by the Party of the Jesuits'. The
editor of *Gazeta Warszawska*, Lesznowski, sued the group of
Jews responsible on the grounds of libel and secured terms of
imprisonment against them of three to four months. The police,
fearing disturbances, forbade articles dealing with the Jewish
question, while the conservative daily in Cracow, *Czas*, refused
to print Lesznowski's apologia. Nevertheless, he found space in
the St. Petersburg *Słowo*, published by a young Pole, Józefat
Ohryszko, but the Imperial government promptly closed down
Słowo for printing anti-Semitic material and imprisoned
Ohryszko, an action which earned it some criticism for interference with the freedom of the press. The Warsaw capitalist,
Leopold Kronenberg, himself a Christian convert from Juda-
ism, was so alarmed by this affair that he bought the paper,
Gazeta Codzienna, to promote the idea of co-operation between
Jews and Poles and induced one of the greatest writers of the
day, J. I. Kraszewski, to come to Warsaw from Zhytomir to be
its editor. *Gazeta Warszawska*, alarmed by the appearance of a
powerful competitor, adopted the attitude that Kraszewski had
sold himself to the Jews. In consequence, when Kraszewski
applied for membership of the Agricultural Society, he was rejected by the anti-Jewish majority among the gentry who
composed it.

It was not merely sneers and prejudice with which the Jews
had to contend. Jews were still subject to a number of frustrat-
ing disabilities. There was some question whether the old rules
governing their place of residence were still in force. There
were 246 towns in which there were no restrictions, but in 207
others it could be maintained that residence was a privilege
and not a right. In ninety towns Christians claimed the right
to refuse a Jew residence, while in thirty-one Jews were obliged
to live in a special quarter. In 111 towns in the frontier zone,
reckoned to be twenty-one vorsts from the frontier line, Jews
from other areas might not settle at all. The Jews hotly con-

tested the old *De non tolerandis Judaeis* clauses, which they claimed had been abolished in the former Prussian areas in 1802 and never upheld in those towns which had formerly been part of Austrian Western Galicia. Equally annoying were the special taxes on Jews, including the tax on Jewish drink shops, the payment by provincial Jews of a residence fee to enable them to stay in Warsaw, and the tax on kosher meat. Politically the Jews had no rights. They could not enter the service of the state, except in a subordinate capacity on the completion of military service. In the former Prussian areas it was still held that the legal procedure of 1796 was in force, under which a Jew could not be a witness in a criminal case where the penalty exceeded six weeks' imprisonment or a fine of fifty thalers. The Russian Director of Internal Affairs, Mukhanov, was unsympathetic to reform, preferring to leave matters where they were. The Jews therefore had legitimate grievances, which invited the attention of enlightened Poles.[1]

There was a certain narrow nationalism among the Polish educated classes inherited from the epoch when Poland had been a great state. The Poles considered themselves superior to the Jews and to the Russians, or Moskale (Muscovites) as they preferred to call them. In Russia Poles were educated in Russian schools and went to Russian universities, where they came to admire Russian vigour and share in the aspirations of the younger generation. In Warsaw in a more purely Polish atmosphere it was difficult to see any good in the Russians, who were too often army officers or unco-operative officials. The Russians were represented as belonging to the Mongolian east, untutored and barbaric. Andrzej Zamoyski, who became chairman of the Agricultural Society, was adept at scoring off the Russians; on the occasion of the Society's inaugural banquet he replied to Mukhanov's toast of 'Aimons-nous!' with the jibe 'Oui, chacun chez soi!' Zamoyski was indeed full of vague phrases which sounded well to Poles, like 'I sense Poland in the air!' Stray remarks of this kind confirmed in the minds of his listeners their belief in the purity of his patriotism. Endowed with a certain handsome austerity Andrzej Zamoyski was the darling of the

---

[1] For a Jewish point of view see O. L. Lubliner, *De la condition politique et civile des Juifs dans le royaume de Pologne* (Brussels, 1860).

szlachta. The same could not be said of the Marquis Alexander Wielopolski, whose political intentions were hardly different from those of Zamoyski. A semi-recluse, Wielopolski brooded on his estates for years upon the best tactics for Poland. For him the supposition that the resurrection of Poland was at hand was idle nonsense and in 1846 he had pronounced in favour of collaboration with Russia in his *Letter* to Prince Metternich, but he had no conception of the emotional appeals likely to attract political support. One *cause célèbre* brought down upon him very great unpopularity. Konstanty Świdziński, a deputy to the diet in 1830–1, who had turned to academic pursuits, left his collection of manuscripts to Wielopolski in his will. Wielopolski decided that it should be housed on his estate at Chrobierz, near the town of Pinczów, instead of at Warsaw, where the materials would be more easily accessible to scholars. Immediately the Świdziński family was in arms to contest the will. The lawsuit became symbolic of the struggle between progressive nationalists and die-hard feudalists. No less offensive to the national spirit was the decision of Wielopolski to send his son, Zygmunt, to serve in the Imperial army. Indeed, many thousands of Poles had worn Russian uniform and some of them are acknowledged as the most resolute of patriots, but the same indulgence was not granted to members of the Polish aristocracy. Memories of the Confederation of Targowica, when the reactionary aristocracy had betrayed Poland, were so strong that Wielopolski's policy of courting Russia was viewed only in the worst possible light. The Agricultural Society won cheap popularity by refusing to accept Wielopolski's son as a member in his father's place on the flimsy grounds that he was not technically a landed proprietor, an act interpreted to mean that the *szlachta* did not think Wielopolski had the best interests of Poland at heart. Even before the crisis of 1861 the Polish gentry had entangled their material interests with their emotions. Fidelity to an unwritten code of national ethics prevented them from accepting without reservation the logical consequence of 'organic work', frank political co-operation with the occupying power. The agrarian problem was the rock on which they were to founder.

Of all the questions which beset the Kingdom of Poland and

the former Polish provinces incorporated in western Russia none was more acute than the condition of the peasantry. The peasant, oppressed by the landlord, rewarded him with cordial dislike. Everywhere the memory of the Galician massacres of 1846 was fresh in the minds of the Polish gentry, who had much to fear from the peasantry, whether Polish, White Russian or Ruthenian. It was equally true that a solution of the agrarian question raised grave difficulties for the Russian government.

Conditions were not uniform in Russia. Some landlords were in favour of reform in order to permit the growth of capitalist farming, while others for want of money preferred delay. In the more remote areas there were owners of estates who could see improvement only in the increase of existing obligations. A compromise had therefore to be found which would reconcile these conflicting interests, without at the same time stirring the peasants to revolt. Extreme caution was necessary in the Polish areas lest a social explosion call into question the validity of Russia's western frontier and produce international complications. At the height of his power Nicholas I had shirked the issue of peasant reform. A secret committee established in March 1835 had recommended a three-stage programme of liberation. In the first instance, labour services were to be limited to three days a week, after which the government was to proceed to the next step by which the peasant was to be tied not to the person of the lord, but to the land itself. The final stage of reform was to be the complete emancipation of the peasant with the right to rent land from the lord. This meant nothing more than emancipation without land, a proposal so fraught with danger that Nicholas I dissolved the committee at the beginning of 1836.

Instead, an indirect approach was adopted. On 11 May 1836 was established the Fifth Echelon of the Imperial Chancery, which in 1838 was transformed into the Ministry of State Properties. The government hoped that by reorganizing its own lands, upon which one-third of the rural population was settled, it would be able through its example to set in motion evolutionary reforms on the private estates, but the general result of its activity was only to bring the state peasants under the closer control of officialdom and arouse as many discontents as it sought to appease. In November 1839 a fresh committee was appointed under Prince Vasilchikov, in which Count Kiselev was the most important figure, to consider once more the problem of reform on private lands. The timidity of the government is shown by the secrecy with which the committee's discussions were surrounded; it was given out that it intended to consider labour services on the state lands in the western *gubernii*, where in any case the interests of Russian landlords were not seriously affected. Kiselev adhered to the principle that the landlord's title to the soil could not be invalidated, but that the peasants had the right to rent land. Among other things he insisted upon a clear definition of peasant duties and an exact measurement of holdings; houses and movable property should belong to the peasants, who were to have the right of appeal to the courts. Even these limited proposals met with opposition in the committee and gave rise to rumours beyond official circles. To prevent speculation Nicholas I in February 1841 told the committee that he did not intend to give support to Kiselev's projects and that he considered that the wishes of the landlords should be the basis of the committee's deliberations. On 11 April 1842 he told the Council of State that he had no intention of freeing the peasants, because in the existing situation of the 1840's social reform could cause only unrest; he was moreover at pains to affirm the principle that the soil belonged to the gentry. The limit of the government's action was the ukaz of 14 April 1842, which permitted landlords to make agreements with their peasants for the lease of lands, which, in effect, meant that the question was shelved. It was hardly likely that Alexander II on his accession would be able from the outset to show greater resolution than his father. The position of the dynasty was not undermined, but it was at least shaken by defeat in the Crimean War.

The proposal of partnership between the crown and the gentry contained in Alexander II's speech to the Moscow nobility on 30 March 1856 did not meet with an immediate response. A means had to be found of familiarizing the Russian landlords with the problems of reform. If co-operation was to be found at all, it was to come from the areas which were socially and economically the more advanced. Those parts of the empire which were ready to adopt a new system of agriculture lay near the markets for produce, especially in the west, in the governor-generalcy of Vilna, and beyond it in the Kingdom of Poland. Here the gentry was not Russian, but Polish, constituting a source of not only internal discontents, but also of diplomatic repercussions.

One Polish institution in the Kingdom of Poland had not been suppressed by Russia and that was the *Code Napoléon*, adopted in the Duchy of Warsaw in 1807 and retained by Alexander I in 1815 as the basis of the Kingdom's legal system.[1] The *Code Napoléon* recognized only two conditions of land tenure, owner-ship and tenancy, and ignored the undoubted belief of the pea-sants that they had a right to the soil, of which they might not be deprived if they rendered their dues to the lord. The Prussian government, when it was restored to possession of the Poznan-ian area in 1815, at first wavered, but in the end restored Prus-sian common law in place of the *Code*. Under Prussian law peasants were assured fixity of tenure, though the subsequent decree of liquidation of 1823 for the Grand Duchy of Posen was not without disadvantages to the smaller peasants. In Galicia fixity of tenure had been upheld ever since the eighteenth century, which to some extent accounts for the trust which the peasants there placed in the Austrian imperial government and the rewards they obtained in 1846 and 1848. The landlords of the Congress Kingdom, therefore, were more favourably placed with regard to their peasants than landlords elsewhere in the Polish areas. The *Code Napoléon*, offering the power of eviction to the landlord, seemed the maximum which the gentry might hope for in the Russian Empire itself. The one restriction upon the landlords of Congress Poland was their lack of capital, which prevented them from taking full advantage of their legal rights. They were, moreover, deterred by the fear of a violent peasant reaction if they had recourse to eviction, for the peasants accepted the theory of the *Code Napoléon* as unwil-lingly as the Irish peasants accepted the English landlord-tenant system. Fixity of tenure was the immediate need of the peasants and the reform they most desired was the grant of a

[1] Cf. R. F. Leslie, *Polish Politics and the Revolution of November 1830* (London, 1956), chapter ii, where this question is discussed at length.

freehold, which would sever once and for all the connection of village and manor. Nicholas I had had an excellent opportunity in 1831, after the pacification of the Kingdom, to settle the agrarian question in favour of the peasant farmers, but he refused to accept it. Instead he ordered that the peasants, who had ceased to perform their services, should resume their normal duties towards the landlord.[1] The question remained unsolved. After the promulgation of the Organic Statute it became clear that the Polish *szlachta* would no longer be considered partners of the government and that in the absence of political activity there was little to occupy their time except the administration of their estates. It was natural in this situation that they should attempt to increase their income by the introduction of more efficient methods. No legal obstacles stood in their way to prevent their rearranging the peasant holdings and consolidating the demesne.

The intermingling of the demesne and the peasant lands was a hindrance to better cultivation of the soil. It meant, as it did in the English open-field village of the eighteenth century, that production was determined by the standards of the peasant farmers. Where peasant services were employed, labour was slack and inefficient. The ideal solution was to separate the lands of the manor and the village and to dispense altogether with labour services, but theory and practice were difficult to combine. Conversion to capitalist farming meant the construction of new farm buildings, the purchase of draught animals and the use of modern implements, which the poverty-stricken gentry lacked the money to buy. Most estates were heavily encumbered as a result of injudicious speculation during the Napoleonic wars and the costs of reconstruction after the passage of the armies across Polish territory in 1812–13. Only the aristocracy with very large estates could afford to undertake experiments. Equally difficult was the problem of peasant tenures. Eviction was possible, but it was a two-edged weapon. Estates needed labour of two kinds, permanent farm-workers and seasonal labour. There was a danger, if evictions were carried

---

[1] *Dziennik Praw Królestwa Polskiego*, XIII, 227–34. Cf. also H. Grynwaser, *Kwestia agrarna i ruch włościan w pierwszej połowie xix wieku (1807–1860)*, Pisma (Wrocław, 1951), II, chapter iv.

to extremes, that there would not be enough labour for hay-making and harvest. There were therefore good reasons for keeping enough labour on estates, because an abundance of seasonal labour would depress wage levels and save the manor considerable expense. Evictions, moreover, were likely to lead to peasant risings. Thus for economic and political reasons the landed gentry of the Kingdom of Poland were inclined to approach the agrarian question with some caution.

The questions of tenures and labour services were closely connected. Labour services might be commuted and a rent substituted in their place, or the rights of the manor might be bought out and the peasant become the owner of his farm. There were therefore two words for economic emancipation, *oczynszowanie*, conversion to rents, and *uwłaszczenie*, conversion to freeholds. From the point of view of the landlords, for whom the *Code Napoléon* was so advantageous, there was much to recommend conversion to rents, because this solution would seem to substantiate their claim that they were the absolute owners of the soil. The rents which they derived from the peasant would furnish them with the capital for the employment of wage labour and the reconstruction of the demesne economy, while at the same time it would compel the peasants themselves to offer their labour in order to obtain money with which to pay the rents. The fixing of rents naturally offered some difficulties because there was a limit to the amount the peasant was prepared to pay, but on the whole there were solid advantages to be obtained from this solution.

Conversion to freeholds was not as attractive to the landed proprietors, but even here they could extract something for themselves. It was essential that the peasant should himself be obliged to pay the redemption dues, both because this would provide the manor with capital for reconstruction and because the necessity of finding ready money would compel the villagers to continue furnishing the manor with labour. It followed that the higher the amount of compensation to be paid by the peasant, the easier would be the lot of the landlord. There were in addition strong political arguments in favour of conversion to freeholds. It was the aspiration of every peasant to own his farm and therefore it could be claimed that the purchase of freeholds would cause much less discontent than any other system of emancipation. To this could be added the dangers of leaving the agrarian question open to the manipulation of left-wing agitators. The Polish Democratic Society's manifesto of 1836, pleading that Poland could be re-established by an appeal to the people upon the basis of granting them their freeholds without the obligation of themselves paying compensation to the manor, had the prestige of being the good old cause of the left wing. From the point of view of the landlords the linking of the national cause with the agrarian question was full of peril. The Democratic Society had known well that it would have to depend to a large extent upon the gentry and had supposed that the landlords should receive compensation in the form of bonds guaranteed by the state, but this was open to the practical objection that the landlords would not easily be able to convert their bonds into money. It was, moreover, feared that the peasants, freed absolutely from their obligations to the manor, would cease to provide wage labour and leave the landlords to their own devices. The Democratic Society's programme offered a solution which in the most favourable circumstances confronted the landlord, though perhaps not with ruin, at least with grave hardships. If it were carried out as a necessary part of an insurrection, in which there would be widespread disorders, revolutionary requisitioning and Russian reprisals, then obviously the landed proprietors were likely to suffer grievous losses from which they might never recover. It was clearly in the interests of the gentry after 1831 to accept the military rule of Paskevich, because the Russian army was a guarantee of stability.

The situation did not remain static. Even without emancipation conditions began to change gradually under the impact of European economic expansion. A distinction must be drawn between the public estates, under which category may be included not only the crown lands, but also the estates of the clergy and the so-called donated lands; the great estates of the aristocracy; and, finally, the lands of the medium gentry, some of whom possessed only one village. Over the crown estates the government exerted a fitful supervision, which offered some measure of protection to the peasants, though even here they were occasionally subject to oppression at the hands of the leaseholders. In the donated lands, confiscated estates which Nicholas had granted to some 138 Russian officers, the owners had the obligation of reorganizing tenures within the course of six years. Peasant lands and demesnes were to be separated, provided that the peasant holdings consisted of at least thirty morgs. The peasants might pay their dues in money or in kind, or, if they wished, in labour, though in this case their obligations were not to exceed three days a week for one holding. Where labour services were converted into rents, a day of manual labour was reckoned at six kopeks and a day of services with animals at twelve kopeks, but it was also permitted to assess rents upon the basis of the income drawn from the holding. These rents were not always equitable, but on the whole they were tolerable for the peasants, who were much envied by peasants on private estates.[1]

The Zamoyski family was most prominent among the aristocracy for the improvements it undertook. Its properties were scattered throughout Poland, but the majority of them lay in the southern regions of the Kingdom in the area of Zamość. This was a relatively backward part of the country, but the personal efforts of the family were to give it as modern an appearance as that in the more highly developed areas in the west. The actual *ordynacja*, a network of estates inherited by the head of the family, contained some 100 demesnes and over 100,000 peasants, but owing to the system of leasing individual properties to tenants the income derived from it was not always as great as it might have been. Leaseholders frequently failed to pay their rents and had to be taken to court. This situation gave rise to the idea that the estate might draw an income direct from the peasants in the form of rents. In 1833 a directive was issued to the effect that labour services might be converted into rents at the rate of one *złp* for a day with animals and half a *złp* for a day of manual labour. As long as the peasant paid his rent he was guaranteed fixity of tenure. The process of commutation proceeded very slowly at first, but in the course of time almost all the Zamoyski peasants opted for rents in preference to

[1] For details of donated estates see J. Kaczkowski, *Donacye w Królestwie Polskiem* (Warsaw, 1917).

labour services. The estate evidently treated the peasants in a cavalier fashion where it suited its purposes. Some of the smaller peasants it simply ejected from their holdings and it gave instructions that none were to be settled on demesne lands leased to tenants, who were obliged to cultivate them entirely with hired labour.[1] Trouble very naturally appeared in the lean years of the 1840's and there was some tendency to return to labour services, but the estate replied by selective evictions to keep the peasants in order.[2]

Other landlords lacked the means to do anything on as grand a scale as the wholesale conversion of the Zamoyskis, but active farmers among them were none the less willing to make changes and attempt experiments. The general tendency on medium estates was for the size of the peasant holding to decrease and the older type of husbandman, the thirty-morg full-peasant or the fifteen-morg half-peasant, to become much rarer. One writer in 1842 in an article with the title of 'A description of the present state of my husbandry, preceded by a frank confession of its historical development and errors committed in it',[3] gives an example of what might happen on an estate in the western regions of the Kingdom in the area of Kalisz. When the writer took over his property in 1821 he was utterly dependent upon labour services, because he lacked the capital to dispense with them. On this estate there were two demesnes and three peasant villages. In the course of time the half-peasants holding fifteen morgs found it very difficult to survive and a score or more gave up their holdings, with the consequence that the landlord incorporated their lands into the demesnes. The village came to consist entirely of small holdings and the peasants rendered only manual labour. The writer added that his peasants were in poor condition: 'Although they work only three days a week manual labour they are not in a prosperous state.' The result

---

[1] Antoni Cyprysiński, the official reponsible for this reorganization, wrote an account of his work, 'Objaśnienie teraźniejszego urządzenia rolników w ordynacyi zamoyskiej', *Biblioteka Warszawska*, IV (1847).

[2] S. Kieniewicz, *Sprawa włościańska w powstaniu styczniowym* (Wrocław, 1953), pp. 28–9.

[3] K.W., 'Opis mego teraźniejszego gospodarstwa proprzedzony wyznaniem sumiennem jego historycznego przebiegu i popełnionych w niem błędów', *Roczniki Gospodarstwa Krajowego*, I (1842), pp. 127 ff.

of this reorganization was that the landlord was able to settle most of his peasants on the edges of the demesnes with one field only and himself to introduce four-field rotation on the rest of the arable. Two thousand Chełm morgs were in the possession of the manor and 1,000 remained to the peasants. The same kind of conditions prevailed across the frontier in Poznania. In Szkalmierzyce, for example, a cottager worked four days a week in return for a house, a garden, less than an acre of arable land, four thalers and three bushels of grain.[1]

On the eastern side of the Kingdom the size of peasant holdings was much larger. One writer called Kruczaj, in asking the revealing question 'How much land ought to be given to the peasant?',[2] came to the conclusion that those who thought that a peasant ought to have enough land to employ two animals on light soil and three on heavy soil, were in fact asking for forty to fifty morgs for the peasant holding, 'which I think seems excessive'. Though the aspiration here was the reduction of the peasant farm, the writer was clearly thinking in different terms from landlords in the west. In the northern parts of the Kingdom, however, contact with East Prussia was promoting commercial farming. Count Stanisław Krasiński began to settle labourers on his land, who in return for a house, free fuel, free pasture and half an acre of meadow were obliged to pay fifty *złp* a year, or work one day's manual labour a week. Krasiński looked upon himself as a public benefactor, because the labourers, whom he settled, arrived with nothing more than the clothes they stood up in, a length of coarse cloth and supplies for their journey in a bag, but within a year they had married, their children soon swelling the family income. Krasiński likewise congratulated himself on not evicting his peasants, but waiting until the peasants could support their burdens no longer and were forced to give up their farms before he embodied their lands into the demesne. This had the advantage of allowing experience in new agricultural methods to be obtained by degrees and did not demand a considerable out-

---

[1] K.G., 'O cząstkowych statystyczno-przemysłowo-rolniczych opisach w W. Księstwie Poznańskiem', *Roczniki Gospodarstwa Krajowego*, II (1) (1843), pp. 1 ff.

[2] K. Kruczaj, 'Jak wiele należałoby nadać włościaninowi ziemi aby i on i właściciel wsi całej i krajowe rolnictwo miały społem zapewnioną, o ile to w mocy naszej, należną prawdziwą pomyślność', *ibid.*, II (4) (1843), pp. 296 ff.

lay at any one particular moment: 'Thus the remaining peasants who perform labour services give up one after another and
today they no longer constitute a very important element on
my lands.'[1] These were the practical consequences of the
absolute power which freedom to evict accorded by the *Code
Napoléon* brought about. If a halt had not been called Congress
Poland would have become in the course of time an area of very
large farms and minute holdings of farm labourers. A substantial
peasantry would have disappeared altogether. It is difficult to
suppose that landlords would have been willing to consider conversion to rents or freeholds at all, if it had not been for political
pressures.

At the head of the movement to consolidate the position of
the gentry stood Andrzej Zamoyski, brother of the head of the
family. Zamoyski believed that the aristocracy of Poland still
had a part to play, principally in setting an example of self-
discipline and public spirit, but at bottom he never departed
from a narrow attitude of class interest. Above all, he was
anxious to combat radicalism, which he considered had been
responsible for so many of Poland's misfortunes in the past. In
the new Poland he wished to preserve the old hierarchical structure of society with the aristocracy at the top. The means was to
turn his countrymen's attention away from politics to the practical problems of agriculture. Since 1835 he had been experi-
menting on his two farms of Michałów and Deszkowice, part of
the Zamoyski property of Klemensów, and had worked out his
own system of rotation, tried new methods of ploughing and
sowing and rid himself of labour services. In April 1842 a group
of leading landlords inspired by Zamoyski founded the agricultural periodical, *Roczniki Gospodarstwa Krajowego*, which gave
him a platform for his ideas. In 1843 and 1845 small exhibitions were organized at Klemensów. The visitors were much impressed by the excellence of Zamoyski's tillage and many drew
the simple lesson that good yields could be achieved only where
labour services had been abandoned. Gradually Zamoyski
established for himself the position of being the leader of the

---

[1] St. hr. K., 'Próby praktyczne ułatwiające włościanom występowanie z dzisiej-
szej nędzy i zapewniające im byt samoistny', *Roczniki Gospodarstwa Krajowego*, iv
(1844), p. 123.

entire landlord class, just as he was the admitted agricultural expert in the Kingdom. Undoubtedly the very name, Zamoyski, was an advantage, for the founder of the family fortunes, the sixteenth-century chancellor, Jan Zamoyski was commonly regarded as one of the architects of *szlachta* liberties. Sentimentally it was supposed that history might repeat itself and Poland regain her liberties under Count Andrzej. Dung, beetroot, turnips, ploughs, distilling, agricultural machinery and the rest, however, were not subjects which required political skill. Andrzej Zamoyski was not the stuff of which leaders are commonly made. He was to allow a mixture of personal vanity, timidity and, very often, spite to cloud his judgement. It was the misfortune of the landlords that he was not found wanting until a crisis arose. In the 1850's he was almost the uncrowned king of the *szlachta* in the Kingdom and generally regarded as the most proper person to represent Polish interests. The freedom of action which he claimed for the noble landlord, however, was to be severely limited by the events of 1846, when the Galician peasants showed that they too had aspirations and, moreover, the will to claim their rights.

The peasants in the Congress Kingdom did not appear to have shown much hostility to the system of labour services after the war of 1831. They returned to their duties without significant protest. In 1833 they co-operated with the Russian authorities in tracking down the partisans of Zaliwski who entered the Kingdom from Galicia. They were equally ready to assist the recruiting officers to root out the soldiers of the disbanded Polish army, whom Paskevich wished to recall to the colours for service in the Russian army. The passivity of the peasants in the 1830's was no guide to their attitudes in the 1840's, when the pressure of the landlords had increased and poor harvests roused them to a keener appreciation of their own interests. The Russian authorities were disturbed by the curious affair of Father Piotr Ściegienny, who in 1842 began to appeal to the peasants in the southern regions of the Kingdom with the aim of raising them in revolt against Russia. His methods were hardly those of the Polish Democratic Society. His first appeal was 'A Bull of Gregory XVI to the Polish People', which declared that the Holy Father commanded them

F

to resist the Russians. His 'Aphorisms on Communal Life', however, demanded thirty morgs for each peasant and laid down the principle that every village should have four 'dictators' to regulate its economic life. His aim, it appears, was a theocratic village of substantial farmers living harmoniously in the love of God and enjoying universal education. A rising was actually planned for October 1844 in conjunction with the Warsaw secret society, 'Union of the Polish People', led by Leon Mazurkiewicz and Władysław Dzwonkowski, but in August Ściegienny came under the suspicion of the police after he had been denounced by a village schoolmaster for possessing subversive literature. He was undeterred by the warning he received and in September called upon the peasants to 'rally around the standard of the Virgin Mary against her enemies and the enemies of the Fatherland and the People'. At his meeting at Krajno on 24 October his followers could find nothing better to do than sing the songs of that most reactionary of Polish Catholic adventures, the Confederation of Bar of 1768! Unable to rouse enthusiasm at Kielce, he was arrested upon the denunciation of a peasant. For all this conspiracy's immaturity it was an ominous sign that the peasants might stir. Followed by the Galician massacres of 1846 it seemed most sinister.[1]

By a miracle the massacres did not extend over the frontier into the southern districts of the *gubernia* of Radom, where conditions were almost identical with those prevailing in the circles of western Galicia. By chance it happened that Nicholas I himself was in the area in May 1846 and took the opportunity to warn the peasants personally that he would not permit them to follow the example of the Galicians.[2] The Viceroy, Paskevich, was inclined to make light of the unrest, professing his belief that the discontents of the peasants had little or no political significance, but were prompted by a primitive desire to plunder the manors.[3] Nicholas I, however, feared lest his personal intervention be insufficient to preserve order. There

---

[1] For details of Ściegienny, see M. Tyrowicz, *Sprawa Ks. Piotra Ściegiennego* (Warsaw, 1948); and M. Żywczyński, 'X. Piotr Ściegienny w świetle dotychczasowych badań', *Sprawozdania Tow. Hist. Kat. Uniw. Lubelskiego*, 1 (1947).

[2] D. Domagalski, *Irlandia i Polska* (Cracow, 1876), pp. 240–1.

[3] *Russkaya Starina*, xlviii (1885), p. 219.

was a great deal of mobility among the peasants in Poland. Seasonal labour in southern Poland included radically minded Russians from as far afield as Lithuania, where they met with Galicians from across the frontier.[1] Failure to act might have led to widespread repercussions. For once Nicholas I cut through the normal procedure of Russian officialdom with its endless reports and appreciations preceding any important decision. On 3 June 1846 a special committee was set up to consider the peasant question in the Kingdom, under the direction of Paskevich, but with orders to come to a speedy decision. On 7 June 1846 was signed a ukaz which went a long way towards undoing the effect of introducing the *Code Napoléon* in 1807.[2] All peasant farmers, whether in villages or private towns, who held more than three morgs of land, were granted fixity of tenure, provided that they fulfilled their obligations to the manor. The landlord could not evict peasants, reduce the size of their holdings, or increase their duties. For the first time the principle was accepted in Congress Poland that there was a difference between noble and peasant land. Vacant peasant farms could no longer be embodied in the demesne, but must be filled with fresh peasants within two years. A promise was, moreover, extended that the whole question of extra duties and miscellaneous rights of the manor would be the subject of a separate decree, while the preamble contained the assertion that it was the government's intention in future to prepare a law settling the entire agrarian question.

It was one thing to issue a law, but another to have it carried into effect. The landlords, as mayors of the rural commune under the law of 1818, were informed confidentially of the ukaz during the course of July 1846. There were not a few who considered that the government's decision to postpone its promulgation until after harvest provided a last opportunity for evictions. The peasants for their part soon heard rumours of the law and began in some instances to refuse services, which in its turn gave the landlords the chance to administer corporal

---

[1] Cf. J.A., 'Opis gospodarstwa w Garbaczu', *Roczniki Gospodarstwa Krajowego*, IX (1846), p. 81.

[2] The text may be found in *Dziennik Praw Królestwa Polskiego*, XXXVIII, and in N. Milyutin, *Izsledovaniya*, II, fascicule 1, pp. 6–8.

punishment to them.[1] On 22 November 1846 a supplementary decree laid down the principle that all duties which were unspecified in time, extent or kind should cease and with them compulsory service to the manor, together with the provision of produce at fixed rates, but duties which were accurately defined were to continue. The landlords, however, as mayors of the communes, were able to draw up their own lists, which the illiterate peasants could hardly check. As long as the Polish landlords controlled the rural administration, even the best of intentions of the Russian government were bound to be frustrated. Nevertheless, the legislation of 1846 did accord the peasants some measure of protection. The landlords considered it yet another example of the government's reactionary policy, modifying the liberal *Code Napoléon* and placing a fresh obstacle in the way of progressive agriculture, but while Paskevich remained Viceroy there was little effort to apply a rigid interpretation of the law. In the question of what action should be taken at the expiry of a rent contract the attempt by the Commission of Internal Affairs to give the law a more specific meaning was lost in the arid discussions among officials. Where loopholes appeared, the landlords took full advantage of them.

There were many ways by which the landlords could circumvent the law. They could embarrass the peasants' economy by closing the woods to them. Where they were the owners of the peasants' draught animals and seed they could withdraw their property. In times of harvest failure it had been the custom for the manors to help the villagers, but there was no formal obligation for them to do so. The landlord could therefore bring about the ruin of the peasant and, when he was compelled to leave his holding, neglect to fill it with another peasant farmer. Fictitious entries could be made in estate registers to cover lands which had been incorporated in the demesne. There were landlords who cared little for legal formalities and continued to evict peasants in spite of the 1846 law. A particularly poor example was set by the Zamoyski family. The British consul-general, Mansfield, reported in 1857 that 'the Ukase of 1846 might have applied in a country where serfdom was the

[1] H. Grynwaser, *Kwestia agrarna i ruch włościan w Królestwie Polskim, Pisma*, II, 122–47.

rule. It was simply an anachronistic or subversive socialistic regulation where serfdom had been abolished.' Though he might represent the law as a retrograde step, he could happily report that it appeared to make no difference in practice:

The Zamoyski family, who probably have 20,000 such farmers, have no written contracts and apparently setting aside the Ukase of 1846 freely exercise the right of eviction when the rent is not paid regularly in advance.[1]

The extent to which the law of 1846 failed to achieve its object may be obtained by a comparison of the statistics published in the almanacs of the Warsaw Astronomical Observatory for 1846 and 1859, and by Milyutin in his official reports for 1863–5.[2] The number of holdings on private estates was reduced from 208,236 in 1846 to 197,903 in 1859, a loss of 10,333. The number of holdings below three morgs, which were not covered by the law of 1846, fell from 30,860 to 11,079, a loss of 19,781. There were therefore many peasants at the time of the rising of 1863 who had only recently lost their holdings.

By the year 1860 the agrarian structure had become highly complex. The figures for 1859 show that there were 453 places officially described as towns, of which the government was the landlord of 224 and private persons of 229. In 4,891 rural communes there were 22,613 villages of which the bulk, 17,837, were held by private persons and the remainder by government and official institutions; because the landlord, or in the case of a crown estate the leaseholder, was the mayor of the commune, the figure, 4,891, represents the maximum number of persons who may be regarded as being landed gentry, though obviously some of the *szlachta* were mayors in more than one commune. There were altogether in the Kingdom in 1859 324,809 peasant farms, of which 208,982 (64·3 per cent) were held on the estates of private persons and 115,827 (35·7 per cent) on government and institutional lands. Of the 208,982

---

[1] F.O. 65/501, Mansfield to Clarendon, 7 April 1857.
[2] L. Wolski, 'Główniejsze wiadomości statystyczne o Królestwie Polskiem na zasadzie akt urzędowych', *Kalendarz . . . na rok zwyczajny 1859*, and 'Materyały do statystyki Królestwa Polskiego na zasadzie akt urzędowych', *Kalendarz . . . na rok zwyczajny 1860*; and N. Milyutin, *Izsledovaniya v Tsarstve Pol'skom*, ii. Cf. also W. Grabski, *Historya Towarzystwa Rolniczego*, and S. Kieniewicz, *Sprawa włościańska w powstaniu styczniowym*.

peasant farms on private estates, 52,506 were held by the payment of rents; 31,636 by a mixture of rents, services and payments in kind; and 124,840 by the performance of labour services.[1] There were in addition 26,166 allotment holders and cottagers. For all the progress being made in agriculture over half the landed peasants still performed labour services.

The size of holdings, however, shows the beginning of the tendency to parcelization. Of the 208,982 holdings on private estates 11,079 were less than three morgs (5·3 per cent); 51,634 between three and nine morgs (24·7 per cent); 59,269 between ten and fifteen morgs (28·3 per cent); 74,334 between sixteen and thirty morgs (35·6 per cent); and 12,666 over thirty morgs (6·1 per cent). Parcelization was most evident in the southern and western districts of the Kingdom, but less pronounced in the north and east. Rents tended to follow the same pattern, being high where parcelization was most intense, but lower where peasant farms were larger. There were, of course, considerable variations within districts according to the quality of the soil. Government and institutional lands show a higher incident of survival for the larger peasant farms and, on the whole, a lower exaction of rents, but the general rule seems to have been that smaller holdings and higher rents applied in areas where conditions offered better opportunities for commercial farming. To some extent a higher yield from a smaller acreage may have compensated for the shrinkage of the peasant farm, but by English standards the Polish peasant holdings were pitifully small. Life for all except a minority of the peasants was hard indeed.

Over the border in Lithuania conditions in places bore resemblance to those in the Kingdom of Poland. Poles were subsequently to protest the purity of their intentions and claim that the desire of the Lithuanian landlords was instrumental in bringing about reform in the whole of the Russian Empire, but an examination of the progress of discussion in Lithuania reveals that this was an altogether too simple a view.[2] The

---

[1] *Kalendarz* (1860), pp. 164–5, 178.

[2] The most modern writings on the agrarian question in Lithuania are those of N. N. Ulashchik, 'Krepostnaya derevniya Litvi i Zapadnoy Byelorussii nakanune reformi 1861 goda', *Voprosy Istorii*, 1948 (XII); 'Iz istorii reskripta 20 Noyabrya 1857 g.', *Istoricheskie Zapiski*, XXVIII (1949); and 'Pogotovka krest'yanskoy reformy 1861 g. v Litve i Zapadnoy Byelorussii', *ibid.*, XXXIII (1950).

gubernii of western Russia were better prepared for reform than most parts of the Empire. Where the old Polish state had extended there was almost no conception of repartitional tenure, which was common in Russia proper. There was therefore an absence of complications which permitted a different approach to the question of liquidation. In 1817–18 there had been an attempt to obtain the permission of Alexander I for reform on the lines of the *Code Napoléon* in the Congress Kingdom and of the Baltic provinces, where the German nobility had reduced their peasants to the status of tenants, but this had been refused, probably on the grounds that reform of this kind would have resulted in too close an assimilation of conditions to those which applied in the Kingdom of Poland, which would have been undesirable on political grounds.[1] There could be no positive Russian action to abolish serfdom without at the same time raising the question of serfdom in the entire Empire. For the moment the condition of the peasants remained unchanged. The landlord retained the right to sell the peasant and his holding, transfer him from one holding to another or move him to another estate, alter the size of the holding and to control his life without undue interference from the government. It was only on 15 April 1844 that Nicholas I decided to take steps to protect the peasants in Lithuania from excessive exploitation. The aim of the Russian government was to give definition to the obligations which the peasants owed their lords, in the hope of producing stability. The general rule adopted by the committees appointed for the purpose of drawing up inventories was that the peasant should not pay to the lord more than one-third of the income from the holding. The tenures were in fact onerous. It was regarded as normal that there should be rendered for the *włoka* (thirty morgs) three days' service with animals by men and three days' manual labour by women, though there were cases in which this scale was exceeded. In periods of heavy work, haymaking and harvest, the peasants normally had the obligation of rendering extra days' labour, up to perhaps twenty-four days in the year, in addition to which there might be compulsory hired labour and carting. Exploitation bore heavily on

[1] Cf. H. Mościcki, 'Sprawa włościańska na Litwie w pierwszej ćwierci xix wieku', *Odbitka z Biblioteki Warszawskiej* (1908).

the peasants and many took flight to escape from it. In 1854 there were 2,646 arrests of fugitive peasants and 2,177 in 1856.[1] Discontent was rife at the end of the Crimean War.

It was not peasant discontent which impressed the Russian government, concerned not so much with the desirability of reform, but rather with the practical political problem of inducing the gentry throughout the Empire to accept reform in principle at all. Lithuania seemed to offer an opportunity of setting reform in motion, though without prejudice to the form which legislation might ultimately take. In 1848 there had been a proposal from the Lithuanian gentry that the peasants should be granted personal freedom, but this had been rejected by the senate on the grounds that it could not accept petitions in matters which lay outside its legal competence.[2] In 1854 the Grodno committee charged with drafting inventories had appended its suggestions for a new approach. The basis of emancipation was that the peasants should be granted their personal freedom, but that all property rights should be vested in the landlords and that henceforth the relations of lord and peasant should be founded upon voluntary mutual agreements.[3] In short, this was an approach identical with that of 1817–18 to reproduce in Lithuania the conditions which had been abolished in the Kingdom by the law of 1846. Nevertheless, it was possible to use the Polish landlords' willingness to consider reform. The governor-general, Nazimov, who in economic matters normally took a pro-Polish point of view, impressed upon Alexander II during his visit to Brest Litovsk in May 1856 the possibility of obtaining Polish co-operation in the emancipation question. During the coronation ceremonies in Moscow in August 1856 the minister of internal affairs, Lanskoy, noted that among the representatives of the nobles the Poles alone were willing to discuss reform. The Poles were asked to present their views, but little advance had been made. The Kovno nobility declared themselves willing to free their peasants, but insisted that they should dispose of the land as they wished, an attitude shared by

[1] N. N. Ulashchik, *Voprosy Istorii*, 1948 (XII), p. 65.
[2] N. Kolmakov, 'Vopros o pochine krest'yanskogo dyela', *Russkaya Starina*, XLVII (1885), pp. 132–3.
[3] N. N. Ulashchik, *Istoricheskie Zapiski*, XXVIII (1949), p. 166.

the nobility of Grodno. In Vilna, the marshal, Domeyko, refused to forward a similar recommendation to Nazimov, not
on the grounds that such a reform would be unjust, but because
he personally objected to reform of any kind.

Discussions in the Secret Committee for Peasant Affairs,
established in St. Petersburg in January 1857, were taking a
different course. Levshin, the deputy minister of internal
affairs, began to insist that emancipation could not for political
reasons be carried out on any other basis than the grant to the
peasant of the messuage in which his house stood and of enough
land to maintain him in a position to feed himself and pay his
taxes. To grant less would be to invite a peasant revolution.
The outcome of the discussions was the celebrated rescript to
Nazimov of 20 November/2 December 1857, which ordered
the creation of committees in the three *gubernii* of Grodno,
Kovno and Vilna, with a co-ordinating committee in Vilna.
Three principles were established in advance. The first bore
the mark of a compromise, that the title to the land was vested
in the landlord, but that the peasants were to be left in possession of a messuage and to be given sufficient land to be able
to discharge their obligations, the principle insisted upon by
Levshin. The second principle was that the peasants were to be
organized in a village commune, over which the landlord
should exercise a patrimonial jurisdiction; and the third was
that in future there must be an efficient system of tax collection. [1]
These conditions did not promise much to the peasants, but one
thing was clear, that the peasants were not to be converted into
tenants without some rights to the soil. The landlords were in
theory vested with full ownership, but in practice a system of
dual ownership was envisaged.

The Nazimov rescript set in motion the consultation of the
nobility all over the Empire and in August-September 1858
the Tsar himself made a public progress to several large cities
to hasten discussions, but the Lithuanians with whom the discussion had begun, far from supporting reform, spent all their
time until the actual signature of the decree of emancipation in
1861 trying to whittle down the principles of the Nazimov

[1] *Khrestomatiya po istorii S.S.S.R.*, iii, 59–61 partially reproduces the text of this
rescript.

rescript. In the *gubernia* of Kovno it was suggested that the land should be divided into two categories, manorial and peasant, selected by the landlord. The lands of craftsmen, fishermen and others were to be incorporated in the demesne. The peasants were to hold no more than twenty diesiatins and any land in excess of this figure was to be incorporated in the demesne; in some places peasants held as much as forty to sixty diesiatins, which shows that the object of the Polish landlords was the partial dispossession of the farmers. There was to be a transitional period of twelve years, after which the Poles proposed that the peasants should be given a 'preferential right' to continue in occupation of their holding, which was an attempt to wriggle out of the grant of hereditary tenure. If the peasant refused to accept a new agreement he might be evicted, while the landlord should be in any case empowered to give a farm to another peasant, if he offered a higher rent. In short, the landlords of Kovno were unwilling to consider the grant of a freehold. The same may be said of the landlords in Grodno and Vilna. When the projects were transmitted to the co-ordinating committee in Vilna a plan was eventually devised in February 1859 under which, after an initial period of conversion, which was to last six years, all peasants holding less than five diesiatins were to surrender their land to the manor, while peasants holding between five and twenty diesiatins were to receive new holdings, or, in other words, to be allotted the poorest land by their landlords. Peasants who failed to honour their obligations to the landlord might be evicted. The aspirations of the Lithuanian Poles were identical with those of the landlords in the Kingdom.

The Polish recommendations made little impression upon the Russian Main Committee in St. Petersburg, which adhered to the principle of emancipation with enough land to support a peasant family, but it was recognized that the *gubernii* of Vilna, Grodno, Kovno, Minsk and parts of Vitebsk, would require a special law on account of their different legal conditions. Two Polish experts, Bronisław Zaleski and Konstanty Giecewicz, continued to press for emancipation without land in one form or another. Even Nazimov, the governor-general, protested in St. Petersburg against violation of the Polish landlords' rights, but the Tsar turned a deaf ear. The Poles were to complain that the Russians sought to conciliate the people against the interests of the nobility,[1] but this was not entirely true. The terms of emanicipation were to be onerous enough for the peasants, but *raison d'état* forbade that a Tsar should make them as onerous as the Poles would have wished.

While reform was under discussion in Lithuania and Russia the same painfully slow process was being undertaken in Warsaw. In April 1856 a committee was appointed in the Kingdom under the chairmanship of General Ixküll to consider what measures ought to be taken to implement Article V of the 1846 law which promised that the government would assist landlords in the task of finding a way to end labour services. The result of the Ixküll committee's long deliberations was the decree of the Administrative Council of 16/28 December 1858.[2] Its recommendations were that the peasants should hold their farms on perpetual leases, but with a revision of rents every twenty years according to the price of corn. Farm buildings, equipment and seed should pass into the possession of the peasants, but the question of woods and pastures should be held over for separate negotiation. If the landlord wished he might retain labour services for a period of up to six years. Fishing and hunting rights, together with the monopoly of distilling and sale of vodka, were to remain his. Peasant holdings might not be subdivided except with his consent. There was, however, no proposal that the government should enforce these suggestions. The negotiation of rents was to be the result of a voluntary agreement by both sides, but a Rent Committee might be appointed for each district, consisting of one official and four landlords, who would assist in the negotiations and obtain a final confirmation of the decision from the official committee of the *gubernia*. In the event of no agreement being reached the existing conditions of tenure were to remain. This was a compromise solution which sought to avoid the hostility of the landlords and prevent unrest among the peasants, but it succeeded in satisfying neither side. The peasants wanted complete freedom from the manor in the form of freeholds, while the

---

[1] Cf. *O wyswobodzeniu włościan na Litwie* (Berlin–Poznań, 1863), p. 21.

[2] *Dziennik Praw Królestwa Polskiego*, LII, pp. 46 ff. Cf. also N. Milyutin, *Izsledovaniya*, II, fascicule B, No. 11.

landlords were not anxious to concede fixity of tenure. The absence of official compulsion meant that very little was done at all to solve the problem.

It was no doubt the slow rate of progress of this system which prompted the government on 31 October 1859 to authorize the Agricultural Society to discuss ways and means of conversion to rents and to publish its findings, subject to the provision that they should first submit them to the censor. To entrust the Agricultural Society with this task was in a way to elevate it to the status of an assembly of the nobility in Russia, but in the social circumstances of the Kingdom of Poland it remained what it was, an association of only a section of the nation. Tomasz Potocki, the brother-in-law of Alexander Wielopolski, wished to see a speedy solution of the problem in order to prevent peasant unrest. He and his fellow landlords in the district of Wieluń worked out a scheme of conversion.[1] It welcomed the possibility of separating the fields of the peasants and the manor and saw rents as a means of progressing towards freeholds, but its calculation of an economic rent was altogether too high; a day with animals was reckoned above the current wage rates for day labourers. The fact that Potocki in effect proposed to cancel the peasants' rights to woods and pastures in itself constituted an insuperable obstacle to the acceptance of the plan. In December 1859 a conference of leading members of the Agricultural Society was held in Warsaw to discuss the recommendation of the Viceroy that the Society should consider the problem of conversion to rents. On this occasion Potocki's plan served as a basis for discussion. The matter was debated again before the whole Society in February 1860, but no progress was made. One delegate, Jan Mittelstaedt, actually produced an idyllic defence of labour services. The problem was again delegated to the committee of the Society in which Andrzej Zamoyski was supreme. Potocki in May 1860 demanded that a specimen rent contract to apply to the whole country be printed. The committee therefore drew up its 'Suggestions for persons drawing up contracts for perpetual leases', which included a draft contract reproducing the proposals in the decree of 28 December 1858. This was only to shelve the matter once

[1] W. Grabski, *Historya Towarzystwa Rolniczego*, II, 159–60.

again. The landlords and peasants had been exceedingly slow
to follow up the decree of 1858. Up to 3 May 1861 only 1,017
holdings had been converted, of which 585 were in the *gubernia*
of Warsaw and 245 in the *gubernia* of Radom.[1] It was abun-
dantly clear that a solution could be reached only if the government applied compulsion, but this was a course it was reluctant
to take, because it was hoped to win the political allegiance of
the landed gentry by giving them a free hand in the agrarian
question. There were, however, some Russian officers who could
think in different terms. For them the people were a potential
ally and the *szlachta* the traditional enemy. Mansfield had noted
that the government might make substantial concessions to the
peasants: 'The chance of such a socialistic and revolutionary
operation in their favour is sure to enlist all the sympathies of the
peasant farmers.'[2] His successor, Simmons, equally faithfully
reported the fears of the gentry:

The general opinion appears to be that the peasants of Poland,
having been encouraged to look to the government as their friend in
opposition to the landlords and to consider the latter as having
interests totally antagonistic to their own, believe that by holding
back from a final settlement the government will at length be induced to decree more favourable terms at the cost of their landlords.
They also appear to be anxiously awaiting the decisions as to tenure,
service &c which must be taken in order to carry into effect the
emancipation of the serfs in Russia.[3]

It was this conviction which some Russians were anxious to exploit. It was also a situation which was more favourable than
any which the Polish Democratic Society had striven to exploit
in the 1840's. The landed gentry of the Kingdom feared not only
peasant passivity, but a threat also from the revived radicalism
of Warsaw.

Although the Congress Kingdom had enjoyed relative peace
under Paskevich it had not entirely been unaffected by revolutionary feeling. Many citizens of the Kingdom had moved into
Poznania in the early 1840's to take up revolutionary activity
there. There had been an intellectual revival in Warsaw with

[1] W. Grabski, *ibid.*, II, 213.
[2] F.O. 65/501, Mansfield to Clarendon, 7 April 1857.
[3] F.O. 65/538, Simmons to Russell, 1 November 1859.

the foundation of the important periodical, *Biblioteka Warszaw-ska*, in 1841 and *Przegląd Naukowy* in 1842. Edward Dembowski had gathered round himself a group of young radicals, which initiated a plot for an armed uprising, but its efforts had been thwarted by the arrest of Father Piotr Ściegienny, which in its turn led to the arrest of conspirators in Warsaw. This set-back accounts for the lack of vigour in the uprising of 1846 when the Polish movement in the Kingdom was speedily crushed by the peasants. Failure, however, gave conspiratorial activity in Warsaw a distinct feature which was not present in other parts of Poland. The direction of the Polish movement passed temporarily into the hands of women, of whom the most prominent was Narcyza Żmichowska. They had little idea of fighting for feminine emancipation, considering that the achievement of Polish emancipation would be sufficient reward, but they spoke with as much determination as men. A half-hearted attitude towards the national cause was likely to deprive the male of feminine regard or favour, while zeal was the way to a woman's heart. Neither feminine nor masculine leadership could have produced a rising in Congress Poland in 1848. Fantastic rumours circulated in the country. The peasants obtained the impression that labour services were about to end. In the district of Łomża youths hid in the woods in expectation of a rebellion and at Kalisz the secondary school closed for want of pupils to attend classes. Paskevich tightened his security precautions and kept order. Narcyza Żmichowska went to Poznań to plead with the Polish National Committee for an attack on the Kingdom, but she was politely rebuffed. With the collapse of the Poznanian national movement in May 1848 all chance of a rising in the Kingdom vanished. Traces were soon discovered of the conspiratorial movement in the Kingdom and numerous arrests followed, including that of Żmichowska herself in November 1849. Terms of imprisonment were imposed and a large contingent of young Poles was sent to Siberia for chastening, whence they were released only after the promulgation of Alexander II's amnesties in 1856.[1]

Paskevich was thorough in his suppression of conspiracies.

[1] Cf. A. Minkowska, *Organizacja spiskowa 1848 roku w Królestwie Polskiem* (Warsaw 1923).

There was scarcely a flicker of activity in the Kingdom during the Crimean War. The landlords were content to make a handsome profit in a period of high prices. The Polish youth had not yet recovered its revolutionary zeal. Polish energies were limited to the emigration. The curious Michał Czajkowski formed a band of Cossacks to fight for the Turks. The poet, Mickiewicz, was sent to Turkey in 1855 to resolve the difficulties which arose in the formation of a genuinely Polish legion between the self-appointed Cossack, Czajkowski, the Democrats who wished to form their own legion, and Władysław Zamoyski, anxious to raise and command a force of his own. The sole result of this episode was that Zamoyski at last obtained his life's ambition, the title of general, from the British government, and Mickiewicz was struck down by cholera in Istambul on 26 November 1855. Efforts of Napoleon III to resurrect the Polish Question with his allies were dropped when peace was in sight. The Crimean War merely confirmed the Poles of the Kingdom in their opinion that there was little to be obtained from abroad. When the milder *régime* came into being in the Kingdom of Poland after 1856 the approach of the radical left was cautious in the extreme.

In the early years the most important activity was led by Edward Jurgens, an official in the Commission of Internal Affairs. Jurgens had been educated at the University of Dorpat and passed as a matter of course into the bureaucracy. He and his friends had not the slightest intention of planning an insurrection. On the contrary they were convinced that the best course to follow at first was to attempt the resuscitation of the Polish nation by the extension of education to the masses. They attached great importance to the two oppressed sections of the Polish community, the peasants and the Jews. To win over the peasants they hoped to induce the *szlachta* to carry out a voluntary conversion to freeholds, but they abstained from any activity which might have brought them into contact with the peasantry. The Jews they hoped to merge with the Poles, just as they extended their friendship to the half-Polonized Germans who formed a substantial section of the Warsaw middle class. The aim of Jurgens was to give the middle class a cohesion which it could not possess as long as it was divided into Pole,

Jew and German. Unity could alone enable it to speak with greater authority to the government. The Jurgens group was thus essentially middle class in outlook with a moderate programme calculated to appeal to the well-established officials and literary men in Warsaw. It was to this element that the returned exiles in general attached themselves. Men like Karol Ruprecht and Agaton Giller, held in high esteem for their sufferings and referred to as the 'Siberians', lent a certain prestige to the policy of Jurgens, because, if respected patriots could be attracted to him, there was no reason why others should not adhere to his course of action. There was, nevertheless, a feeling of uncertainty in the Jurgens group. Narcyza Żmichowska, herself a member of it, warned the émigré publicist, Seweryn Elżanowski, that he must expect no sudden or substantial progress:

The people have expressed themselves only in so far as they have given a vote of no confidence to their masters and the *szlachta*, only in so far, I might say, as they have given a vote of confidence to the Imperial government.[1]

It appeared to be an uphill struggle to make any impression upon Polish society. The pessimistic view of the Jurgens group led to their being called the 'Millenaries' by the extreme left, who laughingly said that they intended to put off the attainment of Polish independence for a thousand years. There were men in Warsaw who viewed with impatience the caution of this comfortably established section of the Polish intelligentsia, secure in their possession of adequate salaries and not inclined to risk their ease in the hazards of revolution. An evolutionary approach did not suit the intellectual proletariat, the makers of revolution everywhere in Europe and nowhere more strongly entrenched than in Warsaw.

For the majority of the educated class in Warsaw life was by no means easy. Far too many men with pretensions to professional advancement were drawn to Warsaw, still the centre of a distinctly Polish social system, though historic Poland no longer existed as a political unit. The hardships of the intellectual proletariat could only be increased by the changes in agriculture.

---

[1] N. Żmichowska, *Listy*, edited by S. Pigoń (Wrocław, 1957–60), II, 380.

One source of employment had always been in the supervision and organization of peasant labour on the large estates, but with the application of modern methods fewer estate officials were needed. In Warsaw there seemed to be opportunities for able men. The city had been connected with western Europe in 1848 with the completion of the Warsaw–Vienna railway and was shortly to be joined with St. Peterburg in 1862. In 1850 the customs barrier between the Kingdom and Russia was abolished, which seemed to promise that Warsaw would develop rapidly as a commercial centre and absorb more of the Polish intelligentsia, but there were always more claimants for well-paid posts than there were posts to give. There was therefore in Warsaw a class of seedy clerks, discontented men with no stake in the community, scratching a living as best they could. Having severed their connection with the rural society, they were careless of the interests of the *szlachta*. Having nothing to lose, they were ready to seek the remedy of insurrection in order to strike off the chains of national servitude, for nothing less than the restoration of the old Poland could rescue them from their present stagnation. The alternative was to accept assimilation with the growing working class of the city, but educated men have no liking for manual work, however much they commend its virtues in others.

There was plenty of combustible material in Warsaw for the extreme left to divert to revolution. The student class was traditionally sympathetic to the left, though in the 1850's there were in fact few students in the city. In 1860 only 290 students were enrolled for courses in the Medical School, 121 in the Marymont Agricultural College and 110 in the School of Fine Arts. Students therefore tended to augment their strength with schoolboys; there were 1,226 pupils in the principal *Gymnazium* and another 1,309 in less exalted establishments which could provide auxiliaries. Educational institutions were the source of the depressed intelligentsia. Their pupils knew that life offered them only bleak prospects and they turned their ears willingly to proposals for insurrection. By themselves they could have achieved nothing, if behind them had not stood the Warsaw working class, which in 1794 and 1830 had shown that it was second only to Paris in its readiness to rise against authority.

G

There was a mystique, inherited from the shoemakers by the workers in the railway yards and in the British firm of Evans & Co., that Warsaw stood in the vanguard of the national struggle. The revival of Polish radicalism was to begin with the vapourings of the very young, but in the end it was the workmen of the city who were to keep Warsaw faithful to the insurrection of 1863.

The politics of the very young were necessarily immature in a country like Congress Poland. Denied by the long rule of Paskevich and its rigid censorship access to political literature, the youth of the country began their thinking from the Polish Democratic Society's Manifesto of 1836, which had the prestige of being the traditional programme of the Left. Congress Poland and imperial Russia still awaited a solution of the agrarian problem and therefore offered a field for the Democratic Society's programme. At the outset, however, the youth of Warsaw thought more in terms of release from the servitude which students daily experienced in their lives under the strictly utilitarian educational system. At the bottom the Russians prescribed a simple curriculum of reading, writing and arithmetic, but as the student advanced he discovered that he could obtain a knowledge of anything which did not savour of Polish nationalism. Medicine, natural history, geometry, physics, chemistry and mathematics were open to him. He was allowed to study the Russian language and its literature, but only the Polish language. In consequence the works of the Polish Romantic poets came to have the attraction of illicit alcohol, more avidly acquired, more deeply drunk and more potent in its effect because it was forbidden. Set before the young man was the ideal of the Romantic hero, the model upon which he should base his conduct. Dreams of action were a pleasant distraction from everyday frustration and limited prospects for the future.

The first real revolutionary activity began with the opening of the Medical School in October 1857. Kurzyna and Jaśniewski, two of its students, began to organize their fellows as a revolutionary cell, but by the spring of 1859 it was obvious to the authorities that academic studies were being neglected and that the probable cause was political activity. In the summer the

Russian authorities decided upon a purge in order to get rid of the more dangerous agitators; they came to the conclusion that examination performances would reveal the exact relation of academic to political work and in June 1859 brought forward the date of the examinations. Those who did not pass were to be sent down and only those who achieved a satisfactory standard were to remain. This action caught the students unawares and no amount of protest could persuade the Russian curator, Tsitsurin, to change his mind. This situation thus produced a split between the adequately prepared, who were the less politically active, being as a rule from the well-to-do families, and those who were not. The latter abused the former for their lack of national spirit and called for a strike against the examinations. Out of 318 students 214 chose the patriotic course of refusing to take the tests and adopted the name of the 'Reds' in contrast with those who submitted, whom they called the 'Whites', the first occasion on which these appellations appeared in the Congress Kingdom to indicate on the one hand radical patriotism and on the other conservative moderation. The Reds to emphasize their patriotism held a demonstration on the field where the battle of Grochów was fought in 1831, a place considered for ever symbolic of the undying hatred of Poles for Russians. The upshot of this affair was that Kurzyna decided to take refuge abroad with his hero, Ludwik Mierosławski, who for the first time established contact with a group within Russian Poland. For the first time there was a possibility of a conspiracy resurrecting the Democratic Society's manifesto of 1836.

In the autumn of 1859 a new man appeared in the Medical School, Karol Majewski, who was never thereafter to be very far from the centre of events.[1] It would appear that Majewski, who had already tried a career in agriculture and failed, was by English standards something of a ne'er-do-well. He certainly did not regard his membership of the Medical School as entailing a pressing obligation to concentrate entirely upon his studies. It was rather a foothold from which to influence the academic youth. Majewski was a born president of a students'

---

[1] For a biography of Majewski, see W. Rudzka, *Karol Majewski w latach 1859–1864* (Warsaw, 1937).

union. His first action was to organize the *Towarzystwo Bratniej Pomocy*—The Self-Help Society, which was to embrace the students of the Medical School, the School of Fine Arts and the Marymont Agricultural College, attracted to it by its excellent service in providing literature forbidden by the censor. Majewski professed his ultimate object to be the calling of an insurrection, but that was not on his immediate agenda. He viewed with suspicion the possible intervention of Mierosławski in the affairs of the Congress Kingdom and tried to keep him quiet by conducting negotiations with him, as if the Self-Help Society held in its hands the threads of a future revolt. From the very beginning Majewski revealed considerable reluctance to encourage the partisans of direct action. His own inclinations led him closer to the Millenary group of Jurgens, to which he, as brother of one of Warsaw's more successful laywers, Wincenty Majewski, instinctively belonged, but already there were signs of a more revolutionary trend among the students and workmen of the city.

Since the spring of 1858 Narcyz Jankowski, a retired officer of the Russian army, had been constructing a more radical association. Majewski did not offer open opposition, but joined with him in the creation of the *Kapituła* (Chapter), the first federation of Warsaw radicalism, but Jankowski was easily played off. He was invited to go abroad to confer with Kurzyna with the result that his passage through Cracow attracted the attention of the Austrian police, who arrested him on his return journey and handed him over to the Russian authorities. Majewski was thus left in undisputed control of the academic youth of Warsaw and could divert their activity along relatively innocuous lines. On the one hand he had to satisfy the emotional craving for action, but on the other he must prevent violence from leading to savage repression by the Russians and to the undoing of the concessions obtained since 1856. It was for this reason that in 1860 he formed an alliance with the Millenary group. Jurgens, Majewski and a schoolmaster, Władysław Gołemberski, constituted the so-called 'Triumvirate', the task of which was to direct the energies of Warsaw towards political activity with the object of convincing the Russian government of the need for reform and at the same time to compel the Agricultural Society to use its position as the one legal Polish institution to extend its attention to matters other than farming. The Triumvirate did not wish to promote a revolution, but merely to accelerate the evolution of reform.

The weapon which the Triumvirate chose was the rowdyism in the streets. Quiescence under Paskevich's rule had given the impression at home and abroad that the Polish spirit was dead and that the system of iron subjection had achieved its purpose. The Triumvirate now proposed to give evidence that this was an incorrect assumption. Political demonstrations might be forbidden, but there was nothing to prevent the populace from showing its respect to the dead, especially if the corpse was symbolic of some national achievement. When Count Wincenty Krasiński died in 1858, a man who had long feathered his own nest by adopting an attitude of subservience to the Russians, the populace chose to remember that he had once been an officer in the service of Napoleon I and turned out to pay exaggerated homage at his funeral, as if he were a national hero. In February 1859 his son, Zygmunt Krasiński, one of the three great Romantic poets of Poland, died abroad in exile and the memorial service in Warsaw attracted large numbers of people. This in its turn gave rise to the idea of a memorial service to all three poets, Mickiewicz, Słowacki and Krasiński, but on this occasion the authorities forbade the service amid angry protests. In this setting the Grochów demonstration of June 1859 assumed a significance it scarcely deserved. The Triumvirate were therefore confident that they could obtain a response from the public and set itself to arrange larger and better organized demonstrations. Thus every funeral turned out to be a demonstration of Polish solidarity. The culmination of this movement was the open demonstration against the monarchs of the three partitioning powers, when they met in Warsaw from 20 to 25 October 1860. There were dangers in this form of political pressure, because the demonstration could easily become not a means, but an end in itself. It was a weapon which the most inexperienced and the least intelligent agitator could use. It could be employed again and again, often without clear appreciation of the political purposes it was expected to achieve. Undoubtedly the young Poles acquired a taste for annoying the Russians. It was understandable that even the simplest Russian soldiers resented being called 'Cabbage Heads' and answered the Poles with a growing dislike.

The rowdiness of the Warsaw streets was reaching its climax precisely at a moment when Alexander II was preparing himself for the signature and promulgation of the decree of emancipation in the Russian Empire. The news of impending decision created a flurry in all Polish political circles, because similar reforms could not afterwards be long delayed in the Kingdom. The attitude of the Warsaw Left was that the Poles ought not to appear to follow in the wake of the backward Russians. It followed that the Polish landlords themselves must take the initiative in order to prevent the peasantry gaining the impression that their real benefactors were the Russians and their Tsar. The Triumvirate therefore decided that the Agricultural Society must be forced at last to make a positive decision in the agrarian question. Nothing less would suffice than a declaration in favour of freeholds to be obtained on generous terms. At the same time the inadequacy of Russian concessions was not to be passed over. The Agricultural Society, though not a parliament, nevertheless had the authority of a semi-representative body. The plan was to organize a great demonstration on the occasion of the Society's conference in Warsaw in February 1861 and to carry away the conservatively minded *szlachta* in a tremendous wave of national emotion. This plan was so widely canvassed in Warsaw that neither the Russians nor the landlords were left in much doubt of the radicals' intentions.

At the end of 1860 a sense of urgency was at last introduced into the situation. The landlords were required to solve the agrarian question, which many of them thought needed no solution. There were almost as many opinions as there were landlords to express them. The 1850's had seen the rise of agricultural literature, both pamphlets proposing reform and monographs in the field of economic history; the researches of Prince Tadeusz Lubomirski mark the beginning of the modern study of Polish agrarian history. In 1860, however, leisurely academic study of an urgent political problem was not possible. There were *szlachta* from the eastern regions of the Kingdom, who had little money to effect a conversion to commercial farming and who feared the abolition of labour services; the aesthetic defences of serf labour from Jan Mittelstaedt might not find much vocal support, but there were those who silently agreed with him. The group which controlled the publication of *Roczniki Gospodarstwa Krajowego* and was entrenched in the committee of the Agricultural Society, led by Andrzej Zamoyski and therefore called the 'Klemensów Party', favoured only conversion to rents. Count Tomasz Potocki, however, was prepared to offer strong arguments in favour of conversion to freeholds. He believed that an emancipated peasant class would develop the same political instincts as the conservative landlords. A conservative Poland could thus be formed which

would be able to shield Eastern Europe from the progress of socialism as once she protected the West from the onslaughts of barbarism.[1]

Philanthropy played as little part in Potocki's thinking as in Andrzej Zamoyski's. Potocki never proposed that the peasants should obtain their freeholds without paying compensation to the landlords. He hoped to retain for the manor the traditional rights of hunting, fishing and the monopoly of distilling. The woodlands and pastures he would have reserved to the manor. His object was to go half-way to meeting the aspirations of the peasants, but to leave them in some degree of dependence upon the gentry.

The sense of danger and excitement at the beginning of 1861 was sufficient to bring Potocki's brother-in-law, Alexander Wielopolski, back into Polish politics. Wielopolski, normally a semi-recluse, advanced upon Warsaw to discover what part he could play in the crisis which was about to mount. Wielopolski's views did not differ substantially from those of Andrzej Zamoyski, at least with regard to the agrarian question. He too was in favour of conversion only to rents,[2] but he realized that the agrarian problem did not constitute the whole Polish question. Wielopolski had the same appreciation of the situation as the Left, but he believed that some political concessions were necessary to draw off the pressures exhibited on the streets of Warsaw, with the aim of diverting national energies into more orderly and

---

[1] T. Potocki, *O urządzeniu stosunków rolniczych* (second edition, Poznań, 1859), pp. ix, 516–27.

[2] Cf. his views expressed in *Biblioteka Ordynacyi Myszkowskiej*, 1 (1859), Introduction p. 62.

constitutional channels. He hoped to put to advantage his long record of willingness to co-operate first expressed in his *Letter to Metternich* in 1846, but his own isolation and his willingness to accept the Organic Statute of 1832 were insuperable obstacles to acceptance of his ideas even by the *szlachta*. At the beginning of 1861 Warsaw stood on the verge of crisis, the Poles prisoners of their own difficulties and emotions. The landlords were divided, the radical movement prepared to put pressure upon them, but not itself to seize power. Only in this situation of indecision could Wielopolski have hoped to influence events at all.

CHAPTER III

The Crisis of February–April 1861

THE Viceroy, Mikhail Gorchakov, was not seriously disturbed by the course of events in the Kingdom of Poland. He was confident that the upper classes would approach the question of peasant emancipation with caution. The displays of discontent in the streets he was inclined to dismiss as the pranks of schoolboys. To Simmons, the retiring British consul, he declared that they were 'foolish exhibitions . . . deserving a good flogging' and he repeated this opinion to his successor, Stanton.[1] There had indeed been no Polish demonstration which the police and the Russian army could not easily have suppressed. In St. Petersburg, however, the chancellor, Alexander Gorchakov, was obliged to take a wider view of the situation. The British ambassador, Crampton, detected in him signs of uneasiness. In a private letter to Russell he reported that the chancellor 'was evidently alarmed at something and although he did not pronounce the word "Poland" I could perceive that this was the subject probably uppermost in his thoughts'.[2] This may have been only an intelligent guess, but it was obvious that serious disturbances in Congress Poland coinciding with the state of tension within the Russian Empire on the promulgation of the decrees of emancipation, which everyone expected to be made on the anniversary of the Tsar's accession at the beginning of March, was the last thing that a Russian statesman desired. If the Russian peasants chose to react violently against the scheme of liquidation, which was in fact to be a partial expropriation of their lands by the landlords, then there was a chance that a crisis in Poland, with its attendant possibilities of inter-

[1] F.O. 65/557, Simmons to Russell, November 1860, and F.O. 65/583, Stanton to Russell, 20 February and 25 February 1861.
[2] P.R.O. 30/22/23, Crampton to Russell, 11 January 1861.

national complications, might be sufficient to threaten the security of the entire Empire. These were, however, considerations which seemed to have troubled Mikhail Gorchakov and his army staff very little. They were confident that they could meet any danger from the side of the Poles.

Russian confidence in their own security from Polish attack was to all appearances correct enough. The Polish populace was unarmed and had no intention of precipitating an insurrection. The leaders of the left-wing Triumvirate, Majewski, Jurgens and Gołemberski, were not directing their efforts against the government, but rather placing pressure upon the Agricultural Society. Their calculation was that no Pole would care to admit in public anything less than the most intense zeal for the national cause. If they could rouse the people of Warsaw to a pitch of patriotic ardour and induce them to demand that the Agricultural Society should take the initiative of declaring its willingness to grant the peasants their freeholds, then the landlords would be swept away in the prevailing emotional tension. They believed that they had only to send a large body of demonstrators into the hall where the Agricultural Society was meeting and they would carry all before them. The nobility of France had been carried away in a gust of sentimental self-sacrifice in August 1789, when they had renounced their feudal privileges. There seemed no reason why the Polish *szlachta* should not be induced to do the same.

Andrzej Zamoyski and the Klemensów group within the Agricultural Society's executive committee had no doubt of what was afoot in the city of Warsaw. They had small inclination for any other solution than conversion to rents and they certainly did not intend to submit to the left wing's pressure for the presentation of a petition to the Tsar asking for the grant of political liberties to the Congress Kingdom, because that course might result in the suppression of the society itself and the destruction of all hope that the gentry themselves would guide and direct the course of emancipation in the Kingdom. Zamoyski and his friends therefore came to the conclusion that the Society should use its initiative while it still had it. The best way out of their difficulties was to hurry through the agrarian business and, when this had been done, to dissolve the meeting before the left wing could assemble their forces in the streets. Thus Polish honour would be satisfied by the declaration abolishing labour services before the promulgation of the Russian decree, conversion to rents rather than freeholds obtained and the landed gentry left with their social hegemony unchallenged.[1] It was small wonder that the Viceroy thought the situation in Galicia more threatening.

The Klemensów party, however, though strongly represented in the committee, was by no means unanimously supported by the rank and file of the membership. An effort was made to achieve uniformity of outlook by calling in the local secretaries of the Society on 18 February for preliminary discussions, but when the Society assembled on 21 February it was obvious that Zamoyski was not to have his way. As president he opened the conference with an address advocating conversion to rents, but he was not long left unchallenged. Węgleński, as conservative as Zamoyski and not hitherto in disagreement with him, stated that something more substantial than conversion to rents was required. Tomasz Potocki came out strongly once more in favour of freeholds. The solution which the Society reached in its sessions of 25 and 27 February was in effect a compromise solution, between the two opposing views among its own members on the one hand and on the other partially approaching the solution required of the Society by the left-wing movement in the city.[2] A six-point resolution was drawn up, declaring that speeding abolition of labour services and conversion to rents was the prime need, though this must be achieved by voluntary agreements between the landlords and peasants. Ultimately, however, the peasants should proceed to the purchase of their freeholds, the capital value of their farms being achieved by multiplying the estimated annual value of the rents by sixteen and two-thirds. The commune and not the individual peasant was to be responsible for the regular payment of the instalments. In order to facilitate the operation of this scheme a request was to be made to the government for a committee to examine the workings of the Administrative Council's decision of 28 December

[1] Cf. F.O. 65/583, two letters of Stanton to Russell, 12 February 1861, which record Zamoyski's views.

[2] For the text see *Roczniki Gospodarstwa Krajowego*, XLIII (1861), pp. 128, 140–2.

1858. This resolution therefore was a document which could permit conversion to rents along the lines advocated by Zamoyski, in which the dogma of the freely negotiated contract between landlord and peasant would give the gentry every opportunity to extract as high a rent as possible without the interference of the state. If the worst came to the worst and conversion to freeholds became necessary, then the capital value of the holdings would be a multiplication of an inflated rent. In the conditions which existed in Congress Poland the plan of the gentry can scarcely be considered a generous gesture towards the peasantry.

While these discussions were proceeding in the Namiestnikowski Palace, private talks were being held in the Europejski Hotel in which the question was posed, whether or not the Society should submit a list of political demands to the Viceroy on behalf of the Polish nation. There was general agreement that Poles could not appeal to the treaty of 1815, because that would seem to recognize the fact of partition and deny the ultimate aim of independence within the frontiers of historic Poland. This fidelity to the national ideal, necessary because adherence to anything less would have destroyed the respect which the Agricultural Society undoubtedly enjoyed among the public in Warsaw, complicated the problem of formulating an address. The emotional need to demand everything destroyed the possibility of presenting the modest requests which would have satisfied the majority of Poles, for the system of 1815 was the very most that the Tsar would restore. Zamoyski refused absolutely to consider the presentation of any form of political demand, because for him the prime necessity in Poland was material and moral reconstruction. Dabbling in politics might lead to the suppression of the Agricultural Society itself, which would exclude the gentry from a voice in the details of agrarian reform. He privately declared that he could not remain president of the Society if its members insisted upon a petition, and his influence was enough to induce them to abandon all intentions of a political nature.[1]

Jurgens and the Millenary group were not completely convinced of the value of a demonstration, but Majewski and his

---

[1] For an eyewitness account of these discussions see A. Wrotnowski, *Porozbiorowe aspiracye polityczne narodu polskiego* (3rd edition, Cracow, 1898), pp. 222–4.

students insisted that they should call for a public ceremony to commemorate the anniversary of the battle of Grochów, 25 January, which should serve the purpose of attracting a large crowd, which could be led to the Namiestnikowski Palace. There an attempt was to be made to put spirit into the Agricultural Society. The Viceroy knew of these plans and was ready to frustrate them. A large crowd was easily broken up by the police in the Square of the Three Crosses. The Agricultural Society was unruffled by the entry of a member crying out that their countrymen were being murdered in the streets and supported the view of Zamoyski that the Society should take no notice of the disturbances. Gorchakov was confident that all was quiet and the situation well under control. Karol Majewski, however, was delighted by the response which he obtained from the Warsaw public and decided that another and larger demonstration should be called for 27 February. He believed that the demonstration of 25 January had been enough to produce a change of heart in the Agricultural Society, because on that day it had admitted for the first time the need for conversion to peasant freeholds. A second demonstration might force it to draw up a petition to the Tsar. Both the Viceroy and Zamoyski were equally determined that such a demonstration should have no chance of approaching the Namiestnikowski Palace. Zamoyski himself requested protection from the government, lest the Agricultural Society's meetings be interrupted by demonstrators.

It was not difficult to assemble a large crowd on 27 February. Rumours had been circulating that a 'virgin Jenike' had lost her life on 25 February, but this was too hollow to be believed. What did attract attention was a memorial service in honour of Zawisza, a revolutionary executed for his part in the Zaliwski expedition of 1833, and Konarski, the emissary of Young Poland, executed in Vilna in 1839. The mood of the city was so excited that any religious procession would have attracted followers. No one was quite clear of its intentions, but from the outskirts of the town the procession made its way into the square before the Castle when it became involved in the purely private funeral of one Lempicki, an official of the Fire Assurance Board. Here, thought the crowd, was the victim of Russian brutality on

25 February. An incredible mêlée ensued, when the crowd and the cossacks, attempting to head off the demonstrators and prevent them from marching up the Krakowskie Przedmieście to the Namiestnikowski Palace, became mixed up with the funeral cortège. A man holding the cross began to use it as a club and when it broke the crowd shouted that the Russians were defiling the holy objects of the Roman Catholic faith. All this would have come to nothing had not the Russian adjutant-general, Zabolotsky, who had no authority to interfere as he did, turned out a company of Russian troops and marched them into the Krakowskie Przedmieście from the opposite end of the street from which the troops and police were trying to clear it. Assaulted with stones and mud, Zabolotsky threatened to open fire, which only drew forth cries of 'You can't! Napoleon has forbidden it!', a reference to the common suspicion that the milder rule in Congress Poland was the result of the Franco-Russian understanding. Others shouted that there was nothing to fear—'Don't be afraid! They will shoot with blank cartridges!' For some reason unknown the Russian soldiers obtained the impression that they had been fired upon and Zabolotsky immediately gave the order to fire into the crowd. The Russian soldiers, who had stood enough from Polish insults, did as they were told, but their standard of musketry was not high. Although fifty-five rounds were fired, only five persons were killed, including two members of the Agricultural Society who had walked down the street to observe the fray. At once the crowd scampered in all directions, carrying with it the corpse of Lempicki.

This incident could scarcely have been attributed to the Viceroy's brutality. Indeed, he was at a loss to discover what had happened. Nevertheless, it achieved for the left wing exactly that result which they had desired. For the first time a mass indignation swept Warsaw. The whole affair was enlarged into a massacre. The five corpses were collected and at length laid out in the Europejski Hotel, where all might file past and pay their homage. Almost the entire middle-class population of Warsaw adopted the dark clothes of mourning, which were retained long afterwards as the mark of hostility to Russia. Never had there been such a display of solidarity. All classes of the community joined together to honour the dead. The only regret was that there were not more victims. A Jew was wounded but to the intense chagrin of his co-religionists he recovered. Thus it was not possible to paint a picture of Jew and Gentile suffering together, but the Jews nevertheless put a good face on the matter and paid their tribute to the Christian dead. In view of the unanimous indignation in the city of Warsaw it was no longer possible for the leaders of the Agricultural Society to pretend that there was no need for the presentation of political demands to the Viceroy. Failure to take action would have turned opinion against the Agricultural Society and against the gentry class as a whole.

There were already signs that the merchants of the Chamber of Commerce were prepared to take independent action if need be without the gentry. It sent a deputation to the Viceroy demanding a public funeral with full honours and insisted that the popular and lenient Marquis Paulucci, a member of the army staff well known for his liberal opinions, should be appointed Chief of Police. A request was made also that the Chamber of Commerce should be allowed to send a deputation to St. Petersburg to present an address to the Tsar.[1] Gorchakov seemed shaken by the turn which events had taken. To Zamoyski he protested his innocence: 'Me prenez-vous pour un Autrichien? Je n'ai donné qu'un seul ordre, celui de ne pas livrer la citadelle, même sur une injonction signée de ma main.' To the Chamber of Commerce he conceded the appointment of Paulucci to a general oversight of the Warsaw police. It appeared that at last the Poles of the Kingdom could now take the initiative.

There followed a critical debate in the Zamoyski Palace between the leaders of the gentry and the prominent members of the Chamber of Commerce. It was easy to realize that a new situation had arisen, but less easy to formulate suggestions for the better government of the Kingdom. At this stage the Marquis Wielopolski intervened with his own suggestions. He had always been in favour of bold action and had insisted that the nobility through their marshals had the right of approach to the Tsar, but there had been few willing to associate themselves with him. He had in the past shown little regard for public

[1] N. V. Berg, *Pamiętniki o polskich spiskach i powstaniach*, pp. 221–3.

opinion. His *Letter* addressed to Metternich in 1846 had too openly pronounced in favour of complete co-operation between Poles and Russians for his views to be entirely acceptable to public opinion, but now once more he returned to the problem, presenting through his brother-in-law, Tomasz Potocki, the plan of a petition to the Tsar, which he asked the Polish leaders to consider. To some his draft seemed audacious. He declared that the Poles were denied all part in the government of their country and were ruled by foreigners who did not understand native conditions. Normal studies were hamstrung by the absence of suitable higher education, while rigid censorship prevented the growth of a healthy public opinion. The Jews were treated as a caste apart, though they were as much inhabitants of the Kingdom as the Christian Poles. These points were simple enough, but they were prefaced by references to the constitution of 1815 and the Organic Statute of 1832, which would have given the Tsar to suppose that the Poles would have been content with the restoration of local autonomy within the frontiers defined by the Vienna Treaty. This contained the implication that the Polish leaders had given their tacit acceptance to the permanence of partition and no longer desired the unification of all Poland within one body politic. Most of the landed proprietors would have been content enough to get back to the system of 1815, but the middle-class element, in closer contact with the rising temper of the Warsaw public, refused to append their signatures to an address of the kind proposed by Wielopolski, lest they lose their authority in the town, in which case the extreme radicals might gain control.[1] The Polish leaders therefore decided to have recourse to a wordy address, which avoided direct demands and which at the same time seemed to express the pent-up emotions of the public.[2]

The address finally agreed upon in the Zamoyski Palace pleaded that events in Warsaw were the manifestation of a unanimous feeling which showed the need for some legal means by which public opinion might be represented, but there was no elaboration of this suggestion with concrete proposals. One sen-

---

[1] For the French and Polish texts of Wielopolski's plan, see H. Lisicki, *Aleksander Wielopolski*, II, 31 f.

[2] *Wydawnictwo materyałów do historyi powstania, 1863–1864* (Lvov, 1888), I, 1–2.

tence at least could be interpreted to mean that the Poles had not surrendered their ideal of complete independence in all parts of Poland:

This country, equal once in the degree of its civilization with other countries of Europe, will not achieve the development of its moral and material resources as long as the principles flowing from the spirit of the Nation, its tradition and history, shall find no expression in the Church, in legislation, in public education, in short, in its entire social organism.

These were not sentiments which were likely to be received with approval in St. Petersburg, where the suspicion would immediately be entertained that an extension of the frontiers to include the *gubernii* of western Russia was what lay at the bottom of Polish hearts. The British consul, Stanton, was actually informed by Zamoyski that the extension of constitutional freedoms to western Russia was essential.[1] The defence of the address adopted by the gentry was that it wisely steered a course between the excited feelings of the public and the hostility of the Tsar, leaving to him to decide the exact extent of concessions.[2]

The Viceroy, Gorchakov, was impressed by the solidarity of Polish opposition. A middle-class committee had taken over the arrangements for a ceremonial funeral of the five victims. All the marshals of the nobility resigned their offices in protest against the shootings. On the morning of 28 February Zamoyski arrived with the Archbishop, Fijałkowski, to present the Polish address to which were already appended 20,000 signatures. At first Gorchakov had supposed that the crisis was by no means serious, merely requesting that a state of siege should be proclaimed and reporting that an address had been submitted to him, the terms of which were 'very liberal', to which the Tsar replied that 'in any case now is not the time to make concessions and I will not make them'.[3] Gorchakov may have hoped that the excitement would gradually die down and that it would not be necessary to make recommendations to the Tsar, but the funeral of the five victims on 2 March, during which a voluntary police force of Poles took the place of the military and

[1] F.O. 65/583, Stanton to Russell, 2 March and 16 March 1861.
[2] A. Wrotnowski, *Porozbiorowe aspiracye*, p. 240.
[3] *Russkaya Starina*, XXXVI, 553–4, 555.

H

uniformed police in maintaining order, was the occasion of so impressive a display of national solidarity that the isolation of the Russian administration could not have been made more plain. Gorchakov attempted to convey the gravity of this situation by sending a copy of the Polish address not to the Tsar, but to the minister of war, Sukhozanet, who would naturally forward it to the Tsar, but the Tsar, to some extent lulled into a sense of security by Gorchakov's earlier telegrams, replied that the address was improper and must be returned.[1] Finally, Gorchakov took his courage into his hands and told the Tsar frankly that the situation was critical and that there was need to send to Warsaw a person enjoying his personal confidence to examine the state of affairs in the Kingdom. On 3 March he again telegraphed to St. Petersburg, asking permission to withhold the rejection of the address until the arrival of Karnicki, a Polish official in the government of the Kingdom, who was charged with making personal explanations to the Tsar. At length the Tsar's resolution began to weaken a little. On 4 March he agreed to await Karnicki's arrival, but added on 5 March that the address was most unsuitable and that orders had been given to the minister of war to send reinforcements into the Kingdom: 'You are not on any account to leave the city of Warsaw. In the event of need bombard it from the citadel.' These were strong words, but a gradual change of policy in St. Petersburg was becoming evident. It is not easy to discover what was the exact state of opinion among Russian ministers, but it is not unreasonable to suppose that caution sprang from the realization that the decree of emancipation for the Empire, signed but not promulgated on 3 March 1861, required tranquillity. The Kingdom of Poland had been denuded of troops to guard against disturbances in Russia and the prospect of widespread hostility in Poland was not one to be faced with equanimity.

The exact nature of the discussions in government circles in Warsaw is likewise by no means clear, but a general agreement was reached that the situation in the city should be handled with tact. It appears that after the shootings of 27 January Gorchakov ordered Julius Enoch, the chief procurator of the Plenum of the Warsaw departments of the Senate, to make a

[1] Ibid., xxxvi, 555-6.

report on the situation.[1] Enoch's appreciation was that Europe was suffering from a revolutionary malaise and that recent events in Italy, the Danubian principalities and the Austrian Empire were bound to have repercussions on the state of feeling in Poland. If the aspirations of the moderates were frustrated, there was a danger that they would be forced into collaboration with the extremists. There was therefore only one course open to the government:

Il est de son devoir d'empêcher la jonction des rouges avec les propriétaires fonciers, jonction qui était à prévoir tant en regard au manque du courage civil de la majorité des citoyens, qu'aux sympathies ouvertes pour les fauteurs du désordre d'un grand nombre entr'eux.

The government could never hope to satisfy the masses, but it might win over the small but influential group of landed gentry and middle class who had much to lose by disorder and who would not join a revolution unless all hope of amelioration were destroyed. They therefore ought to be admitted to some small part in the administration and a number of grievances ought to be removed. The Roman Catholic church might be placed under the control of a Pole rather than an Orthodox Russian. The Poles ought to be given some share in the preparation of legislation. The interesting suggestion was put forward that a university might be established, because otherwise Polish students would study in Russian universities, where removed from parental supervision they would almost certainly pick up subversive ideas; a university in Poland would tend to combat radicalism. The way to attract Poles into co-operation with the authorities was the erection of a local government system, with the qualification that large assemblies of electors should be forbidden and that the franchise be strictly limited and the elec-

[1] For the text see H. Lisicki, *Aleksander Wielopolski*, II, 39–47. Karnicki afterwards called into question the authenticity of this document, declaring that it was drawn up much later in order to leave in the archives a proof that initiative came from the Polish side, cf. *Suum cuique—Kilka słów z powodu niektórych ustępów dzieła p.t. Aleksander Wielopolski* (Dresden, 1878). A. M. Skałkowski, *Aleksander Wielopolski*, III, 14–15, citing Enoch's unpublished reply, *Odpowiedź na dresdeńską broszurę 'Suum cuique'*, upholds its authenticity. Cf. also A. M. Skałkowski, 'Juliusz Enoch i jego pisma w sprawach polsko-rosyjskich 1861–1864', *Pamiętnik Biblioteki Kornickiej*, IV (1947), pp. 197–207.

tions indirect. Gorchakov himself drew up a very similar appreciation on 1 March for transmission to the Tsar.[1] He declared that he could, if an insurrection broke out, take the army out of the city into the country and bombard the city into submission, but that it would be profitable first to try tactful handling of the situation by investigating the shootings, allowing the funeral of the five victims to proceed without interference and giving Paulucci supervision of the police. There were therefore two sides to Russian official thinking in Warsaw. On the one hand friendship was to be extended to the propertied classes, but on the other security precautions were to be strengthened to prevent Polish radicals from obtaining control.

The upper classes, however, did not reveal a corresponding willingness to collaborate with the government. Only one man had appeared to offer any concrete proposals and that was Wielopolski, who had departed into the country to avoid being involved in the funeral ceremonies in Warsaw. It was to Wielopolski that Gorchakov now turned, recalling him to Warsaw and asking him to give a closer definition to his abortive project of an address of 27 February.[2] Wielopolski wished to obtain regional self-government, even though this in some measure fell short of the constitution of 1815. Among his proposals he now included the erection of a council of state charged with the preparation of legislation, a supreme court operating in Warsaw, a senate of Polish notables, with provincial dietines, and a new municipal administration in Warsaw. To deal with the problem of public order he asked for new regulations governing public meetings and for the abolition of military courts. To meet the demands of the liberal bourgeoisie he asked that the Jews should be given equal rights with the Christians. Above all, he insisted that there should be a positive attempt to settle the agrarian question by converting labour services into rents; Wielopolski rejected the Agricultural Society's plan of conversion by voluntary agreement and called for the direct intervention of the state to force a solution upon the peasants. Gorchakov watered down the political proposals of Wielopolski when they came to their agreement on an eight-point programme

[1] *Russkaya Starina*, c (1899), pp. 119–21.
[2] H. Lisicki, *Aleksander Wielopolski*, i, pp. 173–5.

on 14 March. The final result of the negotiations was that they proposed a senatorial council consisting of eight palatines, the bishops and some nominees of the crown, who should meet yearly, hearing petitions and complaints, surveying the operation of the laws, and commenting upon the conduct of the administration; every two years a Plenary Council, composed of the senators and leading officials, was to meet to examine draft plans for fresh legislation. This was a solution which clearly aimed at safeguarding the interests of the landed gentry, though bringing in the urban middle class as a junior partner in the affairs of state. Nevertheless, Gorchakov still considered that it might be more than the Tsar would grant and waited for information on the Polish Chancery's view in St. Petersburg which he expected the official Karnicki to bring back.[1] It was not until 21 March that he transmitted Wielopolski's plan to St. Petersburg, a slowness in informing the Imperial government which was now criticized by the Tsar who was beginning to recognize the need for speed.[2]

During the period between the funeral of the five victims and the Tsar's ultimate decision an uneasy quiet prevailed in Warsaw. The moderate Polish groups, who feared that the extremists of the left wing might get out of hand, did everything they could to keep their unruly fellow countrymen and especially the working men of the city in order. Archbishop Fijałkowski set the tone by ordering a period of unlimited mourning for the five victims, which lent a certain formality and solemnity to Polish hostility. The committee which had organized the funeral sought to keep demonstrations within bounds by organizing a collection on behalf of the dead men's relatives and by establishing a fund for the erection of a statue in their honour. Gorchakov did what he could to assist the civic leaders. On 5 March he permitted the establishment of a 'Municipal Delegation' to advise the government on the handling of the situation.[3] The Agricultural Society circularized its members on 3 March, appealing for the preservation of unity and order. Indeed, the situation seemed tranquil enough for the Society

---

[1] Cf. *Russkaya Starina*, c, 128.   [2] *Ibid.*, xxxvi, 562.
[3] For the minutes of its meetings see W. Przyborowski, *Historya dwóch lat*, ii, 495–514.

to take up the agrarian question, for on 12 March it issued a confidential circular informing its local agencies of the resolutions of 25–27 February, but urging upon them the need to obtain the co-operation of the clergy with the object of avoiding disputes with the peasants; care was to be taken to inform the peasantry only of the first stage of liquidation, conversion to rents, and to avoid mention of the dangerous question of conversion to freeholds. Archbishop Fijałkowski lent his aid to this action, by issuing the slogan of 'Unity among the Faithful' to the clergy. With political reforms uppermost in the minds of the Poles, there was clearly a retreat from the agreement to proceed ultimately with the creation of a completely independent peasantry.

To keep the Poles quiet while reform was being discussed Alexander II agreed to certain prominent persons being informed that changes were about to be introduced, though he insisted that he should not in any way be interpreted to be acting out of a sense of weakness. The adjutant, Meyendorff, was sent from St. Petersburg with the official reply to the address of 27 February, in which the Tsar declared that he rejected it and refused to be swayed by the action of 'a handful of individuals',[1] but verbal permission was given for the nature of the reforms under discussion to be revealed to prominent persons; these reforms were to include the creation of a council of state, the institution of town councils and changes in the system of education. When this news was given by Gorchakov to Zamoyski, Archbishop Fijałkowski and two representatives of the Warsaw bourgeoisie, Leopold Kronenberg and Ksawery Szlenker, on 13 March, they expressed their satisfaction with the prospect of reform, but they objected strongly to the tone of the Tsar's letter of reply to the address, which they feared might have the effect of exciting feverish imaginations in Warsaw. They therefore requested that Gorchakov should not publish the Tsar's letter, but to Gorchakov's request for permission to withhold it there came back the order that it must be published at once. Few Poles ever kept secrets and the news of reform soon made its way round Warsaw and it is doubtful whether the brusque tone of the Tsar's letter impressed the Poles at all. Nevertheless Gor-

[1] H. Lisicki, *Aleksander Wielopolski*, II, 57–8.

chakov felt himself obliged to give colour to the rumours of reform by making a substantial gesture which would convince the public of their truth. He hit upon the happy idea of removing the control of education from the hands of the Director of Internal Affairs, Mukhanov, who was exceedingly unpopular, and giving it to the civil governor of the Warsaw *gubernia*, the Pole Łaszczyński.

Concessions designed to placate the Poles, however, went hand in hand with a strengthening of the security system. On Gorchakov's order, Mukhanov in his capacity of Director of Internal Affairs sent instructions to the civil governors of the five *gubernii* upon the methods which they were to employ against outbreaks of violence.[1] Paragraph IV called upon local officials, in accordance with the security instructions of 1846 and 1848–9, to enlist the aid of the people in the maintenance of order, but because the mayors of the rural communes were under the law of 1818 the landlords within whose estates they fell, or their nominees, it was ordered that this part of the instructions was to be made known to the minor officials of the communes, the *sołtysi*, who were appointed from the peasants. Inevitably this circular soon became known to the public and the inference was drawn that the government was preparing to authorize a massacre of the *szlachta* on the lines of the Galician jacquerie of 1846, which was universally ascribed to the machinations of the Austrian administration. At once there was a public outcry. The Committee of the Agricultural Society felt that the situation was so serious that it issued a new circular pressing for haste in conversion to money rents and, though it still insisted upon voluntary agreements, declared that the purchase of freeholds was its ultimate intention.[2] There was evidently some panic among the officials and officers of Gorchakov's staff, who must have gone behind his back and pleaded with St. Petersburg to dismiss Mukhanov in order that he might take the blame.[3] The promptness with which Alexander II authorized Mukhanov's dismissal is in clear contrast with the

[1] H. Lisicki, *ibid.*, ii, 63–4, prints one version of this circular.
[2] H. Lisicki, *ibid.*, ii, 64–6.
[3] This is the interpretation I place on the Tsar's telegram of 22 March 1861, *Russkaya Starina*, xxxvi, 563.

stout words which he had used at the beginning of the crisis in Poland, which indicates that he had already decided to fall in line with the suggestions which he was receiving from his advisers.

The progress towards reform in St. Petersburg was slow. It cannot be supposed that consideration of the Polish situation alone occupied the attention of the Tsar. On 3 March he had signed the decrees of emancipation for the Empire, which were announced in the churches a fortnight later on 17 March. No doubt the difficulties which he expected in the Empire determined his attitude towards the Polish question, inducing him on the one hand to seek a basis for Russian rule in the Polish propertied classes, and on the other to strengthen as far as he could the security system in the Kingdom. There were, however, limits to the concessions he would make. When Gorchakov's first envoy, the Polish official Karnicki, arrived in St. Petersburg on 7 March, Alexander II's first words to him were—'Dites moi ce qui se passe, qu'est ce qu'on demande à Varsovie. Ce n'est pas une constitution, j'espère!'[1] On 8 March an extraordinary session of the council of state was summoned, at which in addition to Tymowski, the Polish secretary of state, and his assistant, Platonov, Alexander Gorchakov, the minister of war, General Sukhozanet, and the chief of the gendarmerie, Dolgorukov, were present. The outcome of this meeting was that the Polish chancery was ordered to present its appreciation of the situation. The report drawn up in Tymowski's name shows how little would have been granted from the Russian side.[2] It was recommended that elected governments should be set up in the towns, communes, districts and provinces, though in the last two the report insisted upon the principle of indirect election 'because that would be the best guarantee of the election of right-thinking people'. It adopted the plan that a council of state should be resurrected to serve as a means of direct contact with the Tsar. The plan drawn up by Gorchakov and Wielopolski, which proposed a central representative body, was not brought forward from Warsaw until 21 March and was not seen by the Tsar until 24 March. Alexander II, in fact, telegraphed to War-

---

[1] W. Przyborowski, *Historya dwóch lat*, II, 125.
[2] Cf. H. Lisicki, *Aleksander Wielopolski*, II, 47–57.

saw: 'I cannot accept Wielopolski's plan in its entirety.'[1] All elements in Wielopolski's plan which seemed to indicate some degree of autonomy in the Kingdom were eliminated; the senatorial council with its two yearly plenary sessions and even minor suggestions like the redivision of the Kingdom into eight *województwa* instead of five *gubernii* or the restoration of the Alexander University in Warsaw did not meet with approval. Instead, the Tsar granted that the administration of religion and education might be separated from the Commission of Internal Affairs and Wielopolski appointed its director; education might be reformed in order to give adequate facilities for higher studies. The Council of State might be revived as a body drafting laws, but consultation of the Polish gentry and middle classes was to be limited to the creation of councils in the *gubernii*, districts and principal towns.

In Warsaw Gorchakov was nervous lest Easter bring with it a revival of disorders. Hooliganism and serenading of unpopular figures with raucous music had made their appearance. To the black of mourning was now added colour. The idea had gained currency that the frock-coat should be abandoned and that Poles should wear their national dress. Square hats and long boots and all the paraphernalia of traditional clothing appeared, often with ludicrous results. Anxious to maintain order, Gorchakov telegraphed St. Petersburg immediately he received news of reform for permission to release details in the hope that this would have a quietening effect. The Tsar telegraphed back a summary of the changes to be introduced and the Marquis Wielopolski took office as director of the Commission of Religion and Education. The Tsar was, however, under another form of pressure from the military. The russified Pole, General Gechevich, got himself recalled to St. Petersburg to represent the army's point of view, but his stay was short because he was sent back to Warsaw with a sealed letter, the contents of which he did not know, but with which Gorchakov promised to conform.[2] There is every likelihood that Alexander II was preparing the way for some form of repressive action when reform had been granted. In his telegram of 25 March, in which he agreed to make changes, he declared: 'In the event of fresh disorders I

[1] *Russkaya Starina*, xxxvi, 564.   [2] *Russkaya Starina*, xxxvi, 562, 564.

expect energetic measures from your side.'[1] With the departure of Mukhanov the Directorship of Internal Affairs was vacant and it is significant that to this post Gechevich, the man who recommended strong action, was appointed. The letters which Gechevich was sending to St. Petersburg, probably to the minister of war, Sukhozanet, boded ill for the demonstrators. Gechevich, while professing his personal devotion to Gorchakov, saw it as his duty to strengthen his will and, if necessary, to induce him to deal sternly with the working classes. His letter of 3 April contained the ominous sentence: 'Our present position is that of a soldier who takes his weapon into his hands after long standing at ease.'[2] This hint of violent action was not merely the policy of the local military commanders in the Kingdom. It already had the highest approval in St. Petersburg. The formal circular sent to Russian embassies and missions abroad explaining that concessions in the Kingdom of Poland must not be considered to proceed from a sense of weakness[3] takes on a clearer meaning when it is read in conjunction with the letter of the Chancellor Gorchakov to Kiselev in Paris of 31 March 1861, which clearly foreshadowed severe measures:

Le terrain sur lequel nous sommes aujourd'hui est celui du droit qui nous donne doublement la faculté de réprimer sévèrement les tendances qui dépasseraient les limites de la pensée Impériale.

Les télégrammes de Varsovie nous annoncent déjà une impression favorable qui aurait pour résultat de séparer les classes intelligentes de la populace. Si cette dernière remue il en sera fait justice.[4]

The Russian government had already come to the conclusion that it was once more master of the situation in Warsaw. On the next occasion shootings were not to be accidental.

Easter 1861 in Warsaw was turned into a festival of class solidarity. The working men of the city were entertained in the houses of the aristocracy and middle class. Poles and Jews fraternized with one another. No one was in a mood to listen

---

[1] *Ibid.*, xxxvi, 564.

[2] 'Pis'ma generala Getsevicha k***', *Russkaya Starina*, c (1899), pp. 138–9.

[3] H. Lisicki, *Aleksander Wielopolski*, ii, 89–90.

[4] F.O. 64/574, Napier to Russell, 5 April 1861. This is an extract of a document which came into the possession of the British embassy from the printing department of the Russian foreign office.

to Wielopolski. Andrzej Zamoyski might have lent his influence, but as soon as he received the news of the concessions he announced his refusal of co-operation. He conceded that Poles might with profit take part in the government of the Kingdom, because they were citizens of a province of Poland, but that 'there must be some one who should represent the ancient Poland in her historic frontiers. I shall be that man. I shall reserve myself for this task and I can take no official post.'[1] Wielopolski, who could not have found a personal approach to Zamoyski easy, tried to bury their differences by paying a visit to the Zamoyski Palace during the Easter holiday, but was only snubbed for his pains. It was an unpromising beginning to be denied the co-operation of the leading figure in the Kingdom. The clergy likewise took offence. They were annoyed by his speech in which he announced that he would tolerate 'no government within a government', by which he meant to indicate that he would not act as a puppet to be manipulated either by the clergy or by the gentry; as far as they were concerned, they must realize that he would act with fairness towards all other religious denominations. The clergy certainly did not relish his promise to the Jews that they should receive justice.[2] A handbill was published by a small body of priests, who had no scruples about signing themselves as the 'Catholic Clergy of the Kingdom of Poland', declaring that they took their stand upon the principle that the Catholic was the national religion of the Poles.[3] It became patriotic for parish priests to condemn Wielopolski, where they might have exerted a moderating influence upon their congregations. Where Wielopolski failed to obtain respect, it was unlikely that the Russian Gorchakov, however great his reputation for mildness, would succeed in calming the public. His appeal for co-operation of 2 April 1861, issued with full knowledge of the alternatives for the Poles, passed unheeded.

The excited mood of the city seemed artificial by comparison with the tide of elemental discontent which threatened to over-

[1] W. Przyborowski, *Historya dwóch lat*, II, 254–5n.

[2] Cf. his speech to the Jews of Pinczów, H. Lisicki, *Aleksander Wielopolski*, II, 79–80.

[3] For the text see A. Giller, *Manifestacye Warszawy 1861 r.* (Stanisławów, 1908), pp. 75–6.

whelm the countryside. Fear of the consequences of the Mukhanov circular had already driven the Agricultural Society's executive committee to inform the peasants that it approved in principle conversion to freeholds. It was realized that this discussion of a fundamental question would raise a storm of speculation in the countryside, which it would require an effort to restrain, lest there be a repetition of the events of 1846, still hanging like an evil cloud over Poland. The aid of the clergy and the bishops was enlisted to preach the doctrine of national unity and the fraternity of landlord and peasant.[1] A pamphlet was issued over the signature of a peasant named Długoszek, who had been installed as a member of the Agricultural Society as a symbol of the solidarity prevailing in the farming community. This pamphlet likewise called for a display of goodwill between landlord and peasant.[2] Instructions were given to the local representatives of the Society to press on with the work of agrarian reform. Into the midst of all this Wielopolski plunged, brushing aside the plea of the Agricultural Society that the ultimate aim was conversion to freeholds. Convinced that conversion to rents must first be undertaken, Wielopolski on 30 March issued a summons to the clergy to assist in the work of the landlords and the government in converting labour services, thus revealing that there was a division of opinion among the landlords and between the Agricultural Society and the government. It is not surprising that with these announcements the peasants became suspicious of what was happening in Warsaw.

The excitement of the Polish peasants was enormously increased when they discovered that on 17 March there had been an announcement of reform in Russia, even though they were ignorant of its details. The political organization authorized by the laws of 3 March 1861 was uniform for the entire Russian Empire, including those areas in which the Polish gentry were supreme. A rural commune was formed from the peasants who constituted the property of one landlord; these peasants were

---

[1] Cf. H. Lisicki, *Aleksander Wielopolski*, II, 66–75, for the efforts of the administrator in the diocese of Płock.

[2] For the Russian version see A. Podvisotsky, *Zapiski ochevidtsa o sobytiyakh v Varshave v 1861 i 1862 godakh* (St. Petersburg, 1869).

to form an assembly and appoint an alderman (*starosta*) and collector of taxes. A group of communes formed a canton (*volost*) with an assembly consisting of its chairman (*starshina*), officials and collectors of taxes. This system was to come into operation within nine months of the publication of the decrees in the *gubernia*. To settle disputes between landlords and peasants there were established arbitration commissions, appointed from among the local landlords, from whom there could be appeal to the district commission, if either party did not obtain satisfaction. Beyond these two commissions was a commission of the *gubernia*, which acted as the final arbiter.

Two general principles governed the economic reorganization of the Empire. The landlord was granted ownership of the soil, but he was placed under the obligation to grant the peasants a messuage and a portion of the arable land. The peasant remained liable for the payment of dues to the landlord, whether in labour or money. The villagers had to settle their relations with the landlords, which were to be recorded in a regulatory charter within two years of the publication of the decrees in the *gubernia*. Special rules applied within the two areas formerly embraced by the Polish Republic, the northern group of *gubernii*, Vilna, Grodno, Kovno, Minsk and parts of Vitebsk, the area defined as Polish Livonia, and the southern group, the *gubernii* of Kiev, Podolia and Volhynia. In both areas work had been in progress since 1844 to draw up inventories, which could not be ignored. The system of peasant tenure here was different from the Great Russian.

In the northern group all supplementary obligations in kind were abolished and the inventories adopted as the basis of the peasants' dues. The landlord might retain one-third of the cultivated land, on condition that the lands of the peasants were not reduced by more than one-sixth. The peasants could perform their obligations in labour, but if they decided to convert to rents, they were to be assessed on the basis of the inventory with a deduction of 10 per cent, provided that the rents did not exceed three roubles per diesiatin. Rents were, however, to be reassessed every twenty years. If labour rents were retained, they were not to exceed twenty-three days per diesiatin, while the proprietor retained the right to ask for hired labour. If peasants wished to purchase their freeholds, they could do so, but the messuage could be reduced by the landlord to ten diesiatins if it exceeded that size. The government undertook to assist in the purchase of arable land, the peasants paying 20 to 25 per cent of its estimated value as a deposit and the government issuing bonds to the extent of 75 to 80 per cent, which the peasants were required to redeem at 6 per cent interest per annum over a period of forty-nine years. Somewhat similar rules applied in the southern group of provinces, except that the use of the land was granted not to the peasant, but to the peasant family.

This was not a complicated scheme, but it could easily be misunderstood by the peasants and certainly left far too much power in the hands of the landlords, who were charged with the execution of it. They could arrange holdings at will and could demand rents and labour in accordance with the somewhat inflated rates recorded in the inventories. The consequence of promulgating the decrees was an outbreak of peasant disorder, especially in the provinces of western Russia and above all in Lithuania. Lanskoy, the minister of internal affairs, reported on 11 April that

In places, especially in the White Russian and Lithuanian *gubernii*, through a false understanding, the impression created by the manifesto was unfavourable. The peasants said: 'Whether it is two years or twelve, it is all the same. It is clear that the landlords will spin the business out' or 'Why have they excited the people for nothing? Everyone spoke of freedom, but now they once more order us to wait for it.'[1]

In the property of a Zamoyski in the district of Oszmiana, *gubernia* of Vilna, 10,000 peasants ceased work. No less than 2,000 peasants set up barricades in the town of Ivia and offered resistance to the soldiery. Numerous disturbances occurred in the district of Novoalexandrovsk, *gubernia* of Kovno, where there were clashes with troops. In Polish Livonia the situation was tense. Ten thousand peasants were involved in refusal to perform labour services in the district of Białystok. East of Brest Litovsk the countryside was aflame with discontent, while in the *gubernia* of Minsk there was trouble around Mozyr. Only in

[1] *Otmena krepostnogo prava* (Leningrad-Moscow, 1950), pp. 8–9.

backward Samogitia was there calm. In the southern group of provinces there were also disturbances, but not on as large a scale as in the northern group.[1] Everywhere a personal representative of the Tsar in each *gubernia* directed the use of troops and ordered the arrest of peasant leaders. For the Kingdom of Poland the disturbances had considerable significance. They were most violent where conditions bore a close resemblance to those pertaining in central Poland. Quickly the news of the Russian decrees and the Lithuanian peasants' revolt spread along the railway line from the frontier. The peasants professed to believe that the Tsar had intervened to protect his people and preserve their lands to them. On the one hand they saw an apparently beneficent Tsar, on the other the return of what they thought to be a Polish government in Warsaw, associated in their minds with the rule of the landlord. The peasants took that action which alone they could take, the refusal of labour services. After Easter the strike movement spread across the Kingdom of Poland. Up to 20 per cent of peasants holding three morgs or over refused to perform their obligations. These strikes were local in character and there was no attempt to wreak vengeance upon the *szlachta*.[2]

Wielopolski could not know to what lengths the peasants would go. In the midst of this confusion he could see only one solution, that the government should use the army to maintain order and save the gentry from a massacre and the country from economic disruption. It appeared essential that the agents of the Agricultural Society should stop moving round the countryside announcing a different policy from that of the government, because that would merely destroy the authority of the state. The only course therefore was to suppress the Society altogether and invite its leading members to join a government committee to consider the agrarian question.[3] On 6 April 1861 the dissolution of the Agricultural Society was

---

[1] Cf. the selection of reports in E. A. Morokhovets, *Krest'yanskoye dvizheniye v 1861 godu posle otmeny krepostnogo prava* (Leningrad-Moscow, 1949).

[2] H. Grynwaser, *Sprawa włościańska w Królestwie Polskim w latach 1861–2, Pisma*, III (Wrocław, 1951), p. 29. Cf. also S. Kieniewicz, *Sprawa włościańska w powstaniu styczniowym* (Wrocław, 1953), p. 153.

[3] For Wielopolski's motives see his son Zygmunt's pamphlet. *Lettre adressée à M. le Comte Stanislas Tarnowski* (Cracow, 1880).

announced and in its place was promised a new official committee to settle outstanding questions.[1] Two days earlier, on 4
April, the force of special constables, which had been maintained in existence after the shootings of 27 February, was dissolved and with it the unofficial committee of leading citizens
in Warsaw, which had continued to exist in one form or another.
Wielopolski in effect issued an imperious summons to the landlords for their co-operation, but this appeal to a sectional
interest was not appreciated by the public at large, intoxicated
by the apparent national revival of the past month. It appeared
that Wielopolski was destroying Polish institutions and riding
roughshod over national feelings.

An angry mood now pervaded Warsaw. The same demonstrators who on 25 and 27 February had turned out to force the
reluctant landlords of the Agricultural Society to adopt a positive attitude towards the agrarian question now came on to the
streets to protest against its dissolution. On 7 April a large
crowd assembled to render homage to Andrzej Zamoyski and to
present him with a wreath to mark the death of the Society.
Zamoyski, embarrassed by a street demonstration of a kind he
disliked, appeared reluctantly to accept the ovation of the
crowd, which chanted—'Hurrah for the Agricultural Society!
Hurrah for Zamoyski! Long live the King of Poland, Andrzej
Zamoyski!' Zamoyski evidently suggested that the crowd should
go home, but it was not until nightfall that the government was
reasonably secure. The demonstrators obviously intended to
continue harassing the authorities, if only for the enjoyment it
offered. General Khrulev, a Russian officer recently transferred
from St. Petersburg to supervise the maintenance of order, demanded that clear instructions be given for the handling of disturbances. Wielopolski was brought into the discussions, which
resulted in the 'Law on Disturbances' based very largely upon
his suggestions.[2] This measure introduced a procedure similar
to that of the British Riot Act. The authorities were to call upon
the crowds to disperse, giving them three warnings by beating
on a drum. The penalties for failure to disperse increased with
each beating. If the crowd then refused to leave, force might be
used. The merit of this measure was that it at least sought to

---

[1] H. Lisicki, *Aleksander Wielopolski*, II, 80–1.   [2] H. Lisicki, *ibid.*, II, 85–7.

prevent arbitrary shootings by the military of the kind which had occurred on 27 February. Its error was that, not communicated early enough to the Poles, it was not and could not be understood by the crowds which gathered in the streets. The way was thus open for the disciplinary action which the military party in the Castle had been urging upon the Viceroy. The demonstrations were renewed on 8 April. Hymn-singing was conducted in the Krakowskie Przedmieście, led by a young man, Karol Nowakowski, who had a genius for organizing street gatherings. The authorities were not disposed to offer provocation, but in the evening the crowds, following the Lublin post coach, on which the postilion was audaciously playing the old tune of the legionaries in the service of France which has come to be the Polish national anthem, 'Jeszcze Polska nie zginęła', found their way into the square before the Castle, where stood a police guard and its military reinforcements. Khrulev with some misgivings put into operation the new riot procedure, but this was merely laughed to scorn by the crowd. The inevitable tragedy followed. The Russian soldiers, infuriated by the thousand insults which had been heaped upon them and their officers, gladly accepted the order of Khrulev to fire into the crowd. Gorchakov subsequently telegraphed to Alexander II that ten persons were killed,[1] but the Russian historian, Berg, wrote that over two hundred were killed, who were quickly collected by the soldiers and placed in the courtyard of the Castle and afterwards buried in a common grave in the Citadel. Berg says that altogether 484 shots were fired, which would seem to indicate that his estimate and not Gorchakov's was the correct one.[2] The students and working men of Warsaw paid with their blood to discover that the government was prepared to go to considerable lengths to make possible cooperation between itself and the Polish propertied classes. The lesson was for the moment severe enough to cow the demonstrators. Five victims of a purely haphazard shooting incident on 27 February had been sufficient to shake the system of Nicholas I to its foundations. Now over two hundred deaths produced scarcely a murmur. Perhaps the landed gentry and the

[1] *Russkaya Starina*, XXXVI, 568.
[2] N. V. Berg, *Pamiętniki o polskich spiskach i powstaniach 1831–1862*, p. 318n.

I

Warsaw middle class were not entirely sorry to see the working men of the city reminded that there was such a thing as law and order.

The architect of the projected compromise between Russia and Poland, Wielopolski, was certainly not slow to take advantage of the situation. At the first sound of the shooting he drove to the Castle amid a shower of stones and abuse. Finding that the Pole, Wołowski, refused to take responsibility for the application of the Disturbances Law before its promulgation and had resigned his office of Director of Justice, Wielopolski took over his duties. By becoming Director of Justice he could obtain some measure of control over the details of peasant reform. On the other hand, his acceptance of this post seemed to show that he assumed responsibility for the shootings, while Russian officers saw him only as an ambitious man, who grasped at office in order to squeeze further concessions from the government without at the same time bringing to it any great popularity or support from the Polish population.[1] Andrzej Zamoyski refused to exert a calming influence, persisting in his pose of non-co-operation. Invited to take part in the work of the council of state, he declined to take his seat. Gorchakov on Wielopolski's advice suggested to the Tsar that it was best not to exile him, for fear of making him a martyr.[2] Zamoyski was a broken reed and privately many of the leading landlords regarded him as such. Tomasz Potocki, Alexander Jackowski, Tytus Wojciechowski, Alexander Ostrowski, Franciszek Węgleński, Alexander Kurtz, Klemens Krzyżtoporski, Antoni Wrotnowski and the ubiquitous Leopold Kronenberg, names which counted for something in the Agricultural Society and among the men of property in the Kingdom, all consented to take part in the work of the 'Peasant Committee' of the Commission of Internal Affairs. What they would not give Wielopolski was their moral approval of the course he had taken, however much they might admit its utility and accept its advantages. The mystique of Polish nationalism prevented them from adopting the attitude of open supporters of the *régime*. The Church

---

[1] Cf. Gechevich's letters of 15 and 16–20 April 1861, *Russkaya Starina*, c (1899), pp. 142–6.
[2] *Ibid.*, c, 133–4.

had not forgiven him for his policy of toleration and the Warsaw parish priests made common cause with the agitators, refusing to exercise a moderating influence. Warsaw radicalism
never ceased to see Wielopolski as a collaborator of the worst
kind. His explanation of the significance of the Agricultural
Society's suppression, that it was merely to put order into
the work of finding a solution of the agrarian question and
to give leading figures in Poland an official standing, was
received unsympathetically.[1] An almost immediate reaction
of the Left was the 'Message to all Poles on Polish Soil',
which condemned all collaboration with the foreigner, demanding that Poles should not speak to Russians or Germans.
The aim should be the restoration of Poland in the pre-1772
frontiers, an ideal which could not be given up on account of a
temporary relaxation of Russian rule:

Expect nothing from the Government, hope for nothing, take
advantage of everything and serve the country's needs with common
and united strength, and we will all learn when the time shall come
to stand on the field of battle and be victorious in arms.[2]

This handbill, issued from the circle around Agaton Giller, did
not propose immediate armed rebellion and in fact hoped to
combat it, but it did advocate no collaboration with the system
of Wielopolski beyond what was absolutely necessary. What
Wielopolski required was whole-hearted co-operation in order
to secure the enlargement of Russian concessions, but that he
was never able to obtain.

Wielopolski intended to wage a class war on behalf of the
gentry against the peasants. The extension of Polish influence in
the administration served that end. In the countryside the landlord could control the local administration and rule supreme.
The urban intelligentsia might be bought off by the creation of
more opportunities for advancement. Thus the transition to
more modern social relationships could be achieved with the
preservation of the Polish aristocracy's privileged position. In
1861 the main objection of the left wing was revealed to be that

[1] H. Lisicki, *Akeksander Wielopolski*, II, 91–3, for the text of his statement.
[2] 'Posłanie do wszystkich Polaków na ziemii polskiej', in A. Giller, *Manifestacye
Warszawy 1861 r.*, pp. 78–81.

Wielopolski's conception that this could be achieved within the Congress Kingdom was not grand enough. All the talk of appeal to the peasants had been shown to be a mere puff of wind. The manifestations of peasant discontent in March and April 1861 had been allowed to pass by without advantage being taken of them for the simple reason that the left wing had virtually no contact with the peasant masses. If emotional dislike of Wielopolski served a purpose at all, it was that in the course of time the Polish left wing came to realize that they could not get rid of him without putting into practice their theory of linking the cause of national independence with the donation of land to the peasants, but in the summer of 1861 the Polish Left was still very far from that conclusion.

CHAPTER IV

Wielopolski's First Period in Office, March–December 1861

WIELOPOLSKI felt the need for decisive action to avert an immediate crisis. A permanent solution of the agrarian question was not to be achieved in a short time. It would have to embrace not only arable tenures, but also the vexed question of woods and pastures, hunting and fishing rights, the right of the manor to a monopoly of distilling, the organization of village communes and the obligations of the peasants towards the state. In the meantime the strike of the peasants had revealed that they were not prepared to tolerate the existing system. If the government began to frame a comprehensive law, the irritations and discontents of the peasants would remain and give rise to fresh disturbances, which might be prejudicial to a settlement in favour of the *szlachta*. In the first instance, therefore, Wielopolski proposed to remove the irritation of labour services which poisoned the relations of village and manor. With their abolition all tenures would achieve a uniformity. Wielopolski therefore urged that labour services should at the earliest moment be converted into money values, at rates favourable to the manor, pending a permanent settlement. The rents thus established, however, were not to serve as the basis of future rents or of the purchase of freeholds. The whole operation was to be regarded as a temporary measure to ease a tense situation.

The committee of landlords to whom Wielopolski submitted his plan on 1 May 1861 was prepared to offer some resistance. They protested that the rates of conversion were too low and the date, 1 October, too early, declaring that the earliest moment was 1 January 1862.[1] Gechevich, the Director of Internal Affairs, had doubts concerning the wisdom of reform:

A new law at this moment foretells not pacification but greater disorders, because it is a well-known fact that the peasants in certain districts are giving as a reason for stopping labour services the circumstance that the government has given them the freehold of the lands they have tilled up to now. If the peasants put forward this sort of view now, before the promulgation of the projected law, after its promulgation . . . their demands will grow beyond all measure. What today 4,214 peasants demand, tomorrow 270,000 will demand, that is, all the peasants who come under the provisions of the ukaz of 1846. In this way the law will not only fail to obtain its principal aim, that of quietening 4,214 peasants, but may stir up fresh disturbances of 300,000 peasants with demands which the government will not be in a position to satisfy. These disturbances may appear in another way, namely that peasants may cease the performance of labour services immediately after the publication of this law without waiting for the date of 1 October fixed by the government.[2]

Wielopolski nevertheless stood his ground and defended his position.[3] The matter was therefore referred to the Viceroy, Gorchakov, who dismissed the arguments of the landlords and Gechevich. His view was that the Polish peasants had lost faith in their landlords and that action was urgent.[4] The Tsar, not unnaturally, supported his Viceroy in this matter and the ukaz authorizing conversion was signed on 4/16 May 1861.[5]

All labour services therefore came to an end on 1 October according to fixed rates of conversion. The country was divided into four regions and in general the rates were lower in the east than in the west. A day of manual labour varied in value from seven and a half kopeks to twelve, and a day with two animals from twenty to thirty kopeks. The temporary rents calculated upon this basis were to be paid quarterly in advance. Wielopolski ordered that the law should be presented to the peasants as

---

[1] N. Milyutin, *Izsledovaniya*, ɪɪ (iv), 46.

[2] *Ibid*, ɪɪ (iv), 38–46. 4,214 was the number of peasants still reckoned to be on strike.

[3] H. Lisicki, *Aleksander Wielopolski*, ɪɪ, 105–11.

[4] H. Grynwaser, *Sprawa włościańska w Królestwie Polskim w latach 1861–62, Pisma*, ɪɪɪ, 53–5.

[5] For the text see H. Lisicki, *Aleksander Wielopolski*, ɪɪ, 98–103.

an example of the Tsar's munificence, though landlords would have been happier if it had been presented as an example of their own, but the peasants did not receive it with enthusiasm. Frequently peasant officials of the communes, the *sołtysi*, were nervous of admitting that the new law had been read out to them and there were frequent instances of their refusing to sign an admission that this had been done. Nevertheless, the peasants were on the whole prepared to accept the law; 126,358 peasants on private lands agreed to temporary conversion and 7,371 refused. By 1863 96·1 per cent of the peasants on all types of land had converted and labour services had for practical purposes ceased to exist.[1] Acceptance of conversion did not signify that rents were easy to pay. The average rate was 1·52 roubles per morg, which amounted to twice the average rent on private estates where conversion had taken place earlier. In individual districts there were even larger disparities than this. The law therefore did not improve relations between the village and the manor. From October to December 1861 there was considerable discontent in the district of Hrubieszów, where 8,574 peasants refused to honour their obligations. Here there were only 7,000 holdings embraced by the new law, which must indicate that discontent had spread to other types of peasants. Disturbances were reported from other districts, but on a less impressive scale. From 1 October 1861 to 31 March 1863, when revolution plunged the countryside into confusion, there were 13,527 cases of administrative distraint, while from 1 October 1861 to 1864 there were 14,560 court cases arising out of the nonpayment of rents under this law.

Wielopolski's law may not have been entirely satisfactory, but it did give a political status to the peasantry, who for the first time appeared to the educated classes as a whole as a force with which to reckon. A peasant could be battered and beaten to perform labour services, but when labour services were abolished no power on earth could make him offer his labour to the manor if he did not wish or had no need to do so. As yet few radicals within the country were prepared to take active steps to organize the peasants, but there were ugly rumours of agitators moving

---

[1] T. Szczechura, 'Ukaz o okupie pańszczyzny z dnia 16 maja 1861 r.', *Przegląd Historyczny*, XL (1949), pp. 261–76.

around the villages conversing with them.[1] It was realized that the exaction of rents remained as a source of friction between landlord and peasant. The radical priest, Karol Mikoszewski, warned the landlords that a more conciliatory approach was required of them: 'Take no notice of the latest order of the government which raises the rent and puts in your hand a weapon against the people, because it is still one more bone of contention thrown up from Hell between you and the people.' He warned the *szlachta* that the opposition to the Russians in the towns did not mean that they could count upon the support of the country in the fight for independence: 'Demonstrations and patriotic songs are all right in Warsaw and the larger towns, but they carry no weight in the villages.'[2] The general tendency of political writings, however, was to put pressure on the peasants to maintain order and to convince them that the point of view of the *szlachta* was entirely reasonable. Mateusz Gralewski, in a pamphlet composed of articles originally printed in the Sunday newspaper, *Czytelnia Niedzielna*, urged that the payment of rents was required because property rights were vested in the landlords: 'The peasants . . . had a right to the soil, but they lost it, partly through their own idleness and partly, for the truth must be stated, through the injustice of the landlords.'[3] Gralewski's argument was that the peasants in the past had refused to go to war in defence of Poland and had in consequence been obliged to make bigger and bigger contributions to the military caste, who thus came to acquire the ownership of the soil. There were others who appealed to the principles of the Christian religion, which forbade one man to covet his neighbour's property. The peasants were to some extent shielded from the arguments of the educated class by their own illiteracy. There were many who thought that the time had come to promote the education of the rural population in order that they might become more receptive of the arguments employed in the popular press. Others, however, thought that education would give the peasants far too clear an idea of their own rights and that the best course was to keep them in a state of ignor-

---

[1] S. Kieniewicz, *Sprawa włościańska w powstaniu styczniowym*, pp. 168–80.
[2] *Słowo polskiego duchowieństwa do polskiego obywatelstwa* (Poznań, 1861), pp. 19, 20.
[3] M. Gralewski, *Opowiadanie o pańszczyźnie* (Warsaw, 1862), p. 7.

ance, lest ability to read and write develop in them a new political consciousness. An appeal to the peasantry was a course which the Russians also could adopt, but the official policy of conciliating the landed gentry did not make this easy. Nevertheless, when renewed disturbances broke out and in the conditions of a state of siege the junior Russian commanders came into closer contact with the people, they became aware that the peasants were ready to make an appeal to the military for protection against the oppression of the landlords. In November 1861 the staff quartermaster, General Semeka, advised the chief of staff, Krizhanovsky, that 'I consider it useful to maintain the favourable attitude and the trust of the peasants towards the military authorities.'[1]

The problem of whether or not to take advantage of the limited autonomy offered by the laws of 5 June 1861 was to a large extent determined by the gentry's desire to secure some oversight of the conversion to rents.[2] The new laws established a system of self-government in town and country. In the towns were established councils with a magistracy charged with the municipal administration and the control of finance; councillors were to serve for six years, one-sixth retiring annually in Warsaw and a half every three years in other towns. Each rural district was to have a council, with a membership according to the size of the population, elected like the town councillors with one-half retiring every three years. There was likewise a council for each *gubernia*, chosen for six years from the members of the district councils on the basis of one member for each district, while for the whole Kingdom there was a council of state composed of members of the Administrative Council sitting *ex officio*, nominated counsellors of state and members nominated from among the bishops, the councils of the *gubernii* and the administration of the Land Credit Society. The vital aspect of these concessions was the power given to the rural district councils to choose the members of the Peasant Committee, which would supervise the operation of Wielopolski's law converting labour services into rents. The franchise law[3] gave the vote only

[1] H. Grynwaser, *Pisma*, III, 69.
[2] For the text of the law see H. Lisicki, *Aleksander Wielopolski*, II, 144–63.
[3] *Ibid.*, II, 137–43.

to the propertied classes. Landlords, hereditary leaseholders and tenants paying six roubles a year in taxes could vote in the districts, and landlords paying four roubles in the towns, to whom were added persons who could prove a yearly income of 180 roubles, constituted the urban electorate. The voter must be over twenty-five years of age and be able to read and write. Candidates for election had to be over thirty years and be landlords paying taxes of more than fifteen roubles a year in Warsaw and the rural districts, or ten roubles in the towns; other persons could offer themselves for election if they were distinguished by their intellectual attainments, or were merchants belonging to a guild or manufacturers employing more than ten workmen. Under these regulations there turned out to be only 24,820 electors in a population of nearly 5,000,000; of these only 7,188 were eligible for office.[1] In short the landlords were to be given effective control of the economic reorganization.

The landed gentry were at first pulled in two directions. They feared to participate in the elections lest they incur the accusation that they were collaborating with the enemy, Tsardom, but on the other hand self-interest commanded them to secure control of agrarian reform. The radical element in Warsaw was not satisfied with the narrow limits of the representative system and sought to compel the *szlachta* to refuse all part in the elections and thus give an impressive display of national solidarity against the illiberal nature of the constitutional reforms. When the elections began in Warsaw on 23 September 1861 two leaders of the extreme Left, Apollon Korzeniowski, the poet and father of Joseph Conrad, and the sculptor, Szachowski, issued an appeal to the electorate not to cast their votes, but it is significant that Andrzej Zamoyski, for once descending from his pinnacle of splendid isolation, intervened with a speech at the polling booth in favour of participation. The leaflet of Korzeniowski and Szachowski, entitled 'The Mandate of the People', insisted that the electoral law was an attack upon Polish national unity, both in the sense that the franchise was too narrow and that Lithuania and Russian Ruthenia were

---

[1] J. Strumiński, 'Rady miejskie i powiatowe w Królestwie Polskim (1861–1863)', *Czasopismo prawo-historyczne*, IV (1952), p. 328.

denied constitutional freedoms.[1] The Poles who thought like
Zamoyski countered these arguments by declaring that it was
issued by a minority and they had no reason to deny themselves
the opportunity of speaking in the name of the Polish nation
because their fellow countrymen elsewhere were denied it. The
underground newspaper, *Strażnica*, which had just begun to
appear, declared that refusal to accept the new electoral system
might mean that the Russians would obtain the return of candidates subservient to themselves. In general, the left-wing appeal
was ignored and the elections passed off without serious incident, except in the provinces, at Ostrołęka and Włocławek,
where intimidation by the local Russian commanders caused
some resentment. Altogether 80 per cent of the electorate voted.
Out of 615 seats on the district councils, 457 were won by landlords, 62 by leaseholders, and 81 by clergy in possession of
church lands; in seventeen towns which went to the polls, 98
seats out of 184 were filled by landlords.[2] In the towns only
twenty-eight Jews were elected and in the rural districts only
seven peasants, who in view of the high property qualifications
for office can hardly have been representative of their class. It
had been Wielopolski's desire to bolster up the position of the
landed gentry and in this he had succeeded.

Wielopolski would have been better satisfied with his success
if he had been able to conciliate the population of the towns,
where the radicals were capable of bringing about fresh disturbances and giving an argument to those Russian officers, who
looked back with regret to the stern rule of Paskevich to renew
their demands for coercion. Wielopolski was in fact greatly
hampered by that pillar of Polish conservatism, the hierarchy
of the Roman Catholic Church, fighting a battle against its
own radical element, the parish priests, who often shared the
point of view of the left wing. The clergy of the Kingdom had
chosen to regard Wielopolski's declaration when he assumed
office, that he would behave with scrupulous fairness towards
other denominations, as an attack upon the church. For once
the hierarchy and the priests were brought together. The bishops

[1] A. Giller, *Historja powstania narodu polskiego w 1861–1864 r.* (Paris, 1868), II
113–16.
[2] J. Strumiński, *ibid.*, p. 337.

since 1815 had tended on the whole to seek an accommodation with the state, while the lesser clergy since the eighteenth century had supported the cause of national independence, but neither element had doubted that the Catholic religion would continue to enjoy a privileged position in relation to other branches of the Christian faith. It was well within the power of the clergy to use its influence on behalf of Wielopolski, but it withheld its aid. On 22 April he issued a circular to the bishops asking for co-operation in the task of maintaining order and warned them that the Viceroy had issued an order for the arrest of disturbers of the peace, regardless of their status. Archbishop Fijałkowski's reply of 10 May retorted that the Catholic was not a tolerated, but an established church, for which reason mention of toleration in Wielopolski's speech to the clergy on taking office was unnecessary. To give force to his arguments he enclosed a letter which he had received from the clergy of the archdiocese of Warsaw, which indeed might well have been written in another age:

We recognize in the church the authority of the successor of St. Peter and the authority of the bishops, the successors of the apostles; we know that this authority has been given to them from heaven for the government of the church, that this authority ought to be recognized by everyone who is a member of the church.[1]

The implication was that Wielopolski should submit to the church, and not the church to Wielopolski. This letter to Fijałkowski was already circulating among the population in the form of a handbill, which showed that the clergy was expressing its solidarity with the young men who created the disorders. In a country, where there were four times as many priests as schoolteachers and where the priest was accorded a respect far in excess of that warranted by his meagre education, this action amounted to nothing less than a declaration of war on Wielopolski. As if this were not enough, there came a further declaration of approval for the young men of the Kingdom from another conservative source, old Prince Adam Czartoryski, who in a speech on the anniversary of the Constitution of 3 May 1791, his last public utterance before his death on 15 July, loaded

---

[1] For this exchange of letters, see H. Liricki, *Aleksander Wielopolski*, II, 93-4, 95.

praises upon those who gave visible manifestation of public spirit and patriotism so long after the suppression of Polish liberties in the Kingdom.

With the gentry neutral and the church, like the streets, actively hostile, Wielopolski could fall back only upon the power of the Viceroy, Mikhail Gorchakov, but his strength had already begun to fail. Only a sense of duty combined with a fear that another Viceroy might adopt a less flexible attitude had kept him at his post; he had remarked to General Kotzebue in March 1861: 'J'ai beaucoup médité sur ma retraite, et je suis venu à la conclusion qu'il n'y a personne en Russie qui aurait pû me remplacer.'[1] It became evident that he was dying towards the end of May 1861. The russified Pole, Krizhanovsky, took over his duties as commander of the First Army and General Merkhilevich his civil duties as Viceroy of the Kingdom. The fear that the situation might get out of hand on his death prompted the Tsar to send his minister of war, Sukhozanet, himself of Polish descent, to discharge the functions of Viceroy until a permanent appointment could be made. The military party was thus greatly strengthened. Krizhanovsky would have been happier if he had been allowed to declare a state of siege, but Wielopolski insisted that there was no justification for it.[2] The Corpus Christi celebrations passed off without incident and absolute quiet attended the death of Mikhail Gorchakov on 30 May. The *régime* of Sukhozanet which followed could hardly have been satisfactory. Sukhozanet was seventy years of age and past his best, inflexible in the attitudes which he had assimilated under Nicholas I and quick of temper, which was the last qualification for a Viceroy in the tiresome circumstances of Congress Poland. Indeed, the death of Gorchakov may not have been entirely unwelcome to the Tsar, for it provided an opportunity for loosening Sukhozanet's hold on the ministry of war and passing it over into the hands of the more capable D. A. Milyutin. In the meantime, however, the Kingdom of Poland had to suffer the frustrations which the military mind knows best how to create.

[1] N. V. Berg, 'Knyaz Mikhail Dmitrievich Gorchakov, 1791–1861', *Russkaya, Starina*, xxix (1880), p. 793.
[2] *Russkaya Starina*, xxxvi (1882), p. 576.

It was not easy for the Tsar to find a suitable successor, for the senior officers of the army had grown up in the system of Nicholas I and most of them thought that there was only one remedy for street demonstrations and that the application of military force. The Tsar's choice eventually fell upon Count Charles Lambert, who had hitherto been considered only for the comparatively minor post of civil governor of Warsaw. The selection of Count Lambert was on the face of it a good one. Lambert was the son of a French *émigré* who had settled in Russia, but still maintained his connection with France. He was moreover a Roman Catholic, which was thought likely to give the Poles the impression that they would receive from him more sympathetic treatment than from an Orthodox Russian. In fact, his appointment was disliked in Russia because he was regarded as being a corrupt officer of the old school and had fallen under suspicion of malversation during the Crimean War, though this may have meant only that he made the profits normal for a Russian commanding officer.[1] He was moreover in a poor state of health, having recently suffered a severe fracture of the leg. He was himself by no means confident that he had the ability to handle the Polish situation. Napier reported that 'I have reason to know that Count Lambert enters upon his duties with sentiments allied to despondency.'[2] Alexander II was indeed in a sorry plight if this was the best material he could find in his Empire to send to Congress Poland. Nevertheless, Alexander II put a good face on it and made Lambert's departure the occasion of a demonstration of goodwill. In his rescript of 18 August 1861, which was published in the press, Alexander instructed him to use all his influence to make the reforms of 26 March effective and to induce the Polish leaders to co-operate with the government. A promise was held out that all previous transgressions would be ignored, but it was emphasized that no disorders would in future be allowed.[3] Lambert arrived in Warsaw on 23 August 1861 and immediately gave the impression that he would revert to the more liberal policy of Gorchakov and reject the stiff militarism of Sukhozanet. Rus-

[1] F.O. 65/577, Napier to Russell, 12 August 1861.
[2] F.O. 65/578, Napier to Russell, 22 August 1861.
[3] H. Lisicki, *Aleksander Wielopolski*, II, 164.

sian soldiers were removed from the streets and Lambert took good care to pay especial attention on his arrival to Andrzej Zamoyski. The public was disposed to take kindly to him and to the new military governor of Warsaw, General Gerstenzweig,[1] but the situation was once more deteriorating. Even before Lambert's arrival demonstrations had taken place in Warsaw and Vilna on 12 August to mark the anniversary of the Union of Lublin between Poland and Lithuania. Now the Church began to mount its own assault upon Wielopolski's edifice of Russo-Polish co-operation.

The Archbishop of Warsaw, Fijałkowski, was a very old man and could not restrain the impetuosity of his priests. Wielopolski realized that without the co-operation of the church he might easily run into difficulties. If the primate had lost control, there could be no other course than to call upon the bishops to exert their authority. An invitation was therefore issued to them to attend a conference in Warsaw during September 1861, but, though Wielopolski was prepared to go a long way towards satisfying their aspirations, the bishops sensed that they had the full weight of public opinion behind them and instead of issuing an appeal for all Poles to work in harmony for the good of their country, as Wielopolski had hoped, used the opportunity to draw up a long list of grievances for the perusal of Count Lambert.[2] They condemned the law that marriages between persons of the Catholic and Orthodox faith must first be celebrated in an Orthodox church and afterwards in a Catholic. They objected to the clause in the Penal Code of 1847 which laid down that children of mixed marriages should be brought up in the Orthodox faith. They objected to the instruction of the Viceroy of 14 July 1854, which forbade sermons dealing with differences of dogma between the Christian churches and limited them to moral questions only. They demanded that the government should in the affairs of the church confine its activity to administrative matters. They asked for a spiritual department to be established under the chairmanship of the Archbishop. For the bishops there should be complete freedom to hold

[1] F.O. 65/584, Stanton to Russell, 1 September 1861.
[2] For their letter of 25 September 1861, see H. Lisicki, *Aleksander Wielopolski* II, 203–9.

synods. No limitations should be set to the number of people entering religious orders. Sees should be filled by persons elected by the cathedral chapters instead of the choice being left to the Viceroy and the Administrative Council. There should be direct contact with the Holy See in spiritual matters and not, as had been the rule since 1845, through the government. Grievances concerning pensions, ecclesiastical funds, the repair of churches and other administrative aspects of church government should be put right. The final demand was that priests under arrest should be released and that there should in future be no arrest of priests without prior consultation of the ecclesiastical authorities.

Undoubtedly the ecclesiastical policy of Nicholas I had not been enlightened and had been designed to favour Orthodoxy, but the attitude of the Polish clergy in September 1861 reveals that they would have been no more enlightened if the opportunity had been theirs. Their legitimate grievances might have been met, but they demanded more, virtual freedom from arrest of the priests who were encouraging the street demonstrations and, in short, all the advantages of an established church without the compromise with the state which establishment supposes. The bishops seemed to point moral approval to the demonstrations in the streets and churches and to issue an invitation to the public to maintain their attitude of hostility until the Church's and Poland's claims were satisfied. It was small wonder that the death of Archbishop Fijałkowski and his funeral on 5 October were the occasion of an unprecedented display of national mourning. An attempt was made to give an impression of fundamental national unity by bringing in parties of peasants from the districts around Warsaw to render their homage to the archbishop, but a dead archbishop and fraternization between the educated classes and a few selected peasants at his funeral were unlikely to bridge the gap which centuries of oppression had created between the manor and the village. The British consul, Stanton, was distinctly unimpressed.[1] Nevertheless, the episode whipped up considerable excitement and led to further demonstrations of hostility to Russia.

National anniversaries had now become fashionable as

[1] F.O. 65/584, Stanton to Russell, 14 October 1861.

opportunities for nationalist gatherings. On 10 October there was a large assembly at the small town of Horodło on the river Bug, where in 1413 the first act of association between Poland and Lithuania had been drawn up. The demonstrators, with their eye on the international press, announced their refusal to accept anything less than Poland's independence within the historic frontiers. The act of protest declared

we renew the act of Horodło in its entirety. We protest against the violation of our liberties and the servitude imposed by the government. We protest against the arbitrary partitions of Poland and demand the restoration of her independence.[1]

The government's reply to this declaration was to impose a state of martial law on the *gubernii* of Lublin and Augustów, but it did not need much foresight to perceive that now any and every national anniversary would give rise to manifestations of hostility. The anniversary of the death of Tadeusz Kościuszko on 15 October promised to be the greatest of all. Young radicals in Warsaw were calling upon the entire population to render its homage. To maintain order Lambert felt himself obliged to declare a state of martial law in Warsaw, but this did not deter the population. On 15 October the congregations in the churches stood all day singing patriotic hymns. This great demonstration had no political ends, but served merely to underline Polish hostility to Russian rule. The congregations refused to leave when Russian officers with great propriety requested them to go home. In the end the congregations came to blows with the police and the military, when the order was given to clear the churches. Altogether some three thousand persons were arrested for resisting the authorities. Lambert was evidently rattled by the behaviour of the Poles and some incautious words of his seemed to place responsibility for the fracas upon General Gerstenzweig, the military governor, who added scandal to disorder by committing suicide. A state of war was declared and the government reintroduced the strictest military control.

The administrator of the archdiocese of Warsaw, Father

---

[1] 'Protest spisany na pograniczu miasta Horodła Nadbużnego', *Wydawnictwo Materyałów*, I, 16–17.

K

Białobrzeski, evidently believed that the time had come to press the claims of the church. Choosing to regard the entry of police and soldiers into the churches as an act of sacrilege, he ordered that places of worship thus violated should remain closed until such time as the government gave satisfaction:

In the meantime I will await and expect forthcoming administrative arrangements which will give certain and inviolable assurance of security to the faithful in the churches against the armed force of the military.[1]

It was a serious act to close the churches in a Catholic country. For the government it was doubly serious, because, though in normal times they might be confident that the peasants would not collaborate with the landlords, a struggle with the church might arouse the religious fanaticism of the peasants and bring them over to the national movement, in spite of their economic antipathy towards the *szlachta*. Even the Jews, who had little to obtain from Catholic intransigence, closed their synagogues as a mark of respect and solidarity. Wielopolski pleaded for a reopening of the churches, but Białobrzeski persisted in his attitude of non-co-operation:

The closure must remain for some time. During this time the illustrious government will be able to find means of arousing the confidence of the people, and will be able to release all prisoners and give an assurance that there will be no repetition of the regrettable events of these last days.[2]

No government could have tolerated the assumption of the role of moral censor by a priest like Białobrzeski. He was quickly informed that there had been no official confirmation of his appointment as administrator of the archdiocese of Warsaw and that therefore he had no official status. He was moreover exiled to Russia, whence he returned in 1862 contrite and chastened, never again to exert any influence on events and still less to assert the supremacy of the church over the state. The consequence of the clergy's display of hostility was that Count Lambert was dismissed and his place taken once more by Sukhozanet.

---

[1] *Wydawnictwo materyałów*, I, 18–19.

[2] Cf. letter of 17 October 1861 to Wielopolski, A. Giller, *Historja powstania narodu polskiego*, II, 392–4.

Once more the Russian military party gained control. Suk-hozanet soon quarrelled with Wielopolski, whom he regarded as the root cause of all the troubles in Warsaw. This quarrel led in its turn to complaints to St. Petersburg, and the Tsar, always slow to understand what was afoot in Warsaw and inclined to trust the army officer in preference to the civilian, ordered Wielo-polski to present himself at court and instructed Sukhozanet that, if he showed signs of recalcitrance, he should be despatched under arrest. In this way Wielopolski's first period in office came to an end and with it the attempt at compromise between the government and the Polish upper classes. Sukhozanet was shortly replaced by General Lüders, who conducted himself less severely, but who was not empowered to put any new policy into operation.

The significance of these events was not lost upon the Poles in the Kingdom. To the moderate sections of opinion it appeared that the ineffectual demonstrations and sterile hymn-singing could produce nothing but further festivals of coercion. Wielo-polski, though they disliked him as a man, was recognized as having obtained solid advantages for the Kingdom. The Law of 16 May converting labour services was proving difficult to operate, but its difficulties were not insuperable. The rudiments of a representative system might eventually foreshadow the restoration of the constitution. The moderates or 'Whites' had already realized in September 1861 during the local elections that they needed some form of organization to guide public opinion. During this month the capitalist, Leopold Kronenberg, who represented the point of view of the Warsaw merchants, Jurgens of the Millenary group, and two prominent leaders of the disbanded Agricultural Society, Alexander Kurtz and Adam Goltz, had formed a small committee to encourage participation in the elections, but the events of October 1861 convinced them that something more than a loose consultative committee was required. What was wanted was an organization with a political programme, lest the public be captured by the left wing and be diverted to revolutionary conspiracies. In December 1861 a conference was called of all the local leaders of the Agricultural Society, the representatives of the large business houses in War-saw, and the moderate section of the academic youth, which led in February 1862 to the establishment of the 'Directory', composed of Władysław Zamoyski, son of Andrzej, Tytus Wojciechowski, Józef Kołaczkowski, Leopold Kronenberg, Jurgens and Majewski. This was a coalition of the moderates of town and country. The landlords conceded to the middle class the emancipation of the Jews and the granting of social and political equality to all classes, in return obtaining for the *szlachta* toleration in their policy of joining the district councils, which presumably meant that a permanent system of rents was to be created. The formation of the Directory thus constituted a retreat by Jurgens and Majewski towards compromise with the landed proprietors.

The result of this compromise was that the Whites were able to elaborate their programme. Their principal propagandist, the 'Siberian' Karol Ruprecht, in his pamphlet 'The Social Question and the National Cause', called for national unity, insisting that an understanding between the people and the *szlachta* was the basis of success for the national movement and that this could be achieved only upon the granting of substantial concessions to the people by the *szlachta*. He was prepared to admit that labour services could no longer be retained and that the peasants must be granted equal rights, but insisted that the grant of freeholds without compensation being paid to the landlords would be unsatisfactory. Ruprecht was going as far as he dared towards the revolutionary conception of freeholds without compensation being paid by the peasants. Ruprecht's view was that there were two courses under discussion in Poland, whether to follow the course of collaboration laid down by Wielopolski, or whether to have recourse to rebellion, but declared that he himself had found a middle way which was not to slip into half-measures. The voluntary system of solving the peasant question ruled out insurrection, but the social transformation would produce unrest. It would therefore be necessary to win over the peasantry by 'moral action', that is, by educating them in the need for solidarity with the *szlachta*, a form of political activity in which women had a special part to play. There were two things to combat in the peasant: his trust in the Russian government and his distrust of the landlord. To solve the social question 'in the spirit of our national needs' and 'to show solidarity with all portions of former Poland' were the prime tasks, which would permit the nation to gather its moral and material resources for the future revolt. An alluring prospect was offered: 'The armed revolt, independently prepared by our own conscious organic work, behold! this is the creed of this middle party.' Care, however, was taken to add that revolution was not on the immediate agenda, though when it did come it would be 'a revolution without anarchy and internal struggles, an insurrection held in the bonds of our national will'.[1] Talk of an insurrection was therefore merely to sweeten the pill. The practical aim was to secure the exploitation of the concessions which Wielopolski had obtained, though not necessarily with Wielopolski at the head of the government.

The little groups of radicals in Warsaw, who appeared at demonstrations and gave them their sense of purpose, had not in the summer of 1861 been closely organized. The secession of Jurgens and Majewski to the Whites left the field open to the genuine left wing, or the 'Reds', to direct the energies of the academic youth and the workers of Warsaw. The Reds, like the Whites, had come to the conclusion that the path which the demonstrations had taken had led to nothing, but the interpretation which the Reds put upon events was that failure had been experienced only because the nation and the people had not been effectively organized. The answer appeared to be a reversion to the creed of the Polish Democratic Society of 1836, the calling of an insurrection against the occupying power upon the basis of unconditional economic and political emancipation for the people. Shortly after the demonstration of 15 October 1861 an effort was made by the Red groups to unite themselves in one body, the *Komitet Miejski* or 'Town Committee'. This body, however, showed from the beginning a lack of homogeneity and absence of political agreement.

On the one hand there was the group led by Daniłowski, a fatuous young man with an admiration for Ludwik Mierosławski, whom he proposed for the post of commander-in-chief in the coming insurrection. Mierosławski unfortunately had been cutting a poor figure. Critical of the failure to call an insur-

---

[1] K. Ruprecht, *Kwestya socyalna wobec Narodowej Sprawy* (Paris, 1862), pp. 57–8; a similar pamphlet is his *Zadanie obecnej chwili* (Paris, 1862).

rection in the spring of 1861, he had summoned a conference of his supporters at home, which assembled at Frankfurt, with the object of getting himself nominated dictator-designate, but the young men who attended apparently expended all the money they had collected in Poland at the neighbouring casino of Homburg and revenged themselves upon Mierosławski for his objections by decreeing that he was excluded from all part in the affairs of the nation.[1] Another venture of Mierosławski, which brought him little personal credit, was the foundation of a military academy at Genoa in collaboration with Józef Wysocki, who had served in Hungary in 1848-9, with the object of training officers for the insurrection. Personal differences, however, soon led to a split and Mierosławski was obliged to give way, leaving Wysocki in sole command.[2] Mierosławski was already past his best, but at home he was a symbol of the revolutionary struggles of 1846 and 1848-9, at least for the less acute young men in the Kingdom. For this reason he had always a small following among the inexperienced youths and his existence was to serve as a needless complication of the Reds' affairs. For the landed gentry he represented as ever the extreme left wing of the revolutionary movement, whose influence was to be seen everywhere.

A second element associated with the Town Committee was the 'Siberians', of whom Agaton Giller was the most prominent. Giller had suffered for his previous experience of conspiracy and was always inclined to combine his adherence to the revolutionary cause with an extreme caution. He evidently enjoyed the excitement of revolutionary activity, but shrank from its consequences. Giller almost invariably exhibited an inclination to seek an understanding with the Whites, to whom another 'Siberian', Ruprecht, had given his allegiance. Giller was by profession a journalist rather than a man of action, the editor of *Czytelnia Niedzielna*, which was designed to convey simple truths to the people. He was nevertheless to remain almost to the end at the very centre of revolutionary affairs.

The driving force behind the Town Committee was the

---

[1] L. Mierosławski, *Pamiętnik*, edited by J. Freilich (Warsaw, 1924), pp. 14–15.
[2] Cf. W. Mazurkiewicz, *Emigracya polska w 1862 r. (Szkoła Genueńska—zjednoczenie* (Paris, 1862).

Russian-trained element. Ignacy Chmieleński, for example, was the son of a major-general in the Russian army and had received his education in the university of Kiev, whence he departed without leave to travel abroad and make contact with Miero-sławski.[1] His influence was reinforced in February 1862 by the arrival of Jarosław Dąbrowski who was to end his career as the general of the Paris Commune. Dąbrowski, trained as a Russian officer, was sent in December 1859 to the General Staff Academy in St. Petersburg, where he finished his course in December 1861, which enabled him to be posted to the staff of the First Army in Warsaw. Dąbrowski's arrival in the city introduced a certain vigour into the proceedings of the Town Committee, which up to that time had been a supine organization without a clear sense of direction.[2] Dąbrowski came from a completely different intellectual atmosphere in Russia, where revolutionary thought was uncomplicated by the grievance of national oppression and was directed towards the one simple end, the overthrow of Tsarist autocracy. Through his friendship with other Polish officers in St. Petersburg, Sierakowski, Zwierz-dowski, Heidenreich and Miniewski, Dąbrowski was connected with a conspiracy which extended into the First Army itself among the officers and N.C.O.s, the 'Zemlya i Volya' conspiracy of 1862.[3] It is supposed that there were in the First Army some two hundred disaffected officers and men, though this group was not entirely Russian in its national composition. Kaplinsky was a Pole, Arnhold a Latvian of Swedish extraction, Slivitsky a Ruthenian, Rostkowski a Pole and Szczur a Warsaw Jew. Andrej Potebnia, who had contact with Alexander Herzen, was a Ruthenian. This cosmopolitan conspiracy had no qualms about raising a revolution in conjunction with the Poles. Assured therefore of some prospect of support from the Russian army, Dąbrowski set himself to the task of strengthening

---

[1] See the article by E. Oppman in *Polski Słownik Biograficzny*; and S. Wilska, *Pamiętnik o Ignacym Chmieleńskim*, with an introduction by S. Kieniewicz (Wrocław, 1952).

[2] Cf. E. Przybyszewski, 'Jarosław Dabrowski i jego rola w organizacji narodowej 1861–1862', *Sprawozdania z posiedzeń Towarzystwa Naukowego Warszawskiego*, Wyd. II, xx (1927), pp. 12–28.

[3] Cf. J. Kowalski, *Rewolucyjna demokracja rosyjska a powstanie styczniowe* (Warsaw, 1949).

the Red organization in Warsaw and extending its influence to the provinces. From the advent of Dąbrowski a permanent feature of the Red organization began to appear. The leader, who controlled the radical agitation in Warsaw and who could above all issue orders to the working men of the city, became a power independent of the committee which directed the formal political activity of the Reds. The Red Committee, with its frequent changes of personnel and its need to remain undetected, was divorced from its supporters, who gave their loyalty to their immediate commander, the Chief of the Town, as he came to be called. The arrival of Dąbrowski gave the Reds an effective organization for the first time, which was more than to compensate for the lack of financial support which the capitalist Kronenberg could put at the command of the Whites.

By the beginning of 1862 the situation in Congress Poland had changed. Wielopolski was at the moment marooned in St. Petersburg awaiting a decision of the Tsar and therefore removed from internal politics. Within the Kingdom the Whites struggled, without openly admitting their intention, for the realization of Wielopolski's programme. The Reds had laid the first foundations of the future insurrection. In effect, the Whites ought to have looked, though unwillingly, to Russia; the Reds were looking to the people.

CHAPTER V

The Second Russian Attempt at Conciliation

THE temper of Alexander II grew very short at the end of 1861. He had done his best for the Poles and had been rewarded with continued hostility. It did not seem that Wielopolski would obtain a cordial reception in St. Petersburg, but in fact he received the order of the White Eagle. The Russians had invented for themselves a picture of the typical Polish nobleman, elegant, brilliant in conversation, superficially charming, but at the bottom treacherous, foxy and ready to stab the honest Russian in the back. From the very beginning of his stay in St. Petersburg Wielopolski showed that he did not conform to this picture. Bulky, not at all inclined either to charm or to talk and concerned only with everyday aspects of Russo-Polish co-operation, he soon became an object of curiosity and interest and was eventually able to win adherents in the Russian salons. Napier reported that, when he sounded him on the question of whether British diplomatic representations would assist the Polish cause, he made no reply at all, but occasionally he could speak his mind:

He comes up like some marine monster to the surface, spouts and disappears in the abyss. Some one was arguing that though political reforms were rarely unattended with some inconvenience they prevented greater evils belonging to eventual convulsion. 'Oui,' said Wielopolski, 'la réforme est la vaccine de la Révolution.'[1]

In remarks of this kind lay the secret of Wielopolski's success. The liberal Russian nobility were no less anxious than the

---

[1] P.R.O. 30/22/83, Napier to Russell, 6 March 1862.

Polish Whites to see some change in the existing political system. The concept of a *Zemsky Sobor*, which was current in these years, was little different from Wielopolski's limited notions of constitutional reform. The motive was the same, the desire for transition to a more modern state of society with the preservation of the old aristocracy. It was obvious that, if Wielopolski could achieve a success in the Congress Kingdom, there was a chance of a similar extension of constitutional institutions in Russia.

Wielopolski's influence in fact extended to the highest in the land. The Empress took a fancy to him and used her influence to advance his cause. The Grand Duke Constantine Nikolayevich, the eldest of the Tsar's brothers, was attracted by the plans for reform in the Congress Kingdom, which would obtain a greater degree of autonomy and therefore a semi-independent dignity for its Viceroy, a post which he coveted for himself. Constantine was well known for his Slavophil views. It would have been a personal triumph for him if he could reconcile the Orthodox Russians with the Catholic Poles. Behind all this there may have been a thought that one day the Austrian Empire might collapse and he obtain a kingdom in his own right. There were other Russians, among them the Chancellor Gorchakov, who were not moved by daydreams, but by *raison d'état*. To them Wielopolski represented a means and possibly the only means of solving the deadlock in the Congress Kingdom. The stumbling-block was the Tsar himself, who remained suspicious of the Polish nationalist claims. When Bismarck took his leave of the Tsar on 8 April 1862, the conversation turned to Poland. Alexander II stated that Prussia and Russia had a common interest in maintaining the *status quo* in Poland:

In referring to Poland His Majesty remarked that he would always do his best to govern that country well, but he had less hope of succeeding with the co-operation of the Poles than he had previously entertained. He believed that there was not a gentleman in Poland who did not aim not only at the re-establishment of the independence of his country in the limits of 1772, but even at the recovery of the old provinces conquered by the Poles from Russia in the 15th and 16th centuries, and subsequently retaken, provinces essentially Russian, by race and religion, and which by all arguments of nationality ought to belong to Russia. The Poles, His Majesty declared, aimed at Kiew itself.[1]

Wielopolski's concentration upon the interests of the Poles within the narrow limits of the Congress Kingdom showed a greater sense of reality than was evident among the Whites of the Kingdom who talked airily of the claims of Lithuania and Ruthenia, as if such talk did not raise suspicion in the minds of the Russians.

Wielopolski was thus compelled to fight on two fronts, in the Kingdom where his measures were still under discussion and in St. Petersburg where he strove to obtain an extension of concessions from Alexander II. Before he left Warsaw he had launched his plan for the fixing of rents upon a permanent basis by publishing his proposals in his newspaper, *Dziennik Powszechny*, on 26 October 1861. The basis of the temporary conversion of 16 May 1861 had been the evaluation of the peasants' obligations in money, a method which was open to the criticism that it might cause some hardships. Now Wielopolski proposed that the rents should be based upon the average yield of different kinds of soil, from which one-third was to be deducted to cover the maintenance of buildings, elemental disasters and communal obligations, which would not fall upon the peasant, but to it was added a surcharge of 5 per cent to cover buildings, implements and seed provided by the manor. The manor was to retain its traditional rights of hunting and fishing, its monopoly of distilling and its mineral rights. In other respects, the proposal was disadvantageous for the peasants. Where rights to woods and pastures were not based upon a written agreement they were to cease. Empty holdings, for which no tenant could be found, might be embodied in the demesne farm after three years. Conversion was to be supervised by two representatives of the rural district council, obviously landlords, and one official. Wielopolski therefore left behind him a clear indication to the *szlachta* of the aims he would be pursuing on their behalf in St. Petersburg. In the discussions which followed in the commit-

---

[1] F.O. 65/602, Napier to Russell, 11 April 1862. It must have gratified Bismarck to hear this, for he himself had transmitted to Gorchakov in the crisis of March 1861 the opinion of William I that liberal reform was dangerous, cf. *Krasny Arkhiv*, LXI (1933), 'Pisma O. Bismarka A. M. Gorchakovu', no. 2.

tees during his absence Russian officials, especially the new Director of Internal Affairs, Kruzenstern, attempted to modify his proposals in the interests of the peasants, but Wielopolski was able to return for the final discussion in the Council of State on 7 April 1862. The right of the peasant to appeal to the *gubernia* or the government in Warsaw, which Kruzenstern had inserted, was deleted and the final decision left in the hands of the rural district committee controlled by the landlords. The proposal was ultimately transmitted to St. Petersburg in a form acceptable to the landlords.

There was a danger that Russian policy might depart from the lines adopted hitherto and seek a basis for Tsarism by satisfying the Polish peasant. There were proposals that Nicholas Milyutin, who was regarded as being too favourable to the claims of the Russian peasants for his employment in the Empire, should be appointed to administer the Congress Kingdom.[1] A decision did not come as quickly as Wielopolski would have liked and there were times when he would gladly have given up public life altogether. On 19 April he was threatening to resign and go home, because one of his subsidiary measures, the education law, was held up, and had to be persuaded to stay by Gorchakov himself.[2] The peasant question nevertheless kept him to his task; after experiencing a minor defeat on the draft of the education law, he remarked to Napier that he had 'consented to remain a little longer to watch the fortunes of his second great measure, that which is designed to regulate the relations of the peasant and the lord'.[3] In the end he was to triumph. Nicholas Milyutin was not to be sent to Poland, for the Tsar's final decision was once more to attempt to win over the Polish propertied classes.

It was an easy enough matter to settle the affairs of the church. There could be no peace if a man like Białobrzeski were to be appointed to the Archbishopric of Warsaw. At Wielopolski's suggestion the Tsar chose Father Feliński, a priest with a revolutionary past which he lived down in the Roman Catholic

[1] A. Leroy-Beaulieu, *Un homme d'état russe (Nicholas Milutine)* (Paris, 1884), pp. 129–30.
[2] Cf. 'Iz dnevnika V. K. Konstantina Nikolayevicha, 18 Apr.–13 Dek. 1862', *Krasny Arkhiv*, x (1925/iii), pp. 218–19.
[3] F.O. 65/603, Napier to Russell, 16 May 1862.

Academy in St. Petersburg. Feliński was thus sent to Warsaw with the task of reopening the churches and restoring religious life to normal. His arrival in Warsaw on 16 February created no disturbances and his advice to the population to discontinue demonstrations in the churches was for the moment heeded. There were some slight signs of opposition when he entered the pulpit in the cathedral on 10 April, but it was noticeable that the demonstrators did not obtain the same sympathy from the public as they had in 1861.[1] There was another slight outbreak of hymn-singing on the anniversary of the Constitution of 3 May 1791, which caused Russell in London, who was probably watching events in St. Petersburg carefully and had been convinced by Napier's arguments that Wielopolski's tactics were the only feasible ones in the circumstances, to telegraph to Stanton the advice that 'partial attempts at disturbances . . . are very weak and foolish'.[2] Indeed, there was no reason why there should have been a resumption of hymn-singing in defiance of the Russian authorities. The upper and middle classes were watching for every sign of concession from St. Petersburg. Stanton's information was that 'the Marquis will have the general support of the upper classes' if his measures were approved.[3] The Reds for their part were planning a real insurrection and had little time for the diverting but unprofitable pastime of church demonstrations.

The motives which finally induced Alexander II to make his submission to pressure in favour of Wielopolski's system are not yet clear, but it is not unlikely that the discovery of the military conspiracy in the First Army in Poland during April 1862 speeded a decision. There was no means of knowing how extensive the plot was, but any Tsar who considered the history of Russia since the death of Peter the Great might with justice have felt uneasy when it was revealed that even a section of the army was not absolutely loyal. Constantine recorded that in the discussions of 21 May Alexander II was visibly shaken when Platonov, the assistant secretary of state in the Polish chancery, mentioned that the army might not take kindly to the appoint-

---

[1] Cf. F.O. 65/612, Stanton to Russell, 19 April 1862.
[2] F.O. 65/612, Russell to Stanton, 28 May 1862.
[3] F.O. 65/612, Stanton to Russell, 20 April 1862.

ment of Wielopolski and that the meeting ended after an angry and abortive dispute.[1] This may be only a straw in the wind but it seems to indicate a state of anxiety. At all events, the haste with which decisions on Polish affairs were made in May 1862 is in sharp contrast with the lack of resolution which had been evident hitherto.

On the evening of 19 May the committee established to examine conversion to rents gave its final decision and approved Wielopolski's proposal in substance.[2] Constantine recorded in his diary: 'I was terribly happy and satisfied with this result, while Wielopolski's faced beamed as I have never seen it before.'[3] And well it might have gleamed. Wielopolski had obtained a solution which would give him a means of inducing the landed gentry in the Congress Kingdom to co-operate with the government. On 22 May Alexander II, with the almost unanimous approval of his ministers, agreed to the appointment of the Grand Duke Constantine as Viceroy and of Wielopolski as head of the Civil Government. Napier was curious to discover the reasons for the sudden conversion of the Tsar. When Wielopolski called upon him on 28 May, Napier asked whether it was the discovery of the military conspiracy which had hastened the decision, but Wielopolski merely replied that he had known nothing of the decision until 26 May when he had been summoned to Tsarskoe Selo: 'The Emperor then said with tears in his eyes "I had a stone in my heart; it is now gone" and embraced him.' The purpose of Wielopolski's visit to Napier, however, was not to relate these charming details, but to remind him of the dangers to conciliation which might result from indiscreet behaviour on the part of Poland's friends:

The Marquis Wielopolski is firmly convinced of the Emperor's good intentions and asks for time, moderation and the absence of foreign instigations which raise exaggerated hopes in Poland and give no material aid. He evidently desires the sympathy and approval of Her Majesty's government and of England.[4]

This plea, that Poland should not become a matter for diplomatic discussion or public pronouncement, was preaching to

[1] *Krasny Arkhiv*, x (1925/iii), p. 222.
[2] For the text see H. Lisicki, *Aleksander Wielopolski*, ii, 359–402.
[3] *Krasny Arkhiv*, x (1925/iii), p. 221.
[4] F.O. 65/603, Napier to Russell, 28 May 1862.

the converted. Already in February 1862 Russell had replied to Napier's question whether Britain ought to raise the question of Russia's obligations under the Treaty of 1815 and stated that he had nothing to add to what Palmerston had said in 1831:

The best chance for Poland in the opinion of Her Majesty's Government consists in patient and quiet submission to the laws, until an improvement shall take place in the political institutions of Russia. Poland would no doubt ask to share in the benefits of these improved institutions. Nor would it be easy to prevent such a union between liberal Russians and liberal Poles as would tend to the advantage of both countries. For this purpose it is desirable not only to prevent collisions between Russian soldiers and Polish citizens, but also to smooth down any feelings of dislike and animosity which may exist between the two races.

Present peace and future freedom may thus be secured, while violent demonstrations in the churches and streets of Warsaw only give excuse for means of repression. The Russian army will not and cannot allow itself to be defeated by the unarmed multitudes of the Polish towns.[1]

Russell was to repeat this conviction in July and, in commenting upon Gorchakov's statement that if he were a Christian subject of Turkey he would conspire against the Sultan, declared:

It is not in the interest of the established Govts. of Europe to favour the democratic movements which are going on in Italy, in Austria, in Turkey and in Poland. Prince Gorchakov ought to perceive the difference between Constitutional Freedom and Democratic License. The Sultan's Rule is not in our opinion tyrannical or intolerant.[2]

Wielopolski was assured of the goodwill of the British govern-

[1] F.O. 65/595, Russell to Napier, 21 February 1862. This advice was merely to repeat the view of Derby and Malmesbury, cf. F.O. 65/520, Malmesbury to Simmons, 7 April 1858. It was moreover a recommendation which the aged Nesselrode had given to Napier, cf. F.O. 65/574, Napier to Russell, 15 March 1861. Palmerston told Prince Władysław Czartoryski even more bluntly that the Polish tactics were of no avail: 'Je dirai que vous avez provoqué les Russes et n'ayant pas assez pour résister vous avez amené l'état de choses actuel. Vous n'avez gagné que l'état de siège. . . . Vous vous êtes conduits comme des enfants contre un maître d'école, lui faissant des niches sans but possible, ou sans avoir les moyens de l'obtenir.' Cf. *Muzeum X. Czartoryskich*, 5695, f. 333, Conversation of Władysław Czartoryski with Lord Palmerston, 20 March 1862.

[2] F.O. 65/596, Russell to Lumley, 30 July 1862.

ment. From the French little trouble was to be expected. Everything therefore depended upon the reception of the reforms in Poland.

The reforms of May–June 1862 seemed impressive.[1] In addition to the law of 5 June covering conversion to rents, the law concerning public education was signed on 29 May. On 5 June the Jews obtained their emancipation. The whole of the civil administration was placed under Wielopolski as head of the civil government. The nomination of the Grand Duke Constantine was a guarantee that the new *régime* would be free from the arbitrary interference of the Russian military, who would not dare to oppose the Tsar's brother openly. Only for a short time did it seem that the new order would be introduced without crisis. Wielopolski travelled to Warsaw at once, but Constantine remained behind in St. Petersburg to acquaint himself with the correspondence relating to the Kingdom of Poland and in the meantime to master the Polish language; his wife, moreover, was pregnant, which was a good personal reason for delaying his departure. The sudden sense of urgency which was introduced into the situation occurred on 21 June when an attempt was made upon the life of General Lüders, who was performing the duties of Viceroy. There was a natural tendency to blame this event upon a Polish agitator, but there was a strong suspicion that the attempt was in fact organized by officers of the First Army in revenge for the execution of the conspirators, Arnhold, Slivitsky and Rostkowski in the fortress of Nowogeorgiewsk. Suspicion fell upon the Schlüsselberg Regiment and Kowalski, a Pole, and his friends, Zakrzewski and Dmochowski, were arrested. The Ruthenian Potebnia, another officer in this unit, evidently knew more than the authorities discovered, for he fled the country. In this situation it was imperative that the Grand Duke Constantine should leave to take up his duties in Warsaw at once.

The letter of instructions which he received before his departure revealed the limits to which Alexander II was prepared to go even in difficult circumstances.[2] Constantine was told

---

[1] For the texts of these measures see H. Lisicki, *Aleksander Wielopolski*, II, 278–358.

[2] 'Perepiska Imperatora Aleksandra II-go s velikim knyazem Konstantinom Nikolayevichem za vremya prebivaniya ego v dolzhnosti Namestnika Tsarstva Pol'skogo v 1862–1863 gg', *Dyela i Dni*, I (1920), pp. 123–5.

that he must work to establish law and order and make the concessions work in order to frustrate the revolutionary party. To this end he should seek co-operation with the moderates, but Alexander II warned him that he would make no further concessions and that on no account would he consider the grant of an army or a constitution. Constantine was expressly warned not to let his Panslavist feelings run away with him. Panslavism Alexander considered very dangerous for Russia and the monarch in existing conditions and that 'the unification of all Slavs in one state is a Utopia'. He could bring military rule to an end as soon as possible, but he was ordered to resist Wielopolski if he should act in any way contrary to the interests of the monarchy or Russia. Wielopolski was to be shown that he was the servant of the monarchy who might act as a first counsellor, but not as a master. Alexander had indeed come a long way since his speech to the Polish nobility in 1856, but his fundamental conception had scarcely changed. He was first and foremost the autocratic Tsar of Russia, serving his Empire according to his own conception of the monarchy's interests. The interests of Poland were subsidiary. The Polish propertied classes could, if they wished, come to a working arrangement with Russia, as indeed the Poznanians were compelled to accept Prussian rule and the Galicians Austrian domination, but they could not be allowed to squeeze too much from Russia or limit in any way the personal power of the Tsar.

The fundamental assumption of Alexander II was that the Polish Whites could master the situation if they would, but this was to underestimate the strength of the Reds. Jarosław Dąbrowski, who had entered the Town Committee in May 1862, counted upon 7,000 adherents, of whom 2,500 were in Warsaw. With this support he was planning to make a sudden attack on the fortress of Modlin, the chief arsenal of the kingdom, housing 70,000 rifles. He was hoping to put his plan into operation before the end of June, because the Russian army in the Kingdom would be concentrated for manœuvres. If the conspirators' support in the army was to be retained, the rising must be brought about before some units returned to Russia. Confronted for the first time with a plan of insurrection, Władysław Daniłowski, at the head of the academic youth, was struck with

L

horror and decided that he and his followers must frustrate Dąbrowski at all costs. To achieve this end he entered into an agreement with Karol Majewski, who, though a member of the White Directory, kept open his contact with the Reds. Majewski and Daniłowski exerted every form of pressure to get a new Town Committee established in which the moderate left might have control, but they did not succeed in ousting Dąbrowski. The result of the dispute was that the Town Committee reconstituted itself as the 'National Central Commitee' and undertook the reorganization of its supporters. Warsaw was divided into four divisions, each with three circles, while the provinces were divided into palatinates, districts and towns. The heads of the four divisions in Warsaw conferred with the National Central Committee through the Chief of the Town, Dąbrowski, who therefore kept the influence of which Majewski and Daniłowski sought to deprive him. The National Central Committee itself consisted of Daniłowski and his follower, Marczewski, who were opposed to Dąbrowski's plan for an early insurrection, the 'Siberian' Agaton Giller and Bronisław Szwarce, a young man who had been working on the railway line under construction near Białystok and who showed a keener realization of social problems than Daniłowski, Marczewski and Giller. Jarosław Dąbrowski as Chief of the Town represented the extreme left like Szwarce.[1] The position of the Central Committee was indeed curious. Daniłowski, Marczewski and Giller constituted a left-centrist majority, which would have been willing to sacrifice certain of the fundamental points of the Red programme if the traditional policy of political freedom within the historic frontiers of pre-1772 Poland could be brought to fruition. Szwarce and Dąbrowski continued to act upon the policy that independence could be won only upon the basis of complete social justice, for that alone would inspire the insurgents.

For the moment there was a stalemate which was very little to the taste of the ultra-revolutionary group, which was led by Ignacy Chmieleński. On the one hand the Central Committee

---

[1] Cf. B. Szwarce, 'Założenie Komitetu Centralnego w r. 1862', *W 40-tą rocznicę powstania styczniowego* (Lvov, 1903), and W. Daniłowski, *Notatki do pamiętników*, ed. J. Czubek (Cracow, 1908). Chapter XII.

seemed to intend the postponement of a rising, on the other the new Russian concessions, though coldly received, nevertheless stood a reasonable chance of achieving their purpose of bringing the Whites into co-operation with the government. If the Whites threw their support whole-heartedly on the side of Wielopolski, then the law for conversion to rents would be put into operation and the alliance of the *szlachta* and the Russian government firmly cemented. All hope of Polish reunification would then disappear. This seemed to Chmieleński a desperate situation which required desperate measures. He evidently came to the conclusion that the only way to prevent the Whites from achieving a juncture with the government was to ensure the continuation of coercive government, the best means to which was the assassination of the Grand Duke Constantine and Wielopolski. For the attack on Constantine he obtained the services of one Jaroszyński, an almost illiterate workman, but one with a sense of decency, for he refused to shoot at Constantine when he arrived at the station in Warsaw on 2 June because the Grand Duchess who accompanied him was unmistakably pregnant and to kill her husband before her eyes would be an eternal blot on the honour of the Polish nation. On the following day, when the Grand Duke visited the theatre, circumstances were not as favourable and Jaroszyński succeeded only in wounding him slightly with his shot. This attack was followed up with two attacks on Wielopolski, the first by a youth named Ryłł on 7 August and the second by another boy named Rzońca on 15 August, but in neither case did they achieve their purpose.

The Grand Duke was not prepared to indulge the extreme left and restore coercive government. Instead he chose to appeal to what elements of sporting feeling the public might have, for it might well be argued that he had scarcely been given a chance to prove the honesty of his intentions. On 4 June he issued a statement that the reforms would proceed in spite of the attack upon his own person. To some extent he did receive the acclamation of the moderates, but the same indulgence was not shown to Wielopolski who insisted that the time had come to make an example of the would-be assassins, who were not granted a pardon, but executed according to the strict letter of the law, to the evident distaste of the public, which regarded them as being too young fully to appreciate the consequences of their actions. For the moment, however, Constantine believed that he had achieved his purpose and that a section of the Whites at least would co-operate in the work of government; to Alexander II he reported:

From all sides they tell me that the party of Zamoyski is quite disorganized. You know that Zamoyski provides only the name for this party and that its present leaders are considered to be Węgleński and Kurtz, who they say are very able, clever and decent people. Both of them have indicated to Wielopolski their willingness to join the government.[1]

On the one hand he tried to please the public by giving his newborn son the Polish Christian name of Wacław. On the other hand he tried to rout out the Warsaw Reds, who exerted an intolerable tyranny over the minds of the moderates, by improving the efficiency of the police force, for which purpose he obtained the services of two British detectives from London.[2] The last two Russian civil governors, Opperman and Fanshaw, were removed from their posts and Poles appointed in their place, though this step was not entirely approved by Alexander II, who wrote that some restraint should be put upon Wielopolski's plans for the complete polonization of the administration: 'It is advisable that you should remind him how he should understand the autonomy of the administration in the Kingdom and that you should not allow the complete exclusion of the Russian element.'[3] The expected co-operation was, however, not forthcoming as quickly as Constantine would have liked and on 27 August he found it necessary to issue a public appeal for support.[4] The Polish Whites were willing to enter into co-operation with the government. Both Węgleński, a prominent leader of the landlords, and Leopold Kronenberg, the Warsaw financier, were in principle ready to offer their assistance.[5] Zamoyski, however, still stood aside, though he might yet have exerted a sobering influence. Constantine realized that he was incorrigible:

---

[1] Constantine to Alexander II, 14 July 1862, *Dyela i Dni*, I, 136–7.
[2] Cf. *Accounts and Papers* (1863), LXXV, 21–3.
[3] Alexander II to Constantine, 3 August 1862, *Dyela i Dni*, I, 149.
[4] H. Lisicki, *Aleksander Wielopolski*, II, 424–5.   [5] *Dyela i Dni*, III, 71.

He is quite mad. C'est un fou, un rêveur, un utopiste, who is made up of malice and gall. Where he ought to talk business and consider possibilities, he rakes up the past and demands the old Poland and the Dniepr.[1]

Undoubtedly the emotional desire for the extension of Poland to the east played a great part in the thinking of the Polish leaders, but of far greater concern was the revolutionary situation which was beginning to appear within the Kingdom itself. In 1861 it was possible to suppose that national solidarity, at least among the educated classes, could be achieved, but from the spring of 1862 with the extension of the Red organization throughout the countryside the possibility of an uprising prefaced by the announcement 'granting the peasants their freeholds had become more than a possibility. It represented an ever-increasing danger. The Reds at home and abroad were not prepared to accept the thesis put forward by Karol Ruprecht that the insurrection should be postponed until after conversion to rents had been completed. At first the underground newspaper, *Strażnica* (The Watchtower), controlled by 'Siberians', merely directed attention to the national enemy, the Russians, and avoided the peasant question for fear of disrupting national unity. *Głos Warszawy* (The Voice of Warsaw), published by the Town Committee, had however begun to declare that the purpose of the Polish national movement was not to preserve the existing state of social relationships. The Wielopolski laws of May–June 1862 reinforced the need of the Reds to define their own social and economic policy, but the crisis within the Town Committee and the formation of the National Central Committee, bringing the 'Siberian' Agaton Giller into an active share in the direction of the conspiracy, had delayed a decision. The arrest of Jarosław Dąbrowski himself at the end of August likewise tended to weaken the revolutionary spirit of the Committee. Szwarce's view was that 'the whole committee in general feared the peasant question like fire, remembering what happened in Kościuszko's day'.[2] Nevertheless, pressure from below resulted in the Central Committee's

---

[1] *Ibid.*, III, 71.
[2] B. Szwarce, 'Założenie Komitetu Centralnego w r. 1862', *W 40-tą rocznicę powstania styczniowego*, p. 449.

gradually taking a more determined attitude to the peasants. Rafał Błoński, who was active in the provinces, demanded a clear profession of the Central Committee's principles in order to be able to quieten the peasants' fears that the future Polish government would restore the old system of labour services.[1] In consequence the Central Committee issued its instructions of 12 August, its first public pronouncement, which, in addition to promising the abolition of taxes on salt and tobacco, the erection of free schools in order to permit everyone to take full advantage of equality of opportunity, the reduction of military service and the maintenance of churches by the state, touched upon the question of tenures:

5. On the government lands the Polish government will not collect the rents, while on the holdings, on which the peasants are settled, it will give to them in perpetual property right from generation to generation. Peasant lands on the non-public estates, however, the Polish government will restore to the peasants in property right and will pay their rents to the lords in instalments, in order that every peasant in the whole of Poland, Lithuania and Ruthenia may be free and independent with no difference between them and the landlord or townsman. If on the other hand the peasants do not listen to the Polish government and do not assist in driving out the Muscovites and the Germans, none of these benefits shall fall to them.[2]

There was an ominous ring in the last clause which contained a threat to the peasants, without a corresponding warning to the landlords. The implication was that the peasants were still regarded as junior partners in the struggle for national independence. There was, however, enough in this declaration to frighten the landlords. Wielopolski attempted to accentuate their fears by publishing in *Dziennik Powszechny* on 29 August a confidential instruction issued on 24 July by the Central Committee and discovered by the police, in which there was mention of the grant of freeholds to the peasants with compensation to the landlords by the future Polish state. In this way the public at large was left in no doubt of the direction in which the Reds'

[1] R. Błoński, 'Pamiętnik z Augustowskiego 1863 r.', *Polska w walce* (ed. A. Giller, Lvov, 1875), II, 325.

[2] W. Przyborowski, *Historya dwóch lat*, v, 487–8.

thought was moving. The Reds were moreover claiming that their National Central Committee must be considered the only authority representing Poland and must therefore command the allegiance of all Poles.[1]

In the August of 1862 the Polish Whites were required to determine their attitude towards the offer extended by the Grand Duke Constantine to take them into partnership. The appeal of Constantine of 27 August called for an answer, but it was not easy for the Whites to make up their minds or even to preserve their own solidarity. There was evidently a conference of the moderate leaders at which an attempt was made to draft a reply. Some of them were in favour of braving the condemnation of the Reds and, pronouncing in favour of compromise with Russia, but others considered that this course would mean that the Reds would proceed to the organization of an insurrection in which they would totally disregard the claims of the gentry. No agreement was reached, but one group, which collected 200 signatures, published its own manifesto, addressed to Andrzej Zamoyski, who had recently announced his opposition by resigning from the Warsaw Town Council on the flimsy pretext that he could not spare the time, but in reality in a fit of pique that Zygmunt Wielopolski, Alexander Wielopolski's son, had been appointed Town President. In this address the minority declared:

We as Poles will be able to support the government with confidence when that government shall be our own Polish government and when all the provinces which constitute our fatherland shall be joined together by a fundamental law [i.e. constitution] and free institutions.[2]

This declaration was not so much motivated by a real desire to secure the extension of the frontier to the east as by a determination to make a demonstration against the Reds, revealing that the Whites too had the interests of independence at heart.[3] The interpretation which the Reds were invited to place upon it was that they could find valuable allies among the Whites if

---

[1] Cf. the announcement of 1 September 1862, A. Giller, *Historja powstania narodu polskiego*, I, 309. *Wydawnictwo Materyałów*, I, 23.

[2] *Wydawnictwo Materyałów*, I, 26–7.

[3] Cf. F.O. 65/612, Stanton to Russell, 15 September 1862.

only they would show due appreciation of the claims of the landed gentry. Giller did indeed acknowledge the confidential instruction of 24 July, published by Wielopolski on 29 August, by reissuing it in the underground newsletter, *Ruch*, on 17 September. The operative clause stated:

By extending brotherly feeling among all classes of our national community we will use our influence to solve the reform of peasant conditions in a manner which will favour the cause of the insurrection and bring the peasants to complete property rights through a Polish government, which from the general resources of the state shall devise funds for the compensation of the landlords for the rents they have given up.[1]

In other words, the Central Committee undertook not to encourage the peasants to wage a class war against the landlords, to whom it promised that they should suffer no financial loss.[2]

Wielopolski and the Grand Duke Constantine now saw that they could not hope for co-operation upon their own terms. The decision was therefore taken to attack and compel the Whites to enter into the government of the Kingdom. On the one hand, it had to be shown that the government could not be made to yield further concessions. This had been the clear meaning of Alexander II's instructions to Constantine. An example was therefore to be made of Count Andrzej Zamoyski, though all sides recognized that he no longer played any decisive part in the affairs of the Kingdom. The address of the minority Whites nevertheless provided an adequate excuse. He was called to leave the Kingdom and present himself before the Tsar to answer for his conduct. Alexander II's comment was that he was a nonentity, 'un rêveur incorrigible', and gave him permission to travel abroad: 'Pour lui dorer la pilule je lui ai dit que c'était pour empêcher qu'on ne se serve de son nom contre sa volonté.'[3]

It was easy enough to send Zamoyski abroad, but it was not from the Russian point of view a simple matter to induce the Whites to commit themselves to the task of making limited autonomy a reality. As long as the pressure of Red agitation

---

[1] W. Przyborowski, *Historya dwóch lat*, v, 483.
[2] I follow here S. Kieniewicz, *Sprawa włościańska w powstaniu styczniowym*, pp. 223–35.
[3] *Dyela i Dni*, iii, 86–7.

persisted, the Whites would adopt an equivocal attitude and keep open the possibility of co-operation with the radical movement. Wielopolski had come to the conclusion that the only way out of the impasse was to destroy the Red organization altogether. The means lay in the renewal of conscription in the Empire and the Kingdom. By carrying out a selective conscription of the youth in the towns the Red organization could be broken and the Whites permitted to join in the work of implementing the reforms without fear of their patriotism being questioned or the peasants being stirred to revolt. There was in this conception a major political error. There was no indication in September 1862 that the Reds, led by the Central Committee in which Giller was the most prominent figure, intended to do more than play at conspiracy. If less impatience had been shown the Whites might have drifted into collaboration and Wielopolski's object have been achieved. To attack the Reds was to invite their submission or drive them to more violent action.

CHAPTER VI

The Proscription and the Genesis of the Insurrection of January 1863

CONSCRIPTION in the Russian dominions could not have been delayed for ever if the Tsar wished to exert an influence in international relations. General Dmitri Milyutin at the ministry of war was anxious to get away from the barrack-square methods of Nicholas I and train a new army. The 1860's were a period in which all European states needed to depart from the tactics which had won the battles of Leipzig and Waterloo. New and younger men were needed to restore the fighting spirit of the Russian army. Although Russia had a paper strength of 1,594,340 men, it would have been difficult, according to Milyutin, to muster more than 500,000 men on the western frontier, which would have been insufficient to deal with Prussia, let alone a European coalition.[1] In Russia and Poland the normal method of conscription had been to take the strongest of the landless peasantry as recruits for the army. The novelty of Wielopolski's suggestion in 1862 was that recruitment should apply for the most part to the towns, the centres in which the Polish Reds possessed their greatest strength, and that there should be a strict control of the exemptions which hitherto it had been easy to obtain. There were indeed strong arguments against applying conscription to the peasantry at a time when a measure of agrarian reform was being put into operation, lest the agricultural economy, already subject to stresses and strains, should collapse altogether. Alexander II himself was doubtful of the wisdom of exempting the peasantry, a course which had already been suggested by General Lüders,[2] but he allowed him-

---

[1] A. V. Fedorov, *Russkaya Armiya v 50–70-kh godakh xix veka—Ocherki* (Leningrad, 1959), p. 27.

[2] *Dyela i Dni*, III, 69.

self to be persuaded to adopt the course suggested by Wielo-polski. Though Wielopolski intended that the main weight of the conscription should fall upon the towns, he did not exclude the possibility that certain classes of the rural population should be called to the colours. These were elements which might respond to Red propaganda, the labourers who were only employed casually, estate officials and petty *szlachta*. His object was to carry out a proscription and it mattered little where his enemies lived as long as they might feel the threat of being transported away from home and kept within the bonds of military dis-cipline. The announcement of the conscription was published on 6 October 1862 in *Dziennik Powszechny*, but without indica-tion of the actual date upon, which the recruits would be re-quired to report for duty. The young Reds were therefore invited to evade conscription by taking refuge abroad, which would have served Wielopolski's purpose equally as well as their being drafted to units in the Russian Empire. There were, however, too many young conspirators for them all to go abroad. The majority could do nothing but remain in the Kingdom.

At the beginning of October 1862 the National Central Com-mittee lacked firm direction and control. Agaton Giller and Padlewski, a young man from the military academy in Genoa, who had recently been appointed Chief of the Town in suc-cession to Dąbrowski, had gone to London to discuss with Her-zen the possibility of a united front with the Russian liberal movement against tsarist autocracy. From the Polish point of view this visit was crowned with success. Herzen took their de-clarations of solidarity at their face value and wrote his 'Letter to Russian Officers in Poland', of 10 October, calling upon them not to take up arms against the Poles and printed in *Kolokol* an appeal purporting to come from Russian officers serving in the First Army, entitled 'To the Grand Duke Constantine Nikola-yevich', which demanded that Russians should not be compelled to suppress a Polish revolutionary movement. The Poles for their part renounced the ancient system of *szlachta* privilege and as-serted that they were seeking alliance with the Russian revolu-tionaries to their mutual advantage. They announced their economic programme to be the endowment of the peasants with complete property rights. As far as the national question was concerned, they aimed 'at the reconstruction of Poland in her old frontiers, leaving to the nations which dwell in them, that is, the Ruthenes, the Lithuanians and the Ukrainians, the complete freedom of remaining in union with Poland or making arrangements according to their own wishes'.[1] It is difficult to see what purpose these declarations were designed to achieve, for they did not advance the cause of the Polish insurrection one jot. The expedition of Giller and Padlewski in September 1862 can only indicate that they did not consider the situation at all urgent and could spare the time to make a long journey. The announcement of the conscription thus came while they were absent from Warsaw.

The news that the government intended to carry out a proscription of the Reds not unnaturally was greeted with dismay by the followers of the National Central Committee. In the midst of the heated discussion there was issued from a source purporting to be the Committee itself the so-called 'Note on Conscription', which declared to the members of the Red organization that the execution of the recruitment would be the signal for an insurrection. Everyone supposed that this note had the authorization of the Central Committee and it would have been fatal to its prestige to have disowned it. Bronisław Szwarce, determined to get to the bottom of this matter, discovered that it had been issued by the supporters of the 'Revolutionary Committee', which unknown to the Central Committee had been set up by Mierosławski's supporter, Narzymski, who was working for the recognition of Mierosławski's claim to be dictator when the insurrection broke out. It was likewise revealed that two members of the Central Committee, Daniłowski and Koskowski, were actually members of the Revolutionary Committee, while Edward Rolski, who was carrying out the duties of Chief of the Town, was involved in the distribution of the 'Note'. Revolutionary indiscipline had in this way produced a situation in which the Russian government could give the signal for the Red insurrection.

The Central Committee was in a state of confusion when Giller and Padlewski returned from London. It was committed

---

[1] Cf. the pamphlet, *Centralny Narodowy Komitet Polski w Warszawie i Wydawcy "Kolokoła" w Londynie* (London, 1862).

to carrying out an insurrection by the Mierosławski group, though it had not yet amassed the resources to wage war with the Russians. Daniłowski could be purged, but the Committee had now no alternative but to behave as if a rising were about to take place. The first step was on 18 October to decree a levy on all inhabitants of the Kingdom for the purpose of organizing the revolt, the sums to be paid within a month; this tax was assessed at ½ per cent on property and 5 per cent on salaries, but the assessment was left to the donor, which did not promise that this measure would yield large sums. In the meantime, the Committee did its best to hamper the conscription. The supervision of recruitment to the army under Wielopolski's system rested with the rural district and town councils. The Committee therefore issued an order through its underground newspaper, *Ruch*, on 12 October that rural and municipal councillors should resign rather than assist the government in the conscription, but with very few exceptions the landed gentry chose to remain in office and ignored the Central Committee.

Greater success attended the Committee's efforts in other directions. Oscar Aweyde, a lawyer who had studied in Berlin and St. Petersburg and who had become a deputy member of the Central Committee in October, established contact with the Red Committee in Vilna, which promised a chance of co-ordinated action in Lithuania, though the Polish movement there was weak and divided by internal feuds. The Galician Reds, the so-called Galician Council, announced on 16 October 1862 that it had submitted to the control of the Central Committee in Warsaw.[1] Within the Kingdom the clergy offered its support. Father Mikoszewski, who passed under the revolutionary name of Sixtus, was organizing the parochial clergy of Warsaw. In the provinces, at a gathering at Bodzentyn in the Świętokrzyskie Hills, a body of the clergy gave its formal support for the policy of resigning from town and district councils.[2] Only in St. Petersburg, where Padlewski journeyed in search of support, did the Committee meet with refusal; there the Russian conspirators were downcast after the arrest of Serno-

---

[1] *Wydawnictwo materyałów*, vol. III, is a collection of this organization's addresses and orders.
[2] W. Przyborowski, *Historya dwóch lat*, v, 493.

Solovievich and Chernyshevsky and could not promise any form of action before the summer of 1863. Nevertheless, the early winter of 1862 saw a remarkable extension in the authority of the Central Committee. To frighten the *szlachta* and the middle classes Wielopolski printed in *Dziennik Powszechny* the manifesto of Mierosławski's Revolutionary Committee side by side with the Central Committee's decree for a financial levy. The Central Committee, having no wish to be connected with Mierosławski, promptly published a reply in *Ruch* disclaiming association with him.[1] This action gave some annoyance to Mierosławski, who replied in kind by criticizing the agreement with Herzen in London, as a surrender of the former eastern provinces to Russia, but it is doubtful whether Mierosławski's newspaper, *Baczność*, came into the hands of many people in Poland. The sole result of Wielopolski's action was to secure a wider publicity for the Central Committee and left no one in doubt that an insurrection was now actively being planned.

At the beginning of December, however, the Central Committee began to have second thoughts. The government held the initiative in its hands and could carry out the conscription in the depths of winter, which would mean that the insurgents took the field in the least favourable season of the year. Rather than ask its supporters to revolt during the winter, the Committee decided that the rising must be postponed until May 1863, but this left unsolved the problem of the young men who had been selected for enlistment. Giller suggested that they should move out of their home districts, the time-honoured method of evasion, and lie up under the insurgent organization's supervision, the cost of their maintenance being borne by the landlords. The lower ranks of the Reds were becoming surly and discontented. There was great doubt whether the mass of the insurgents could in fact remain undetected. There was every danger, if Giller's plan were adopted, that they be discovered and marched off to join the Russian army, which would wreck the Red organization. On the other hand, the Central Committee was coming under strong pressure from its military experts not to undertake a revolt. Weapons, other than sporting guns, were almost non-existent in the countryside and the revolt

---

[1] W. Przyborowski, *Historya dwóch lat*, v, 305–8.

promised to be a pitiful affair. Zygmunt Miłkowski, better known under his literary name of Jeż, who was to undertake the revolt in the Ukraine and Lithuania, did not rate the chances of success highly. Caution was urged by Marian Langiewicz, a former Prussian officer, who had been an instructor at the Polish military academy at Cuneo until its suppression, and by Edmund Różycki, whose father had led the Volhynian revolt in 1831. Force was added to their opinion in December. The financial levy had not yielded vast sums, but the equivalent of £10,000 was sent to Paris to a munitions committee under Józef Wysocki and Ćwierczakiewicz. This money was spent in purchasing obsolete firearms, which the European armies were scrapping as they rearmed with breach-loading weapons, but even this effort came to nothing because Ćwierczakiewicz was arrested by the French police on 20/21 December who gave the Russian ambassador, Budberg, full details of Polish activity. Of this mishap the Central Committee learned on 24 December, when Zygmunt Sierakowski, rejoining his unit in the Russian army, returned from Paris on his way to Russia. On the day before, the police had discovered the printing shop of the underground newspaper, *Ruch*, in the home of a relative of Bronisław Szwarce, who himself fell into a police trap and was imprisoned in the Citadel. The prospects were black indeed.

The Central Committee, reorganized after Szwarce's capture, now consisted of Giller, Oscar Aweyde, who was close in his views to Giller, Zygmunt Padlewski, Jan Maykowski, J. K. Janowski and Father Mikoszewski, the last three being still unfamiliar with the general details of the Red organization. At a meeting on 29 December 1862 Aweyde presented to them the exact state of preparedness. The Kingdom had been divided into eight districts, corresponding to the *województwa* of 1815. In each district there was a commander and a commissar, the latter maintaining contact with the Central Committee. The total strength of the Reds was about 20,000, mainly intelligentsia and workmen in the towns, except for the *gubernia* of Płock, where there was a substantial following of petty *szlachta*. The landed gentry, however, could not be counted upon. In Vilna and Kiev there were Polish committees. The Vilna Committee appeared to be a little piqued because the district of

Białystok, formerly part of Prussian Poland, but since 1807 annexed to Russia, had been brought under the authority of Warsaw, but the Kiev Committee under the influence of Stefan Bobrowski had agreed to accept the leadership of Warsaw.[1] Giller's view was that there could be no other course than to postpone the rising on the grounds that the Committee's strength was totally inadequate. The one member of the Central Committee who favoured a rising was Zygmunt Padlewski, the Chief of the Town, for he stood nearest to the insurgent rank and file and understood their feelings. Against Giller's plan for mass evasion he opposed his own scheme for the withdrawal of their supporters from recruiting points and their concentration in three zones in preparation for armed insurrection. Padlewski's arguments in favour of action were reinforced by pressure from the lower ranks of the insurgent organization. While the Central Committee was carrying on its discussions, the provincial commissars had come together in the Hotel Polski. There it was decided that there was no other course but to revolt, and the youth Leon Frankowski was delegated to present their ultimatum to the Central Committee. If the Central Committee did not call for a rising, they and their followers would withdraw their allegiance. The Central Committee had no alternative but to capitulate and on 2 January the decision was taken to revolt. After some hesitation Giller resigned from the Committee, which passed under the control of Zygmunt Padlewski and Stefan Bobrowski, the student from Kiev, who had arrived in Warsaw by way of Paris on 3 January. Both these men were eastern Poles, of far greater determination and higher morale than Maykowski, Janowski and Mikoszewski, whom Giller had brought into the Committee. Thus after considerable fluctuation in its membership the Committee passed out of the control of the left-centrists like Giller and came under the hand of two genuine revolutionaries. The wavering was over and the insurrection was certain.

Political developments in the Kingdom had not been without their counterpart in Lithuania, though the development of a revolutionary organization had not proceeded with the same speed. In 1862 a 'Lithuanian Committee' was formed by a

[1] J. K. Janowski, *Pamiętniki o powstaniu styczniowym* (Lvov, 1923), I, 15–16.

schoolteacher, Wacław Przybylski, subsequently transferred to Vologda on the pretext of giving him a better post, and a conspirator of 1846–9, the 'Siberian' Franciszek Dalewski. The Lithuanian Committee soon developed views too radical for Dalewski who transferred his allegiance to the Lithuanian *szlachta*. The direction of the Committee, therefore, fell into the hands of the Reds, the chief of whom were Ludwik Zwierzdowski, an officer of the general staff in Vilna, and Konstanty Kalinowski. Both of these men were agreed that the revolution must be based upon the traditional programme of granting freeholds to the peasants, but they differed upon the important question of the status of Lithuania in the new Poland. Kalinowski believed that Lithuania might assume a separate role in the insurrection and that the Committee should not place itself under the Red Central Committee in Warsaw, of which Kalinowski had formed an unfavourable opinion. Zwierzdowski, however, considered that the revolution must be one of all Poland and refused to listen to what he considered the claims of Lithuanian particularism, in which he was supported by the representative from the Warsaw Committee, Nestor du Laurent. From this dispute Kalinowski emerged triumphant because papers of Jarosław Dąbrowski, arrested in August 1862, revealed a connection with Zwierzdowski. Nazimov held Zwierzdowski in high esteem and gave him the benefit of the doubt, transferring him to the Moscow military district. Thus Kalinowski was left in control.

In the meantime the Lithuanian Whites were considering what course they ought to adopt in the light of the growing tension in the Kingdom. In December 1862 Count Wiktor Starzyński, marshal of the *szlachta* of Grodno, Count Zyberg-Plater and Jakób Gieysztor went to Warsaw to reconnoitre the situation. In the Kingdom the White Directory found itself in a state of complete disarray, surrendering initiative entirely to the Reds. The conference of December 1862 with the representatives from Lithuania, together with spokesmen for Poznania and Galicia, produced no decision. The Whites of the Kingdom tended to think that there was nothing to do except wait for what Wielopolski might bring them. The only positive action taken by the Whites was the issue of a valedictory address to the

M

prospective conscripts, 'A Word of Farewell to those involved in the Proscriptiòn'. In January 1863 Piasecki, a follower of the Directory from Lublin, found a confused state of affairs in Warsaw. He ran across a friend, Maykowski, a member of the Red Central Committee, and Padlewski, the Chief of the Town, who clearly expected a revolt, but their views were pooh-poohed by Jurgens and Kronenberg. Kronenberg declared:

There will not be a rising so soon. . . . We will try to get a hold on the young people. At the present time we must work along the mapped-out path of improvements in the administration and education. Try, sir, to extend your organization of the peasants.[1]

The Whites did not desire a rising, but they took no steps to prevent an outbreak. At the meeting in December 1862 Jakób Gieysztor, the Lithuanian, protested that the Whites would find themselves in a position in which they would be compelled to take part, if only for honour's sake,[2] but a conference of 150 landlords at Kovno on 22 January decided to follow the example of the Whites in the Kingdom and take no action to meet an emergency. The outbreak of the insurrection in the Kingdom on 22 January found the propertied classes in the Kingdom and in Lithuania totally unprepared and not a little ashamed lest they be standing idle while their countrymen were engaging the Russians. They expected Wielopolski to be master of the situation, but the Reds were to prove them wrong.

The Reds at least knew their own mind, but it was difficult to decide upon the tactics to be employed. Bobrowski was in favour of a coup in Warsaw, by which the insurgents were to seize the Grand Duke, but there were strong arguments against a revolt in the city. The Russians might easily concentrate their army around and in the city and the insurgents would be compelled to capitulate. From prison Jarosław Dąbrowski advised the Committee to seize the fortress of Modlin and establish themselves in the countryside, where they could declare themselves the legal government of Warsaw. It was this latter plan which was accepted in principle, but time was already growing

---

[1] F. W. Piasecki, 'Od 6 do 26 stycznia w Lubelskiem', *W 40-ta rocznicę powstania styczniowego*, p. 338.

[2] J. Gieysztor, *Pamiętniki . . . z lat 1857–1865* (Vilna, 1913), I, 188–9.

short. The Grand Duke Constantine and Wielopolski had decided upon action. On 13 January the movement of soldiers in Warsaw and elsewhere indicated that the conscription was about to take place. On 14/15 January the authorities rounded up such recruits as they could find. The Reds had long given out that this would be the signal for the rising and the public half-expected that there would be an immediate outbreak of mass violence, but nothing happened. The Whites began to congratulate themselves that all was well and that their own inactivity had been justified. The Red menace had been proved to be a mere chimera. It was now safe to co-operate openly with the government and for once Wielopolski experienced a moment of triumph. All the candidates for office came round to offer their congratulations and to express their goodwill. It seemed that all the struggle and unpopularity which had been endured by Wielopolski was now to have its reward. The Kingdom of Poland was apparently safe for the Whites.

The action of the government in fact disposed of the last doubts and hesitations of the Reds. To withdraw now would be to surrender the people into the hands of the propertied classes, who would solve the social question to their own satisfaction and give up all idea of independence. Padlewski declared that this could not be permitted:

The handing over of recruits today is to leave to the Muscovites the solution of the peasant question which the *szlachta* committee [i.e. the White Directory] has wanted from the beginning. Indeed this is the complete rejection of the people, in other words, of the salvation of Poland. It is to hand over the people to the *szlachta* school. Therefore my opinion was and is—Sacrifice the youth . . . for the people, solve the peasant question through the Polish nation itself, lay the foundations of a great people's war to save the whole nation. That is my conviction and for it I will die.[1]

These were brave and noble words, but the circumstances in which a revolt could be called were hard indeed. Already there were modifications of the original plan. Modlin, it appeared, could not easily be taken, but it was hoped that the insurgent forces would be able to seize Płock, which would become the seat of the revolutionary government. The establishment of a

[1] B. Limanowski, *Historia ruchu narodowego od 1863 do 1864* (Lvov, 1882), II, 241.

government by young men who had been compelled to hide their identity for fear of arrest itself presented a difficulty. In these circumstances it was an error for Padlewski to leave Warsaw to lead an insurgent band, for it left Bobrowski isolated in the Central Committee. The immaturity of the other members produced a strange solution. Turning back to the revolt of 1830 they decided that the revolutionaries had been at fault in not having their own insurgent government ready to take power and in leaving Adam Czartoryski and the conservatives to assume direction. Nevertheless, they needed some prominent person whose name was known to all Poles. Władysław Janowski, who had come up from the south to take part in these discussions, was of the opinion that the only course was to set up a military dictatorship under Ludwik Mierosławski. Bobrowski and Aweyde, who had a clear impression of Mierosławski's limitations, objected strongly, but they were overruled by their colleagues, Maykowski, Mikoszewski and J. K. Janowski, for whom Mierosławski seemed an eminently suitable choice. Władysław Janowski was appointed to convey to Mierosławski the news of his appointment, though he needed an assistant, Stanisław Krzemiński, because he himself had never in his life left Poland and knew neither French nor German. In a country which had not been subjected to suffocating control, in which a more normal political life had been allowed and left-wing leaders were known to the public, Mierosławski, the failure of 1846 and 1848, could never have emerged to lead the nation, but in emigration without contacts of importance with the country he was a symbol. In a normal situation there would perhaps have been no revolt at all, but these were abnormal times and mistakes were easily made by young men, however clear their conception of ultimate duty.

Within the country the insurgents had a simple plan. The Central Committee transformed itself into the 'Temporary National Government', consisting of Mikoszewski, Aweyde, Maykowski and Janowski, which was to go into the country to await the moment when the insurgent forces had cleared an area in which it could function. In Warsaw an executive committee was left behind, under Bobrowski, as Chief of the Town, assisted by the Mierosławski men, Marczewski and Daniłowski;

Agaton Giller was invited to help, but for the moment he held back, because he objected to the nomination of Mierosławski, though he remained in close contact with affairs and was subsequently ready to play his part. Under the military plan the country was divided into four districts; Płock under Konrad Błaszczyński and Podlasie under Walery Lewandowski, two areas which were thickly wooded and where there were concentrations of petty *szlachta* who sided with the Reds, while in the south in the old *wojewódtwo* of Cracow Apolinary Kurowski was to take command, and in the area of Sandomierz, Marian Langiewicz, who could draw upon the assistance of the Poles in Galicia. The main effort was to be made to seize Płock.

The appeal which the revolutionaries made to the Polish public was no more original than their selection of Mierosławski. It was little more than the old Democratic Society's programme rehashed. A grandiloquent manifesto declared that the National Central Committee was the only legal government of Poland and appealed for all Poles, Lithuanians and Ruthenians to join in the common struggle, but it avoided making any suggestion that the Poznanians and the Galicians should rise in sympathy. The revolt was to be against Russia alone.[1] A second manifesto, drawn up in the form of a decree, declared that the Central Committee in its capacity as the Temporary National Government granted the peasants their freeholds:

Every kind of landed possession, which any husbandman has possessed up to this time whether by labour services, rents or other title, together with the messuage which belongs to it, dwellings and farm buildings, as well as rights and privileges attached to it, from the date of this decree becomes the exclusive and hereditary property of its present possessor, without any form of obligation whatsoever, whether gifts in kind, labour services or rent, upon the sole condition of paying the taxes falling upon it and rendering the required services to the country.

This decree was to cover both government and private property, but the landlords were assured that they would obtain compensation for the losses they incurred.[2] A supplementary decree

[1] For the English text, see T. Filipowicz, *Confidential Correspondence of the British Government respecting the Insurrection in Poland, 1863*, pp. 12–13.
[2] *Ibid.*, p. 37.

extended the promise to the landless labourers and farmers of dwarf holdings that they would obtain lands from the government estates of at least three morgs in extent, provided that they served in the insurgent forces in defence of the revolution.[1] The revolutionaries were in theory rising in the name of the traditional policy of freedom, equality and fraternity, to which they had added some measure of economic justice. It was fundamentally an agrarian programme. When the revolutionaries contemplated the people, they could conceive only of those peasants who in 1863 held land. To the landless they offered land if they joined in the struggle, but only from the government estates. The manifestoes were therefore as important for what they did not say as for what they promised. The landed gentry were to continue to hold their estates. No mention was made of the land which had been taken from the peasants and incorporated in the demesne. The implication of the manifestoes was that only the landed peasants had anything to gain from the Polish victory. No material rewards were offered to the working class of the towns, which in Warsaw at least had been the mainstay of the National Central Committee. There was nevertheless a positive side to the Red manifestoes. The Russian government through Wielopolski was attempting to win over the Polish upper classes by a conversion to rents which contained innumerable clauses and loopholes, which the gentry might exploit to wage a class war on the peasantry. The manifestoes at least brought the attack upon the peasants to an end. That was an achievement of far greater importance than the theoretical considerations of the manner in which the decrees might have been made more comprehensive, for it gave the peasants an immediate measure of relief.

For the landed gentry the manifestoes contained all the disadvantages which they had foreseen if an insurrection were called. It was true that they were left with their estates, which were not liable to revolutionary confiscation, but they were expected to forego the income which they drew from the peasants at least during the insurrection. The decrees promised compensation, but when and upon what scale they did not pronounce. Added to their uncertainty was the realization that the period

[1] *Wydawnictwo Materyałów*, I, 35.

of rebellion would demand that the manors supplied from their own stocks the insurgent forces within the country. Appeals to the peasant masses were to invite attacks upon the manors, which the official government would scarcely suppress if the *szlachta* whole-heartedly supported the revolt. The willingness of the Reds to preserve the principle of private property in land was a small compensation for the immediate ruin which threatened to overwhelm the gentry. It cannot be wondered that the attitude of many a landed proprietor towards the revolt contained many reservations.

The revolt broke out on 22 January and the decrees of the Central Committee bear that date. The revolt scarcely seemed serious at all. Out of 144 places garrisoned by Russian troops only seventeen were attacked. The action of the Reds seemed to be only extensive rioting. The students of the *Szkoła Główna*, the higher educational institution which Wielopolski established for want of a university, met in the anatomy theatre and drew up a declaration that they would have no part in a revolt. There was no sudden elemental upsurge of the peasants to take advantage of the revolutionary decrees. It was the British consul Stanton's view that the government still retained the initiative and could extricate itself from the situation by an appeal to the Whites:

It is to be hoped that the Government will avail itself of this opportunity of gaining them to its side by some well-timed concession; and as the socialist nature of the movement can hardly now be doubted it is highly probable that very many among them would be glad of a pretext for siding with the government were such offered them.[1]

The Russian military commanders were by no means convinced that the revolt would dissolve into a series of minor disturbances. The main insurgent effort to capture Płock was a miserable failure, but in the south, in the region of Sandomierz, the ex-Prussian officer, Marian Langiewicz, was able to hold his own and for the moment elude the Russian soldiery. General Ramsay, the general officer commanding the troops in the

[1] T. Filipowicz, *Confidential Correspondence*, p. 14, Stanton to Russell, 29 January 1863.

Kingdom, feared the consequences of allowing the insurgents to launch attacks upon small Russian units dispersed throughout the countryside. The Russian soldiers were trained to fight in masses and had been slow to adapt themselves to the loose formations required by modern war or to show that degree of individual initiative which would be needed to combat elusive partisans.[1] Ramsay pressed upon the Grand Duke Constantine the need to concentrate his forces, to which he agreed on 23 January after some hesitation and by 3 February the army had been brought together in larger units of at least two battalions strength.[2] The military concepts of the Poles argued in favour of this step. The Poles believed that the aim of the revolt was to assemble a national army and defeat the Russians in the field. It could therefore be pleaded that the Poles, if allowed themselves to concentrate, would assemble larger units which could easily be destroyed. The Polish movement was moreover of urban origin. If the towns were held it might be possible to paralyze the revolt.

Ramsay's calculations were in fact to prove correct when it came to fighting the larger Polish units, but the countryside was left open to the smaller insurgent bands. The withdrawal of the frontier guards to places of safety meant that arms could be brought in freely from Galicia. The local administration in the Kingdom came under the control of the insurgents, who could thus exercise a quasi-official authority over large tracts of territory and enforce their revolutionary programme. The revolt, which might have petered out in disillusionment if the Russians had maintained the dispersal of their garrisons, now achieved a permanence. The Whites, still with the possibility of joining Wielopolski's government, found themselves deserted in the countryside by the authorities and completely at the mercy of the insurgents. At the time of the conscription they had con-

---

[1] Cf. F.O. 65/475, Mansfield to Clarendon, 9 December 1856, which records his conversation with General Buturlin, then quartermaster-general of the First Army. Buturlin was convinced of the value of drill and was suspicious of the new tactics made possible by improved infantry arms. His observation was that 'battles were never won by skirmishers' and that 'attempt to make all men good shots is useless'. Mansfield, who was to be chief of staff of the British forces in India during the Mutiny, thought that these were 'such obvious truths'.

[2] For the order of 11/23 January 1863, see G. Gesket, *Voyennye Dyeistviya v Tsarstve Pol'skom v 1863 g.* (Warsaw, 1894), pp. 388–91.

gratulated themselves on the success of their policy in awaiting events. Now they were forced to recognize the bankruptcy of their position. The British consul, Stanton, reported that there was a meeting of the landed gentry in Warsaw, but no decision was reached: 'It was agreed at their last meeting that, no general determination being possible, each proprietor should act on his own view of the case.'[1] In spite of itself the National Central Committee had been able to raise the standard of rebellion and substantiate its claim to speak for the entire Polish nation. Isolated disturbances in Poland were the concern only of the Tsar. A rebellion invited the attention of the great powers which had signed the treaty of Vienna.

[1] T. Filipowicz, *Confidential Correspondence*, p. 36, Stanton to Russell, 6 February 1863.

CHAPTER VII

The Failure of Diplomatic Intervention in the Polish Crisis

THE morale of the Polish insurgents was sustained by the prospect that the signatories of the Vienna treaty of 1815 would intervene on their behalf. The Russian government, for its part, could not at the outset disregard the feelings of western Europe and proceed openly to a policy of terror. The situation in Russia itself was uneasy. The prospect of intervention in the Polish question seemed to add a complication to an already complicated situation, which inclined the Russian statesmen to persist in their attempt to seek an accommodation with the Polish Whites until that moment when they could be certain that there was no danger and that it was safe to resort to drastic methods to bring the Polish revolt to a close. In the summer of 1863 Alexander II experienced many uncertainties, which coincided with the rise of Polish hopes. In this struggle all the signatory powers of the Vienna treaties had a part to play.

In theory all powers which had signed the final act of the Congress of Vienna in 1815 had an interest in the Polish crisis. The exact interpretation of Article 1, however, remained disputed even in 1863. The Russian point of view was that the treaty of 1815 had given the Tsar the Kingdom of Poland in full sovereignty and that Alexander I had as a concession granted the Poles a constitution; though this constitution was required by the treaty, the exact terms of it were entirely the concern of the Tsar and alterations in it entirely within his power to make. In this way Nicholas I had been entitled to abolish the constitution of 1815 and substitute the organic statute of 1832. The Poles were not according to the Russian interpretation empowered to revolt or break with the Tsar. It was on the other hand contended by the powers which professed a friendship for the Poles that, though the Tsar had an undeniable international right to the Kingdom of Poland, he was nevertheless obliged to maintain a constitutional *régime*. The signatory powers which adhered to this interpretation, above all Britain, were never entirely convinced in their reading of the treaty, nor indeed was Russia completely confident that she could act without regard to western susceptibilities. The importance of the controversy was that the western powers could press their interpretation and the Russian government must count upon the possibility of their raising difficulties. When Russia was strong or useful, the signatory powers could conveniently forget the Poles, but when there was a need or an opportunity to weaken Russia the Polish question was raised. In the long run it was not the actual interpretation of the Vienna treaty which was important, but the use it could be put to in international relations. Poles naturally insisted upon the letter of the treaty where it favoured them, but even for them the treaty provided merely a debating point. No Pole ever considered that the petty Kingdom of Poland was an end in itself. Their ultimate object was to tear up the treaty of Vienna, which was no less a partition of Poland than the partitions of 1772, 1793 and 1795. Certainly no Pole of the Red organization in Warsaw thought of the constitution of 1815 as the basis for reorganization.[1]

The outbreak of an insurrection in Congress Poland naturally gave some concern to the Prussian government and on 24 January orders for strict security measures were ordered in Poznania. It was obvious that the Prussian frontier offered an easy refuge to insurgent bands and the Russian ambassador, Oubril,

---

[1] In 1861 the British government laid before parliament its correspondence with France and Russia on this subject, cf. *Accounts and Papers* (1861), LXV, 349 ff. Palmerston's private opinion in 1863 was that Britain had not emerged entirely successful from her effort to establish her position, especially after Lord Durham's visit to St. Petersburg in 1832. 'In past times personal influence did much to embarrass the action of the British govt. Mad[ame)] Lieven had great influence over Lord Grey and put much water into my wine, while at Petersburgh Durham's inordinate vanity and desire to be well with the Russian court entirely gagged him as our mouthpiece about Polish affairs; and accordingly we do not, I think, stand quite satisfactorily as to our language and course in those times.' P.R.O. 30/22/22, Palmerston to Russell, 26 February 1863.

inquired in an audience with William I whether Russian troops would be given facilities to pursue rebels into Prussian territory and whether in general Russia might count upon the good offices of Prussia. This gave Bismarck his opportunity to fish in troubled waters. His original intention was to send General von Alvensleben to Warsaw, but it was unlikely that he would receive a warm reception from the Grand Duke Constantine and Wielopolski if he proposed to them some form of Russo-Prussian co-operation on the frontiers, when they were seeking to reduce tension. It seemed better therefore to send Alvensleben to St. Petersburg for direct conversations with the Tsar and perhaps turn him away from the policy of co-operating with France and seeking a compromise with the Poles. Constantine, indeed, had more than enough troops at his command to deal with the uprising, for on 1 January (O.S.) there were in the Kingdom sixty-six battalions of infantry, twenty-five cavalry squadrons, sixty-two cossack hundreds and artillery with 184 guns, in all 100,000 men.[1] Constantine had good reason to be confident of being able to suppress the badly armed insurgent bands. There appeared to be no need to change the course of Russian policy and in this the Chancellor, Gorchakov, agreed with Constantine. Alexander II, however, professed to be delighted to know that the King of Prussia offered his assistance when he received Alvensleben on 5 February.[2] Gorchakov thus found himself in the unhappy position of being likely to disagree with the Tsar. He realized that any agreement with Prussia could cause only unfavourable reactions in France and Britain, and would give the impression that Russia was in a very weak state indeed if she needed the aid of Prussia.[3] Alexander II, however, did not listen to the objections of Gorchakov, but insisted that an agreement should be signed with Prussia for the preservation of order on the frontier. Unable to resist, Gorchakov was compelled to accept, with only minor alterations, the draft convention dictated by Alvensleben, which was signed on 8 February. The so-called Alvensleben conven-

[1] V. G. Revunenkov, *Pol'skoye Vosstaniye 1863 g. i evropeyskaya diplomatiya* (Leningrad, 1957), p. 126.

[2] Cf. *Die auswärtige Politik Preussens, 1858–1871*, III, 549.

[3] V. G. Revunenkov, *Pol'skoye Vosstaniye*, p. 130.

tion permitted the troops of the Russian army in the Kingdom or the Prussian army in the frontier regions to cross into one another's territory and to co-operate with one another in pursuit of insurgents, under the supervision of officers designated for the task; the two powers undertook moreover to keep one another informed of political intrigues in their respective Polish territories, but this article was not to be disclosed.[1] Alexander II had compelled his Chancellor to sign an agreement of which he entirely disapproved and which was certainly not to the taste of his brother, Constantine. Gorchakov was exceedingly nervous lest the agreement to cross the frontiers be taken up by France or Britain as a pretext for intervention in the Polish question. His advice to the Grand Duke Constantine was that he should not hasten to implement the agreement with Alvensleben:

In view of the deference which the Emperor Napoleon reveals towards public opinion and the weakness of the English ministry before Parliament, we should not show excessive caution, if we were to confine the co-operation, offered to us with such readiness by the Prussian cabinet, to the narrowest limits of absolute necessity. I should be happy if we did not have the need to put it into operation.[2]

It quickly became apparent that Bismarck did not intend the convention to become a dead letter, but hoped to enlarge it to permit Prussian troops to enter into the Kingdom of Poland and co-operate actively with the Russians in the suppression of the rebellion.[3] Bismarck's view was in fact far less sanguine than that of Constantine and the Russians generally, who expected the revolt in the Kingdom to offer few difficulties. He professed to believe that the insurgents would be able to drive out the Russians, which would present Prussia with the problem of an independent Polish state on her eastern frontier. He now began to talk of the possibility of a Prussian occupation and even of the establishment of a Prussian *régime* in the Congress Kingdom.[4] This was indeed more than Alexander II had fore-

[1] For the text see K. Lutostański, *Les partages de la Pologne et la lutte pour l'indépendance* (Lausanne-Paris, 1918), pp. 598–9.
[2] Gorchakov to Constantine, 22 February 1863, quoted by V. G. Revunenkov, *Pol'skoye Vosstaniye*, p. 136.
[3] *Cf. Die auswärtige Politik Preussens*, III, Oubril to Gorchakov, 12 February 1863, p. 241.
[4] *Ibid.*, III, 271.

seen and Gorchakov was authorized to send reminders to Berlin that the Alvensleben convention was designed only to cover cases in which frontier posts might find themselves in danger. Rash talk of annexation or temporary occupation soon began to excite intense interest in Britain and in France, which was the last event which the Tsar had desired.

Unrest in Poland gave rise to grave difficulties for Napoleon III and his advisers. They were not at the outset anxious to become involved in questions arising from the Polish insurrection, lest their fragile understanding with Russia of 3 March 1859 be shattered. As long as the Russian government continued in its effort to satisfy the claims of the Polish Whites, it was possible for the French government to argue that the disturbances in Poland were the work of an unscrupulous minority and that the sensible course was to avoid creating unnecessary complications which might force the Tsar to take drastic action and withdraw his reforms. On 5 February Billault advised the Poles to maintain the policy of seeking concessions from the Tsar, but this was not an easy argument to sustain. The Poles were an oppressed nationality and Napoleon III had a reputation for assisting national movements. For the clericals the Poles were the great Catholic nation of eastern Europe. For the Bonapartists the Kingdom of Poland was the lineal descendant of Napoleon I's Duchy of Warsaw. The Alvensleben convention seemed to point the way out of the government's difficulties. Pressure could be put on Berlin rather than upon St. Petersburg. Bismarck was informed in a stiff note of 17 February that he had no business to intervene in the affairs of the Tsar and his subjects.[1] The French despatch to Russia, however, avoided all reference to the Alvensleben convention, but pointed out the difficulty in which any French government might find itself if public opinion became excited by the Polish question, though France for her part would never do anything to encourage revolutionary or anarchic tendencies in Europe.[2] Thus was Russia invited to remember the delicate state of affairs in France. There was a hint of the 1815 treaty in the note, but this was only to remind the Russians that the placing of the Polish

---

[1] British and Foreign State Papers, LIII (1862–3), pp. 825–7.
[2] Ibid., LIII, Drouyn de Lhuys to Montebello, 18 February 1863, pp. 827–8.

question at the head of the Final Act was an indication of the importance attached to it at Vienna and the complications to which it might give rise. All that Drouyn in effect asked for was tact from the side of the Russians which might permit France to maintain her neutral attitude.

The effect of the French move in Berlin upon the Poles in Poland and abroad was immediate. The right-wing faction of Prince Władysław Czartoryski had up to this stage consistently advised the right wing at home that the insurrection was useless: 'God is too high and France too far.' The news of the French note, however, caused the Hotel Lambert to telegraph urgently to Cracow on 16 February that the orders given to its courier were cancelled: 'Everything changed. Consider G.F.'s instructions as void. Necessary to carry on the struggle as long as possible. Further advice by letter.'[1] The Hotel Lambert followed up this advice with the recommendation that the revolt should take on the appearance of an anti-Russian national reaction and that all suspicion that it had a revolutionary character should be avoided.[2] Thus the Polish gentry were encouraged for the first time to abandon their attitude of passivity and throw the whole weight of their influence behind the insurrection.[3] Napoleon III had in fact made no final decision at this stage, but there were already many wild schemes in the air in court circles, where the idea was gaining currency that the Polish situation should be used to secure the reorganization of Europe. Pressure was being placed upon the Emperor both by Prince Napoleon and by the Empress Eugénie. Prince Napoleon was suggesting a union of Congress Poland, Poznania and Galicia as an independent state, the cession of Venetia to Italy with compensation to Austria in Germany, a wholesale reorganization of the Balkans with the conversion of Constantinople into a Free City, and, not least, the acquisition by France of territories on the left bank of the Rhine.[4] On 22 February the Empress Eugénie unburdened her heart to the Austrian ambassador, Metternich, in a three-hour conversation. She suggested that the time had come for an entente between Austria, Britain

[1] Stanisław Koźmian, *Rzecz o roku 1863* (Cracow, 1894–6), I, 24.
[2] *Ibid.*, pp. 29–30.   [3] See below, Chapter VIII.
[4] E. d'Hauterive, *Napoléon III et le Prince Napoléon* (Paris, 1925), pp. 356–7.

and France with the object of a similar reorganization of the map of Europe. Russia was to be compensated for losses in Poland at the expense of Turkey. Austria was to cede Galicia to the Kingdom of Poland and Venetia to Piedmont, but to provide the new independent Polish state with an Austrian archduke for its king, obtaining herself compensation in the northern Balkans and southern Germany. Prussia was to cede Poznania to Poland and Silesia to Austria, but to receive in return Hanover, Saxony, if Austria should decline to provide an archduke for Poland and the King of Saxony were made king of Poland instead, and all the German duchies north of the Main. France for her part was to advance to the right bank of the Rhine, though leaving Belgium her independent existence.[1] Loose talk of this kind in influential French circles no doubt impressed the Poles in Paris, but it was inevitable that it should arouse the suspicions of experienced diplomats. On 20 February Drouyn de Lhuys informed the British ambassador, Cowley, of his intention of inviting Britain to associate herself with France and Austria in an identic note to Berlin on the subject of the Alvensleben convention.[2] A similar suggestion was made to Austria on 23 February. It appeared that Britain and Austria were to be induced under the cover of assisting the Poles to further French aggression in the Rhineland.

Since the close of the Crimean War the policy of the British government had been to offer Russia a certain tolerance in her dealings with the Poles. In the autumn of 1862 Napier had suggested to Russell that an article inspired by Gorchakov in the *Journal de St. Pétersbourg*, restating the position of Russia in Poland in accordance with the accepted Russian view that the administration of Congress Poland was her own business, ought to be answered with a statement of the British view. Russell responded to Napier's suggestion, but withdrew his despatch by telegram[3] when Palmerston had declared his opinion that an article in an official gazette could not properly call for official action: 'We should in truth be only weakening our position by

[1] H. Oncken, *Die Rheinpolitik Kaiser Napoleons III von 1863 bis 1870 und der Ursprung des Krieges von 1870-71* (Stuttgart, 1926), I, (Akten) 3-6. Metternich to Rechberg, 22 February 1863.
[2] T. Filipowicz, *Confidential Correspondence*, pp. 56-8.
[3] F.O. 65/597, Russell to Napier, 30 October 1862.

seeming to think that it can be shaken by an article in the Peters-burgh Gazette.'[1] There is no evidence to show that Palmerston considered raising the Polish question before the outbreak of the insurrection. News of the fighting in Poland was bound to rouse British opinion and change the situation. Sentimental sym-pathy for the Poles was closely allied to rabid russophobia, which reports of the Alvensleben convention could only excite. In the fluid conditions of British politics in the 1860's it was always possible for a group in the House of Commons to gain the ear of the majority and shape the policy of the government, or, if the government failed to respond, to bring it down. Władysław Czartoryski's cousin, Władysław Zamoyski, enjoyed an entrée into most aristocratic salons in London and had wide contacts among the middle-class chauvinists. In February and March he was able to exert considerable pressure upon members of the House of Lords and House of Commons in favour of Poland, which was embarrassing for the government. Within government circles, however, there was little disposition to fall into line with the French proposal of an identic note to Berlin. Queen Victoria, solicitous for her German relatives and by nature inclined to caution, warned against falling into a trap set by France.[2] There were moreover some misgivings among members of the cabinet, especially Gladstone, Granville and Sir George Cornewall Lewis. Indirect evidence of their views may perhaps be obtained from Cornewall Lewis's brother-in-law, Clarendon, who held the view that the geographical position of Poland ruled out any concrete aid to the insurgents and that, if a despatch were sent to St Petersburg, it must be phrased in a manner acceptable to Alexander II, lest he be obliged to draft a sharp reply and excite still further public opinion in both France and Britain. Claren-don's opinion was that much blame might be laid at the door of 'that frantic idiot Bismarck'.[3] The matter could not however be allowed to pass by default. The debate in the House of Commons on 27 February revealed to the government that there was

[1] P.R.O. 30/22/14, Palmerston to Russell, 27 October 1862.
[2] Cf. *The Later Correspondence of Lord John Russell*, ed. G. P. Gooch, II, 302–3, General Grey to Russell, 22 February 1863. Cf. also *Letters of Queen Victoria* (ii series), I, 66–7, Queen to Granville, 23 February 1863; cf. also *ibid.*, I, 69.
[3] For expressions of Clarendon's views see his letters to Cowley, 26 February, 28 March and 29 April 1863, F.O. 519/179.

N

considerable strength of feeling in favour of Poland, which could not be ignored. Palmerston and Russell were therefore compelled to find a solution which would ease their own internal political position and at the same time avoid playing into the hands of France.

There could from Britain's point of view be no question of an identic note. Palmerston himself conceded that there was some justice in the Queen's arguments:

The Queen of course wishes to keep all safe in Posen, but in fact there is much to be said against any formal representation to Prussia either separately or conjointly with France. These poor Poles are almost sure to be cut down and shot down and have their houses and villages burnt; any representation to be useful to them must be friendly and informal to the Russian government.[1]

The more Palmerston turned his mind to the question, the more he came to the conclusion that the main direction of the British government's attention must be Russia, declaring on 25 February:

It seems to me that France is acting on the Italian saying *chi non può battere il cavallo batte la sella*. Russia is the real culprit and to her as the origin of the evil any real and useful representation ought to be addressed.[2]

On 26 February he had come to the conclusion that he must act on the grounds that 'public opinion in this country as well as in France is getting strong upon this subject and we shall not stand well if we do not do something'.[3] The debate in the Commons on 27 February confirmed in him the view that public opinion demanded that Russia and not Prussia should be the recipient of British representations:

The House of Commons was unanimously Polish and Seymour Fitzgerald actually warlike. There was not a dissentient opinion as to the conduct of Russia.[4]

The course of action was now obvious to the cabinet. In his despatch to Cowley of 28 February Russell politely rejected the

[1] P.R.O. 30/22/14, Palmerston to Russell, 23 February 1863.
[2] P.R.O. 30/22/22, Palmerston to Russell, 25 February 1863.
[3] P.R.O. 30/22/22, Palmerston to Russell, 26 February 1863.
[4] P.R.O. 30/22/22, Palmerston to Russell, 27 February 1863.

French suggestion of an identic note to Prussia on the grounds that there was already reason to believe that the Prussian government would set the Alvensleben convention aside, but it was agreed that the situation in the Kingdom of Poland did suggest that the provisions of the Treaty of Vienna were not being carried out. It was on this basis that Britain invited France and Austria to associate themselves with her and France was asked to consider similar action to that which Britain now proposed to take at St. Petersburg.[1] The British note to Berlin of 2 March was sharp in tone, declaring that the Prussian government by signing the convention had engaged in an act of intervention, but pointed the way out to Prussia by suggesting its cancellation and ending tamely by requesting information of what action was taken.[2] Palmerston was obviously satisfied with the despatch to St. Petersburg of 2 March; congratulating Russell on his draft: 'I think you have very well interwoven the *utile* with the *dulce*.'[3] Though it appealed once more to the treaty of Vienna and to the rights of the signatory powers, it was stressed that Britain approached Russia 'in the most friendly spirit . . . and with a sincere desire to promote the interests of all the parties concerned'. Its positive suggestions were that an amnesty might be granted and that the restoration of the constitutional settlement of 1815, including a diet and a national administration, might make a contribution towards restoration of tranquillity.[4] This note showed absolutely no understanding of the actual situation in the Congress Kingdom, where the insurrection was being directed by the Red Central Committee, which aspired not only to an extension of the frontiers to the east, but also to a more democratic system than that established in 1815. In this Palmerston and Russell can hardly be blamed. For years the consuls in Warsaw had given them information which represented only the views of the Polish Whites, while from St. Petersburg Napier had argued in a similar vein. From the very beginning therefore British diplomacy was unreal in relation to the Polish situation, but astute enough in relation

[1] T. Filipowicz, *Confidential Correspondence*, pp. 97–9.
[2] *Ibid.*, pp. 126–7.
[3] P.R.O. 30/22/14, Palmerston to Russell, 27 February 1863.
[4] T. Filipowicz, *Confidential Correspondence*, pp. 103–5, Russell to Napier, 2 March 1863.

to the subtle international intrigue which was being played in Paris.

The purpose of the British notes in fact was to placate public opinion at home and at the same time side-step the French proposal of an identic note to Prussia. Palmerston was evidently exceedingly pleased with the ingenuity of the British solution, writing to Russell on 2 March that 'it is rather amusing to think that we have baffled the French scheme by adopting their own Polish professed feelings' and repeating his opinion on 3 March that 'the French probably thought that Prussia would not or could not back out of their agreement with Russia, and that if she did not do so upon the representation of England, France and Austria, France would have a fine opportunity of occupying the Rhenish provinces, ostensibly as a measure of coercion, but intending that measure to end in conquest'.[1] Indeed the Prussian government had backed down. Bismarck and Gorchakov vied with one another to avoid taking the responsibility of dropping the Alvensleben convention, which did not increase their mutual regard. Alexander II's view was that 'one must admit that our dear Bismarck is a terrible blunderer',[2] but his blunders could not have been made if Alexander II had not in the first place overriden Gorchakov and allowed the convention of 8 February to be signed. He now found himself in the position of having to face a possible *démarche* of the signatory powers which was being set in motion by the British refusal to be drawn into an identic note to Berlin.

The French government had every reason to feel displeased with the way in which its suggestion had been received. Austria like Britain had refused to take it up.[3] No French statesman was ever much enamoured of the treaty of 1815 to which the British

[1] Cf. P.R.O. 30/22/22, Palmerston to Russell, 3 March 1863. Cf. also F.O. 519/195, Layard to Cowley, 2 March 1863. The Poles were warned of the British attitude, Palmerston and Russell telling Zamoyski of their suspicions: 'Il [i.e. Russell] a, comme L. P[almerston] avait fait samédi dernier, affecté de ne voir dans la "proposition" de la France qu'une "petite manœuvre" contre la Prusse.' Cf. *Muzeum X. Czartoryskich*, f. 5695, W. Zamoyski to Koźmian, 5 March 1863.

[2] R. H. Lord, 'Bismarck and Russia in 1863', *American Historical Review*, XXIX (1923–4), p. 42.

[3] T. Filipowicz, *Confidential Correspondence*, pp. 135–8, Rechberg to Metternich, 27 February 1863.

note of 28 February referred, nor was there much pleasure to be derived from the implication that Britain by sending a note to the Russian government was more solicitous of Polish welfare than France. Montebello had doubts about the wisdom of reading to Gorchakov the despatch of 17 February, which contained an oblique reference to the Treaty of Vienna, but Drouyn replied that he had no need to change it: 'Nous désirons ne pas être irritants, mais nous voulons être sincères. Vous allez recevoir une lettre de l'Empereur conçue dans ce sens.'[1] The Emperor's letter evidently contained the suggestion that the Tsar should grant an amnesty and make further concessions to the Poles. The Russian tactics were to attempt to keep France out of an association with Austria and Britain. The Russian ambassador in Paris, Budberg, had been giving out that his government would for the sake of the entente with France yield to her requests for concessions, but would resist pressure from the three powers in concert. Gorchakov for the moment was prepared only to offer an amnesty after the restoration of order in Congress Poland, though he guaranteed that the existing reforms would be maintained.[2] He had no wish to put France in a position where she must take decisive action on behalf of the Poles, but already the Emperor was yielding to the suggestions of a European reorganization. On 26 February the Austrian ambassador, Metternich, reported that Napoleon III was excited and seemed to see a possibility that Austria might, if she took her opportunity, gain more than she lost in 1859.[3] On 5 March he actually put forward the suggestion himself that Austria should surrender Galicia to the Poles and cede Venetia to Italy in return for a free hand in the east and in Germany,[4] though on 8 March he was willing to whittle his proposal down to an entente between France and Austria, by which they undertook to reach a common understanding in the Polish question and combine to maintain the peace, or, if it should be threatened, to concert measures for their mutual defence.[5]

[1] F. Charles-Roux, *Alexandre II, Gorchakoff et Napoléon III* (Paris, 1913), pp. 337–8.
[2] *Ibid.*, pp. 338–9.
[3] H. Oncken, *Die Rheinpolitik Kaiser Napoleons III*, 1 (Akten) pp. 6–8. Metternich to Rechberg, 26 February 1863.
[4] *Ibid.*, pp. 10–13, Metternich to Rechberg, 5 March 1863.
[5] *Ibid.*, pp. 13–14, for the Empress's letter of 8 March 1863 conveying this suggestion.

It was now the British government's turn to put pressure upon Napoleon III with Russell's despatch of 5 March 1863 proposing formally that France, Austria and Britain should combine to advise Russia to restore order in Congress Poland upon the basis of the 1815 treaty.[1] Palmerston's motive was evidently the desire to obtain some reinsurance against the resurrection of French plans for an attack on the Rhineland. His comment on the draft of the despatch of 5 March declared:

> The French govt. are evidently most disappointed that we have not fallen into the trap laid for us and that we have not joined them in laying the ground for an attack by France on the Prussian Rhenish provinces. But we ought to play their game back on them and urge them more strongly perhaps than is done in the despatch, of which I have a draft just now, to join us in making a representation about Poland to the Govt. of Russia. The Convention between Russia and Prussia may now fairly be considered a thing of time past.[2]

Palmerston was in fact taking a short-sighted view. The advantages to Britain of diverting France to make representations in St. Petersburg were outweighed by the alluring prospect which an identic note to Russia raised of re-creating the Crimean coalition of Austria, France and Britain, which was by no means unacceptable to Drouyn de Lhuys and Napoleon III. It was not as attractive as an identic note to Berlin, but it was a good substitute. The French government therefore accepted the British proposal and every effort was made to associate Austria in their action.

Gorchakov adopted a conciliatory attitude in the face of imminent western pressure. When Napier saw him on 9 March he was at pains to accept the British note of 2 March at its face value and, though declining to express an opinion on the provisions of the treaty of 1815, nevertheless urged that the reforms undertaken in the Congress Kingdom in 1861–2 did in fact meet its requirements. The revolutionary movement in Poland he put down to an international conspiracy and claimed that the peasants had sided with the Russian government, while the landed

[1] T. Filipowicz, *Confidential Correspondence*, pp. 143–4. Russell to Cowley, 5 March 1863.
[2] P.R.O. 30/22/14, a note of Palmerston to a covering letter of Edmund Hammond, 2 March 1863.

proprietors had taken refuge from the insurrection by coming to Warsaw. From Russia's point of view the danger of the revolt was that it aimed at nothing less than the restoration of the pre-1772 frontiers of Poland and thus at robbing Russia of a population which was ethnically not Polish.[1] Gorchakov evidently thought that by adopting a reasonable attitude he could weather the storm. His comment to Constantine on the British notes was that 'I have the impression that this is not a serious démarche, but a formal note to quieten the parliamentary conscience. Neither France nor England wants to go too far.'[2] For him all that was required was a moderate attitude upon the part of Russia. Constantine for his part was convinced that the rebellion was no longer serious and that an amnesty might be announced.

In official circles in St. Petersburg, however, two different policies were contending with one another for supremacy. Alexander II was by no means certain of Russian strength in the Kingdom and on 29 March appointed at D. A. Milyutin's suggestion Count Feodor Berg to assist Constantine in the work of crushing the insurgents. Berg was a general with wide experience of Poland and was well known as being in favour of energetic action by the army to bring the rebellion to a close.[3] Steps were taken to increase the numbers of troops stationed in the three military districts of Warsaw, Vilna and Kiev, which in the first half of April already stood at 270,194 men, over a third of the Russian peace-time establishment. With this policy of toughness was combined a policy of reasonableness. On 10 April Alexander II at length agreed to the proclamation of an amnesty on 12 April to cover not only the insurgents in the Kingdom, but also in Lithuania, which had now broken out in rebellion.[4] The amnesties were moreover part of the Russian diplomatic game. In this way the Tsar hoped to modify the attitudes of Austria, France and Britain and prevent the delivery of an identic note, or at least to forestall such a note by making concessions of his own volition. Concessions to the Poles were not, however, the

---

[1] T. Filipowicz, *Confidential Correspondence*, pp. 220–4, Napier to Russell, 9 March 1863.
[2] V. G. Revunenkov, *Pol'skoye Vosstaniye*, p. 218.   [3] *Ibid.*, p. 220.
[4] For the texts see T. Filipowicz, *Confidential Correspondence*, pp. 404–6.

limit of Alexander II's willingness to withdraw in the face of opposition. A diplomatic defeat might have given the domestic critics of Tsarism courage to question the whole system of autocracy in Russia. Valuyev, the minister of the interior, was therefore instructed to draw up a plan of a constitution, which as he admitted in his appreciation was made necessary by the Polish situation and the persistence of demands for a *Zemsky Sobor* made by Platonov, the representative of Tsarskoe Selo in the St. Petersburg assembly of the nobility.[1] Valuyev's proposals to the Tsar of 13 April 1863 amounted only to a state council drawn mainly from existing assemblies of the nobility, which should exercise advisory functions only. There was to be no change in the existing method of legal sanction. Alexander II was prepared, if difficulties arose, to conciliate only the upper ranks of Russian society and buy off the high nobility. The plan of Valuyev came to nothing and is interesting only as an illustration of the Tsar's lack of self-assurance in the spring of 1863.[2] The internal weakness of Russia must indeed have been very real, if the Tsar were willing to consider even the slightest modification of his own autocratic power.

If Alexander II had had a clear impression of the state of mind existing among his potential adversaries abroad, he would no doubt have felt more confident in his own strength. Russell was already beginning to feel a little nervous and on 18 March warned Cowley in Paris, who was to draw up the note to Russia with Drouyn de Lhuys, that 'we must not make any representations the rejection of which will put us in the alternative of war or humiliation'.[3] On the following day he returned to this theme:

I hope that you and Drouyn will hit upon some mild, strong, conciliatory, threatening, saying more than it means and meaning more than it says form of note, to which all the powers who have none of the booty of Poland in their purses can subscribe. I ask myself, what then? The only answer I can give myself is that if the Poles can make

[1] K. L. Bermansky, '"Konstitutsionnye" proyekty tsarstvovaniya Aleksandra II', *Vyestnik Prava*, xxxv (1905), kn. 9 (November 1905), p. 224.

[2] Valuyev's scheme was taken out and given a dusting in 1880, when the *régime* of Alexander II once more ran into difficulties and constitutional reform had to be considered, but the assassination of Alexander II and the accession of Alexander III brought discussions to an end.

[3] F.O. 519/200, Russell to Cowley, 18 March 1863.

any how an independent Poland it ought to be acknowledged. But I do not think that we ought to spend 100 millions of money in restoring Poland. There is no saying where we should apply our efforts, who would be our allies, nor what sort of govt. it would be possible to set up in place of the Russian despotism.[1]

Russell confessed himself quite surprised when on 25 March Baron Gros, the French ambassador, actually suggested to him that the French government was toying with the idea of asking Britain to join in a proposal to Austria that an independent Poland should be reconstituted on the basis of the union of the Kingdom with Poznania and Galicia; 'this seems so much that I was quite confounded'.[2] Great Britain had no intention of being drawn into hostilities against Russia and this Russell made clear to Cowley:

War we must avoid and I hope the Emperor Napoleon will agree with us in keeping it at a distance. If he were to begin a new way of playing his game and try to get the left bank of the Rhine he would fall more rapidly & as completely as Napoleon 1st. I think he is persuaded of this.[3]

In fact, it was by no means easy to come to any agreement upon an identic note. The French government disliked any idea of a representation to Russia upon the basis of the 1815 provisions, which aroused in Palmerston's mind a very strong distrust:

. . . there are obvious reasons why the French govt. have no particular wish to invoke the provisions of the Treaty of Vienna which is the great millstone about their neck, and which they are always repudiating, and upon every occasion trying to get rid of, while to us on the contrary that treaty is our main security against encroachments by France. All these reasons shew that we cannot present an identic note with France. The French may hint threats which we are not prepared to make and we appeal to the Treaty of Vienna which the French would wish to tear to tatters.

La Caita's report of what the Emperor said to Nigra is very curious, but it opens only one of the many pigeon holes in the Emperor's mind. Antwerp is quite as much in his thoughts as Brussels and his real object and that which lies at the bottom of his heart,

---

[1] F.O. 519/200, Russell to Cowley, 19 March 1863.
[2] F.O. 519/200, Russell to Cowley, 25 March 1863.
[3] F.O. 519/200, Russell to Cowley, 1 April 1863.

as well as that of every Frenchman, is the humbling of England, the traditionary rival of France, and the main obstacle to French supremacy in Europe and all over the world.

The Emperor would wish to bring us upon our marrow bones in the most friendly manner if we would let him do so and it is our business by making ourselves strong to render it hopeless for him to attempt doing so in any other way.

Nevertheless, Palmerston thought the present diplomatic action should be persisted with in order to satisfy public opinion: 'Depend upon it. The feeling at this moment among the Middle and Lower classes in this country is intense interest in favour of Poland.'[1] This was Palmerston's policy in 1863, an attempt to bluff Russia into further concessions to the Poles, taken in company with the power which presented the greatest danger to Britain's interests, for the purpose of appeasing public opinion.

The Austrian government was equally unwilling to appeal to the provisions of 1815. As Palmerston wrote to Russell: 'There is much force & truth in Drouyn's remark that the Devourer of Cracow could not be expected to invoke a return to the arrangements of 1815 about Poland.'[2] The most that Rechberg would agree to under pressure of visits from the British and French ambassadors on 29 March was a simultaneous despatch.[3] Russell's proposal of 30 March therefore was that Britain and France should send identic but separate notes to St. Petersburg. The British note, however, came in for very severe criticism from the Queen, who declared that 'it seems too abrupt & peremptory in the commencement, to be unnecessarily offensive in its allusions to the past govt. of Poland by Russia, to be in the claim of a right to interference by the English Govt. under the treaty of Vienna, "in any way Her Majesty may think proper", a threat which Russia will well know there is no intention of acting upon'.[4] She therefore returned the draft for alteration, which Palmerston executed, praying that it

---

[1] P.R.O. 30/22/14, Palmerston to Russell, 7 April 1863.

[2] P.R.O. 30/22/14, Palmerston to Russell, 28 March 1863.

[3] T. Filipowicz, *Confidential Correspondence*, pp. 297–8, telegram, Bloomfield to Russell, 29 March 1863.

[4] *Letters of Queen Victoria* (ii series), i, 82, Queen's memorandum of 7 April 1863. P.R.O. 30/22/14 contains the original draft with the Queen's comments.

might satisfy her and hoping that he would not have to leave Broadlands to attend to official business, for 'it would be a horrid bore to be summoned up to a Cabinet during the few days of Easter'.[1] Thus the British despatch went off in its emasculated form on 10 April, insisting upon the British interpretation of the treaty of 1815, that the Tsar held the Kingdom of Poland by a title different from that by which he ruled in Russia and that he ought therefore to conform to the stipulations of Article 1 of the treaty, but in fact making no concrete proposals to deal with the present emergency.[2] The Russian ambassador in London, Brunnow, on the same day asked Russell whether the intention of the British government was pacific, to which Russell replied that 'it was, but that as I did not wish to mislead him I must say something more. Her Majesty's government had no intentions that were otherwise than pacific, still less any concert with other powers for any but pacific purposes. But that state of things might change.'[3] In fact, Russell had no intention of giving substance to this implied threat. He had indeed no faith in British action, writing to Cowley on 11 April that if the insurrection continued much longer Britain and France would have to take some action: 'But what if Russia and the U.S. together wish to make war upon us? Absit omen! These are grave matters, but I cannot shut my eyes to them. Russia will give us no satisfaction of course.'[4] When he received the news of the Russian amnesty he replied officially that it was insufficient, but privately he considered that there was little that could be done for the Poles:

As to Poland I hope the Emperor will stay his hand & allow the Poles to try the issue themselves. I believe they will be defeated, but if not, the case for general European remonstrance & our intervention would be far stronger than it is now. My belief is however that three months will see the insurrection crushed. Poor Poles! It is a very sad fate.[5]

The notes of the three powers were presented to Gorchakov

[1] P.R.O. 30/22/14, Palmerston to Russell, 8 April 1863.
[2] T. Filipowicz, *Confidential Correspondence*, pp. 346–8, Russell to Napier, 10 April 1863.
[3] *Ibid.*, pp. 348–50.
[4] F.O. 519/200, Russell to Cowley, 11 April 1863.
[5] F.O. 519/200, Russell to Cowley, 23 April 1863.

on 17 April.[1] The simultaneous delivery of notes by three powers was indeed serious for Russia, but the notes were not identic, which invited Gorchakov to suppose that they were by no means united in their aims. Britain referred to the treaty of Vienna, but France and Austria spoke only of establishing in the Polish provinces 'les conditions d'une paix durable'. The Russian replies were therefore to invite the powers to offer their own suggestions for the pacification of the Kingdom.[2] Britain was informed that 'the Imperial Cabinet is ready to enter upon an exchange of ideas upon the ground and within the limits of the Treaties of 1815', requesting only that the reforms already instituted by the Tsar should be taken into account and that the constitution of 1815 should not be regarded as a panacea. In effect, Gorchakov threw back the question at the three powers and asked them to see whether they could in fact find a closer measure of agreement. The effect of the *démarche* on Russian opinion, however, was disturbing, especially when rumours began to circulate concerning the possibility of a French attack. A French attack was not possible without the aid of either Britain or Austria. Appreciations were drawn up of the ways in which Russia could be attacked by her enemies.[3] There were even hostile rumblings in Sweden, which seemed to show that an expedition to the Baltic might have a base near at hand. This situation produced in Russia moods varying from depression to patriotic exaltation.

The first steps taken by France in reply to the Russian invitation were indeed alarming. On 4 May the idea of a general European congress was canvassed in the form of a *conversation écrite*, but Russell brushed it aside as unworthy of consideration, in which Palmerston fully concurred with him, declaring that a conference with no definite agenda was useless. Palmerston declared that:

[1] The text of the French and Austrian notes are given in *M. d. A-E, Documents Diplomatiques* (Paris, 1863), pp. 9–10, 13, Drouyn de Lhuys to Montebello, 10 April 1863 and Rechberg to Thun, 12 April 1863.

[2] *British and Foreign State Papers*, LIII (1863), pp. 892–7, Gorchakov to Brunnow, 26 April 1863, and *M. d. A-E, Documents Diplomatiques*, Gorchakov to Budberg, 26 April 1863, pp. 16–18, and Gorchakov to Balabin, 26 April 1863, pp. 23–4.

[3] V. G. Revunenkov, *Pol'skoye Vosstaniye*, p. 233, for the appreciation of the Quartermaster-General Verigin.

As things at present stand your three points seem to be good landmarks for us, namely agreement with Austria and of course with France as long as possible; the treaty of Vienna and the Kingdom according to the limits established by that treaty.[1]

The British government therefore argued that the Russians had invited the advice of the three powers and that they were entitled to receive it.[2] The two western powers in fact found it difficult to formulate concrete proposals and readily fell in with the suggestions made by Rechberg on 10 May that six points might be presented to the Russian government: a general amnesty, the establishment of a national representative institution similar to the Galician provincial diet, administrative autonomy with officials drawn mainly, but not exclusively, from the Poles, entire liberty of conscience and worship, Polish as the official language and, finally, a system of organized and regular recruitment. This was not entirely in accordance with the British view that the administration should be handed over to Poles, the Russians confined to certain selected fortresses, and an armistice concluded for one year. Palmerston and Russell were, however, quite willing to accept the Austrian six points, but they continued to insist upon an armistice, which they considered essential for the proper execution of the Austrian proposals.

Undoubtedly in May 1863 Palmerston and Russell began to take far too sanguine a view of the prospects of the Polish revolution and the weakness of the Russians, but they never dreamed of an independence for Poland on the scale which the insurgents demanded. On 15 May Palmerston saw Władysław Czartoryski, who had succeeded to the direction of the Hotel Lambert after his father's death, and his uncle, Władysław Zamoyski. The Poles were anxious to obtain from Palmerston an admission that Russia, having failed to observe the Treaty of Vienna, had forfeited her title to the Kingdom of Poland, but Palmerston reminded them that the basis of western diplomatic activity was insistence upon the treaty rights of the Poles and that to deny Russia's title would in effect only free her from

---

[1] P.R.O. 30/22/14, Palmerston to Russell, 5 May 1863.
[2] Cf. F.O. 519/200, Russell to Cowley, 6 May 1863. Cf. also *ibid.*, Russell to Cowley, 9 May 1863, Russell's note on the copy of the *conversation écrite*.

her obligations, which Britain and France were attempting to force Russia to observe. Palmerston asked them if they would in fact accept an armistice, but discovered that 'they did not like to acknowledge the Poles would be satisfied with anything short of an independent Poland, including the Kingdom, Posen, Gallicia, Volhynia and Lithuania'.[1] Asked to sound the insurgent government in Warsaw on its views, Zamoyski was able to report on 1 July that the armistice would be accepted 'provided that it extended to the whole of Polish territory placed under the dominion of the Tsar by the treaty of 1815; provided that the National Goverment is not called upon to give any opinion as to the other suggestions made by the three powers in reference to the future settlement of the political condition of Poland; and that a representative of the National Government should be admitted into the conference'.[2] This was in fact a much toned-down version of the National Government's letter of 13 June, which insisted upon four essential points, an armistice for all areas held by Russia, the withdrawal of Russian troops to the fortresses, a summons for a Diet and an international commission in Warsaw to supervise the execution of the armistice.[3] When the future historian, Alexander Kraushar, suggested in a series of articles in the Warsaw underground newspaper, *Prawda*, that something less than complete independence for all the areas of Russian Poland might in the first instance be accepted, he received a stern warning from the National Government to desist from such discussion.[4] The limits to which Palmerston himself was willing to go are revealed in his letter of 28 May to Russell. Expressing his view that the situation had reached such a pass that there was now no chance of a permanent compromise between the Poles and the Russians, he declared that an armistice was necessary and should be followed by a conference of the signatory powers of the Vienna

[1] P.R.O. 30/22/14, Palmerston to Russell, 15 May 1863.

[2] P.R.O. 30/22/78, Władysław Zamoyski to Russell, 1 July 1863.

[3] *Polska działalność dyplomatyczna w 1863–1864 r.*, ed. A. Lewak (Warsaw, 1937), I, 23–5. These demands were somewhat modified later in the letter of 10 July, *ibid.*, pp. 26–7.

[4] Cf. *Prawda*, 8–11 (12, 19, 26 June, 6 July 1863). Cf. also A. Kraushar, *Kartki z pamiętnika Alkara* (Cracow, 1910–13), I, 61–97; *Publicystyka tajna warszawska w dwuleciu przed powstaniem styczniowym i w roku 1863* (from *Placówka*) (Warsaw, 1919). Cf. also *Rozkaz Dzienny Naczelnika Miasta*, No. 16 (3 July 1863).

Treaty, but that France and Britain must first reach an understanding on their aims:

> If the foregoing principle were admitted considerations of policy would suggest limited application, not because such limitation would be in itself the most desirable arrangement, but because it would be the most practicable, and we might propose that the new state might be confined to the limits assigned to the Kingdom of Poland by the Treaty of Vienna with the addition of the territory & town of Cracow, that town being the burial place of the former kings of Poland & venerated on that account by the Poles.[1]

Over this kingdom might rule an Austrian archduke. Thus the limit of Palmerston's willingness to depart from the Vienna settlement was the severance of the dynastic tie between the Kingdom of Poland and Russia and the restoration of the independence of Cracow in a slightly different form.[2] Even the most pro-Polish of British ministers scarcely approached the demands of Polish nationalism. Palmerston may have played with the idea that an Austrian archduke might rule the Kingdom, but he never gave encouragement to the naïve notion of the Czartoryski faction that Poland's cause could be furthered by the withdrawal of Russia's sanction to rule in the Kingdom and granting the Poles belligerent rights. In Palmerston's opinion this would be to destroy the whole basis of British intervention on their behalf and to give the Russians a free hand; on 4 June he warned Prince Władysław Czartoryski that he would have nothing to do with the idea: 'Non, jamais, non! Cette sanction retirée, l'Angleterre ne pourrait plus rien pour la Pologne.'[3] The new Poland of Palmerston's creation would have been only a slightly enlarged successor state of the Congress Kingdom, which the Poles would not have accepted as a final solution. Even if it had been accepted as a stopgap solution, it was unlikely that the Poles would in their mood of 1863

---

[1] P.R.O. 30/22/22, Palmerston to Russell, 28 May 1863. Palmerston was at this time ill with gout and did not present this idea to the cabinet.

[2] Russell might have gone a little farther, cf. F.O. 519/200, Russell to Cowley, 28 May 1863: 'I should like to have an Austrian archduke King of Poland on the Vistula and the King of Italy on the Brenta with a guarantee for Austria for Dalmatia &c. I suppose your Emperor would agree to this, but then we ought to leave Rome as part of this arrangement and it could not be effected without war.'

[3] *Muzeum X. Czartoryskich*, 5696, No. 22.

have accepted an Austrian archduke as king and the narrowly conservative institutions which he would have brought with him. It is difficult to argue that Palmerston had a practical solution for the Polish question and it was perhaps fortunate for his reputation that his ideas were never put to the test.

The cardinal error of many diplomatic histories of 1863 is the supposition that Palmerston and Russell directed British foreign policy. Major policy decisions had to be referred to the cabinet and the Queen, though attempts were made to evade such control. Clarendon, who was close to the moderate opinion in the cabinet, declared that he could get no information from Russell and that there were murmurings among the ministers, who complained that they were receiving news too late to give adequate thought to the Polish question; Russell had apparently said that 'Poland and I get on very well without the cabinet.'[1] Clarendon himself had come to the opinion that British public opinion extended no more than good wishes to the Poles.[2] For his own part he doubted the capacity of the Poles to produce a stable *régime*: 'The Poles are no more capable than the Irish of acting together or of resisting any opportunity to sell each other.' It was indeed difficult to deal with a Polish government which no one knew, and he already detected an unwillingness in Britain to undertake hostilities: 'There is the greatest possible indisposition here to go to war for a matter so indifferent to us as Poland.'[3] He had evidently been impressed by a review article in the *Quarterly Review*, which argued that the complaints of Poland in fact amounted to the one-sided arguments of the Polish upper classes which sought to perpetuate their oppressive rule in the Kingdom.[4] The Queen for her part gave warnings that due consideration should be given to Napier's despatches from St. Petersburg.[5] She insisted that it would be unwise to make representations alone with France if Austria refused to agree to an armistice.[6] Britain's policy, she declared, must be to

[1] F.O. 519/179, Clarendon to Cowley, 3 June 1863.

[2] F.O. 519/179, Clarendon to Russell, 29 April 1863.

[3] F.O. 519/179, Clarendon to Cowley, 6 May 1863.

[4] *Quarterly Review*, CXIII (1863), pp. 448 f. The author was Lord Robert Cecil, afterwards Marquis of Salisbury.

[5] P.R.O. 30/22/14, Grey to Russell, 15 May 1863, and copy of the Queen's memorandum of 19 May 1863.

[6] P.R.O. 30/22/14, Grey to Russell, 31 May 1863.

restrain France and not to be carried along with her against her will.[1] These were views which were shared by the Duke of Argyll, the Lord Privy Seal.[2] The wide distribution of political power in Britain during the 1860's compelled Palmerston and Russell to exercise restraint in their public statements and their conversations with Poles. It was only between themselves that they discussed possible modifications of the Vienna treaty. In this they differed sharply from the influential personages of the French Second Empire who gossiped freely concerning their plans for Poland and gave the Poles the impression that far more would be done for them than was actually intended. The Czartoryski organization in Paris was consistently given the advice that the insurrection must be sustained, though French leaders were vague concerning the nature of the aid to be given and the course which French policy would follow.[3] Prince Napoleon freely discussed with Czartoryski the need for an expedition to the Baltic for a landing in Samogitia. On 26 March Napoleon III agreed with him that 50,000 men would be enough 'pour écraser la Russie'.[4] On 31 March 1863 Drouyn de Lhuys told Czartoryski: 'C'est cruel à dire, mais je ne puis m'empêcher de vous dire: Durez!'[5] As late as 29 August Czartoryski was advised by a high French official that 'L'Empereur serait encore prêt à faire la guerre.'[6] The joint representations of the powers in fact fell very far short of the encouraging statements made to the Poles in Paris.

On 17 June the French and British notes were sent to St. Petersburg and on 18 June Austria despatched hers.[7] The British version put forward a demand for a complete and general amnesty, a return to the constitutional system of 1815, which

[1] P.R.O. 30/22/14, Grey to Russell, 1 June 1863, and copy of the Queen's memorandum of 3 June 1863.
[2] P.R.O. 30/22/26, Argyll to Russell, 26 May 1863.
[3] Cf. *Muzeum X. Czartoryskich*, 5712, the Emperor's secretary, Mocquard, on 10 March 1862 impressed upon Władysław Czartoryski the need for endurance: 'M. M[ocquard] finit par dire que la durée et extension du mouvement était la condition indispensable de succès.'
[4] *Ibid.*, 5712. Account of an interview with Napoleon III, 26 March 1863.
[5] *Ibid.*, 5712, pp. 23-4.   [6] *Ibid.*, 5712, pp. 40-1
[7] For the French and Austrian texts, see *M. d. A-E, Documents Diplomatiques*, IV (1863), 27-9, Drouyn de Lhuys to Montebello, 17 June 1863 and Rechberg to Thun, 18 June 1963. For the British text see *British and Foreign State Papers*, LIII (1863), Russell to Napier, 17 June 1863, 32-4.

the Austrian version did not demand, the admission of Poles to public office, full liberty of conscience, the use of the Polish language in official business, and, finally, the establishment of a regular system of recruiting. On this basis negotiations might be conducted. A provisional armistice must first be proclaimed and a conference of the eight signatories of the Vienna treaty called.

In his private letter to Napier, however, which accompanied the official note of 17 June, Russell gave expression to his real views of the situation:

There is no question of war. The Russians seem to wish for it, but there is certainly not here & I believe not in France any intention to indulge them. The reason is plain. While there is no smoke of battle men see clearly over the field & they perceive the anarchy of Poland, & the inability of Russia to govern to ensure obedience, to collect taxes, to put an end to the guerrilla warfare. But if European war were to spring up, the obscurity and the embarrassment would be transferred to us. How could we make or recognize an Executive to which aristocrat and democrat wd. alike submit? How could we induce the Kingdom to keep within its boundaries & not intrigue & subvert Lithuania, Podolia and even Gallicia and Posen? If we tried to reassemble the disjected members of old Poland, who are the Poles, who are the Ruthenians, who Germans? Where are the limits of Poland, & still more where wd. be the limits of a war to reduce Russia to its original insignificance?[1]

In this letter Russell was expressing a point of view which was very close to that of Clarendon. Evidently the original Russian request of 26 April for advice had given an impression of weakness, but now the nearness of war induced a more sober appreciation. In other words, British policy invited Russia to submit to a conference, but did not in the last resort intend to compel submission. For Britain the note of 17 June was the end, but the French regarded the renewed *démarche* as a beginning. On 20 June the French government proposed to Austria and Britain that they should sign with France a diplomatic instrument defining their attitude in the event of a Russian refusal to accept their representations,[2] but even in their pro-Polish moods

[1] P.R.O. 30/22/114, Russell to Napier, 17 June 1863.
[2] *M. d. A-E, Documents Diplomatiques.* IV (1863), 36–7. Drouyn de Lhuys to Gros, 20 June 1863.

Palmerston and Russell were not prepared to tie themselves to French policy. Russell refused to consider the matter and merely circularized the cabinet with information of the proposal, knowing that he would obtain approval of his action.[1] He informed Cowley in Paris that 'the cabinet will not accept the French proposition which smells of gunpowder dreadfully. Austria & England are pacific'.[2]

Britain held the key to the diplomatic situation in 1863. Austria would not move without her and France could not. It would be easy to argue that Russia was alone and by presenting a bold front exposed the British bluff. Alexander II's letter to William I of 1 June, speaking regretfully of the old amity of the three conservative monarchies and asking for his good offices in restoring Austro-Russian amity, to which William I replied on 17 June that he could promise nothing but benevolent neutrality, certainly gives a picture of dangerous isolation.[3] Diplomatic despatches are not the only means by which British governments make known their opinions. Ministers are called to account in Parliament and must there explain their views in terms which have met the approval of their cabinet colleagues, and which give some guidance to the course of conduct they will take. The parliamentary statements of Russell and Palmerston were known to Gorchakov who could hardly have failed to notice that they were couched in altogether different terms from the British diplomatic exchanges with Russia. On 8 June Russell declared in the Lords that British policy was limited to the mitigation of the Polish lot:

For my part, I can see no advantage that could arise from armed intervention on behalf of Poland. I can see nothing, but confusion and calamity likely to arise from an interruption of the peace of Europe. I cannot see what clear or definite object, which a British government could propose to itself, would justify them into entering into such hostilities, and I must enter my protest against engaging in any such contest.[4]

Palmerston in the debate on Polish affairs on 22 June, while the

[1] P.R.O. 30/22/27, Russell's memorandum, 22 June 1863.
[2] P.R.O. 519/200, Russell to Cowley, 24 June 1863.
[3] *Die auswärtige Politik Preussens*, III, 596–8, 626–9.
[4] *Hansard*, CLXXI (1863), 488.

despatches of 17 June were still on their way to St. Petersburg, committed the indiscretion of revealing their contents. Already there was considerable anxiety in the Commons concerning the nature of the *démarche* to be made and Palmerston to quieten the Commons announced that an identic note was not being delivered and that therefore concerted action need not necessarily follow a Russian refusal of the powers' demands. In replies to questions asked by speakers, Palmerston touched on one of the vital points, at least from the Polish point of view:

I think it would be rather a strong proposal to make to Russia, that she should organize a Polish army, to be officered by Poles.[1]

Russell was to repeat in the Lords on 13 July, the very day on which Gorchakov was to send his reply, that Britain could not make war on behalf of Poland:

When you are told that a war on behalf of Poland would be justifiable, the question arises, what is Poland? There is the Poland of the Treaty of Vienna, well defined, in regard to which the powers of Europe have certain rights of interference or remonstrance. But that is not the Poland which is looked to by those who are urging war on its behalf.[2]

Russell could not imagine that Britain, France or Austria would enter into a conflict to establish Poland in the frontiers which existed before 1772, nor would they be justified in imposing Polish rule in areas where the Poles were a minority. There were moreover grave objections to establishing a Polish government at all in view of the character of the insurgent organization.

If it was not a monarchy and if the democratic party in Poland should get the upper hand, are those who intervene in their favour to assist in establishing the democracy? These monarchies—England, France and Austria—might well hesitate in so doing.[3]

Russell's opinion was the 'government must have a clear object before they can venture to come down to parliament and propose war against Russia on behalf of Poland'. What Russell did in 1863 was to put into his public speeches the opinions which he wrote in his private letters covering his despatches. When

---

[1] *Ibid.*, CLXXI, 1265–8, 1274.   [2] *Ibid.*, CLXXII, 630.
[3] *Ibid.*, CLXXII, 631.

Gorchakov received the notes of the powers, it must already have been clear to him from Russell's speech of 8 May and Palmerston's revelations of 22 June that Britain, the most important of the powers making representations to Russia, was engaged in a policy of bluff, while Russell's speech of 13 July must have been added comfort to him.[1] It was in fact translated into Polish and published in the Warsaw official gazette, *Dziennik Powszechny*, in order to demoralize the Poles.[2]

From what is known of Gorchakov's character it is apparent that he was not the man to refuse a diplomatic triumph. There is no doubt that he did triumph in 1863, but the nature of the evidence must invite the question why the Russian government in fact showed extreme caution. To some extent this was caused by the reports sent by the Russian ambassador, Brunnow, from London. Brunnow had at the beginning of the eastern crisis in 1853 made the mistake of exaggerating the peaceful intentions of the British government. He was evidently determined not to make the same mistake again, especially when Palmerston appeared to become enthusiastic for the Polish cause in May 1863. He therefore did not commit himself entirely to the view that the British government was pacific, but warned Gorchakov that Palmerston was likely to take a more hostile attitude towards Russia.[3] Gorchakov informed Brunnow that he did not believe in war in 1863, but that he would not rule out the possibility of Palmerston's adopting a more difficult position. Gorchakov was compelled moreover to bear in mind the poor state of the Russian army. By the end of July no less than 690,000 men were under arms in European Russia, of whom 342,000 were based upon Warsaw, Vilna and Kiev, but D. A. Milyutin did not consider that his forces were enough to suppress the insurrection in Poland and at the same time offer resistance to a European coalition.[4] Gorchakov did not himself take the decision upon the attitude to be adopted by Russia, but submitted his drafts only after the council of ministers on 8 July had pronounced upon general policy towards the *démarche* of the three powers. The final decision therefore was taken by

---

[1] Cf. H. Wereszycki, *Anglia a Polska w latach 1860–1865* (Lvov, 1934), pp. 139–46.
[2] *Dziennik Powszechny*, Nos. 170–2, 29–31 July 1863.
[3] V. G. Revunenkov, *Pol'skoye Vosstaniye*, pp. 295–6.   [4] *Ibid.*, pp. 297–8.

the Tsar and his ministers, but Gorchakov as signatory of the despatches was to appear the hero of the day.

The object of Gorchakov's despatches of 13 July was to prevent a rupture of diplomatic relations and leave the way open to further negotiations. They contained a great deal of propaganda which had the object of presenting the Russian case to the West. In his note to Brunnow Gorchakov declared that the insurrection was a minority movement, which owed much to foreign aid. The insurgents were not, as the powers suggested, asking for an amnesty and autonomy, but for full independence. Nevertheless, Russia was willing to enter into an understanding with the two other partitioning powers, Austria and Prussia, to find a solution for the better government of the Kingdom, but it must be understood that order must be restored before further measures could be adopted.[1] This was not from the point of Palmerston and Russell a satisfactory answer, but the debate in the House of Common on 20 July passed off without much display of passion. The Polish sympathizer, Horsman, in a long speech put forward the favourite idea of Władysław Zamoyski, who was active in organizing feeling in Britain in support of Poland, that the time had come to annul the provisions of the Vienna treaty in respect to Poland, but he failed to convince a poorly attended House. Layard's account of the debate was that:

The Polish debate was a very flat business. Horsman spoke like a pamphlet which sent many people to sleep in a very thin house. The members who were present felt that the question is too difficult even for House of Commons manipulation and that there was no practical recommendation in Horsman's speech. It is easy to criticize the Govt's acts, but not easy to suggest an alternative. Disraeli & his friends at the request of Derby abstained from taking any part in the debate. People are dissatisfied with the Russian answer and yet no one wants to quarrel with Russia with the chance of war.[2]

No more had Gladstone or Palmerston practical suggestions to make for the enforcement of the six points of the despatches of

---

[1] *British and Foreign State Papers*, LIII (1863), pp. 901–7, Gorchakov to Brunnow, 1/13 July 1863. For the despatches to Budberg and Balabin, see *M. d. A-E, Documents Diplomatiques*, IV (1863), pp. 37–41, 47–50.

[2] F.O. 519/195, Layard to Cowley, 22 July 1863.

June. Diplomatic action was thus to dissolve into an ineffective exchange of notes. In Russia defiance could safely be pronounced, but as Cowley wrote to Layard:

It is very easy for the Russians to say they are prepared to go to war when they have *all* but an official assurance that we do not mean to go to war with them.[1]

The matter was nevertheless not over. While Britain blew cold the French blew hot and proposed to Britain that she should join in an identic note to Russia,[2] but Palmerston's view was that the Polish affair was coming to a close:

An identic note is good for a definite and positive demand, on the failure of compliance with which the Parties signing the identic note are prepared to take identic steps. But that does not seem to be our case. Each power received a different answer from Russia, to which each power would naturally make a separate reply to them. . . . The utmost we could do would be to ask the French govt. to let us see the kind of note which they would propose to us to send. But we have *made our siege* already.[3]

Russell perhaps was still inclined to join with France,[4] but the cabinet decided otherwise, to the satisfaction of Queen Victoria who had consistently opposed an identic note.[5] The French remained anxious for joint action, but on 3 August Palmerston wrote:

I see by a telegram that the French are still urgent for an identic note to Russia, but I conclude that you hardly think it necessary to summon the cabinet to reconsider their decision on that matter.[6]

The correspondence with Russia was therefore carried on without further agreement between the powers, though there was some measure of co-operation between Britain and Austria.

---

[1] Add. Mss. 39,106, f. 405, Cowley to Layard, 24 July 1863.
[2] *M. d. A-E, Documents Diplomatiques*, IV (1863), p. 51, Drouyn de Lhuys to Gros, 29 July 1863.
[3] P.R.O. 30/22/22, Palmerston to Russell, 30 July 1863.
[4] Cf. F.O. 519/195, Layard to Cowley, 1 August 1863.
[5] P.R.O. 30/22/14, Grey to Russell, 1 August 1863. This did not prevent the Queen warning Palmerston again on 11 August that no decision on Poland must be taken without her consent during her absence in Coburg—cf. *Letters* (ii series), I, 102.
[6] P.R.O. 30/22/22, Palmerston to Russell, 3 August 1863.

Lord John Russell had not come out of the previous exchanges with much credit to himself, though it had not been entirely his fault that Britain had received a rebuff from Russia. Renewed representations on behalf of the Poles on 11 August[1] met only with Gorchakov's request in his despatch of 7 September that the controversy should not be prolonged.[2] This was in effect to ask Russell to give a formal recognition to the fact of Russia's diplomatic victory. This demand evidently gave Russell cause for annoyance and on 26 September, while on holiday in Scotland, he made a speech at Blairgowrie which hinted that the Tsar might forfeit his title to the Kingdom of Poland,[3] exactly the point which Palmerston had refused to concede to Czartoryski and Zamoyski. Having committed himself in public, Russell then proceeded to give substance to his views in a despatch to St. Petersburg. Napier was warned by telegram that he would receive an important communication and the despatch was actually sent.[4] In the final paragraph Russell declared:

Her Majesty's Government have in the despatch of the 11th August and preceding despatches shown that in regard to this particular question the rights of Poland are contained in the same instrument which constitutes the Emperor of Russia King of Poland. Her Majesty's Government cannot doubt that it is the intention of the Emperor of Russia to acknowledge these rights and to fulfil his international obligations. The government of the Emperor must be aware that until this is done, it may be agreed that the sovereignty of Russia in Poland cannot claim an international sanction.

This view met with the strong objection of Rechberg and produced second thoughts in Palmerston, who returned to the argument which he had made to Czartoryski and Zamoyski that refusal to recognize the Tsar's title was merely to release him from his obligations under the treaty of Vienna.[5] He confessed moreover that he had not paid sufficient attention to the draft, though he did recollect that he had originally offered an objection to the offending paragraph.[6] Poor Russell was thus obliged to

[1] British and Foreign State Papers, LIII (1863), pp. 911–16.
[2] Ibid., LIII, 916–17.   [3] The Times, 28 September 1863, p. 7.
[4] F.O. 65/625, Russell to Napier, 8 October 1863.
[5] P.R.O. 30/22/22, Palmerston to Russell, 8 October 1863.
[6] P.R.O. 30/22/22, Palmerston to Russell, 9 October 1863. He was correct in his recollection, cf. ibid., Palmerston's memorandum of 5 October 1863.

telegraph to St. Petersburg the instructions that the despatch of 8 October should not be presented. Instead he was compelled to send the despatch of 20 October, in which he declared that 'Her Majesty's Government have no wish to prolong the correspondence on the subject of Poland for the mere purpose of controversy' and ended tamely with the first sentence only of the passage to which objection was taken:

Her Majesty's Government have in the despatch of the 11 August and preceding despatches shown that in regard to this particular question the rights of Poland are contained in the same instrument which constitutes the Emperor of Russia King of Poland.[1]

Napier reported to Russell that Gorchakov knew all about this episode.[2] To Berg in Warsaw and to Brunnow in London Gorchakov wrote that he was completely unperturbed.[3] The measure of his confidence was the publication of Russell's Blairgowrie speech and an account of the withdrawal of the final paragraph in the despatch of 8 October 1863 in the Warsaw newspaper, *Dziennik Powszechny*.[4] Not even the Poles were left in any doubt that Russell had not followed up his words with action. Altogether Russell had cut a very poor figure at home and abroad. It was small wonder that he was not prepared to be cordial towards Gorchakov when the Polish episode was thus formally closed: 'I cannot rouse myself to saying anything very sweet at Petersburg.'[5]

Władysław Czartoryski thought that he could use the abortive despatch of 8 October 1863 as a lever against the British government and proposed to Prince Napoleon that he should secure a copy of it from Drouyn de Lhuys for publication, but Prince Napoleon warned him that he would hardly improve the chances of the Poles:

Il ne serait pas difficile de faire tomber Palmerston, mais nous ne savons pas ce que nous gaignerons avec Derby. Il est même à

[1] *British and Foreign State Papers*, LIII (1862–3). pp. 917–18, Russell to Napier, 20 October 1863.
[2] P.R.O. 30/22/84, Napier to Russell, 28 October 1863.
[3] V. G. Revunenkov, *Pol'skoye Vosstaniye*, p. 343.
[4] No. 254, 25 October/6 November 1863.
[5] F.O. 519/200, Russell to Cowley, 31 October 1863.

craindre que le Cabinet Derby ne se tourne contre la France à la première occasion où elle serait engagée.[1]

There were indeed other fish to fry in the autumn of 1863 and the spring of 1864. Germany seemed to have reached a new phase in her development with the congress of the princes at Frankfort in August 1863. At any moment the Slesvig-Holstein question might create international difficulties after Frederick VII died on 15 November. On 4 November Napoleon III had proposed to Queen Victoria a European congress for the revision of the map of Europe. There were other things to consider than the claims of the Polish insurgents who were almost at the end of their resistance. The western powers had revealed very little understanding of the struggle in Poland, but their action had served to keep alive the hope that the insurgents would receive military aid. The Russians for their part had been to some extent compelled to hold their hand. In the Lithuanian *gubernii*, which none of the powers denied were part of Russia, it had been possible to let loose Mikhail Muraviev with a policy of severe repression. In the Kingdom of Poland, where the Russian government professed only the purest intentions, General Berg, who was assigned to play the same role as Muraviev, had for the moment to hold his hand. The failure of the western powers to make their intervention effective was the signal for coercion of the most severe kind to begin there also.

[1] *Muzeum X. Czartoryskich*, 5712, pp. 54 ff. Account of discussion with Prince Napoleon, 13 February 1864.

CHAPTER VIII

The Politics of the Polish Insurrection, January–July 1863

ON the night of 22/23 January 1863 the Polish Reds launched their insurrection against the Russian Empire. It was a heroic and desperate struggle against appalling odds. Even though it was greatly assisted by the Russian concentration of the army, the original plan of establishing a seat of government at Płock could hardly have succeeded. The members of the National Central Committee, designated to form the Temporary Government, arrived at Kutno on the Prussian frontier in the belief that they would be well placed to receive Mierosławski when he made his appearance but the rising in Kutno had not been prepared. Russian security precautions and the suspicions of the police showed that they could not remain in Kutno. On 27 January they decided to leave, Mikoszewski and Janowski making their way by devious routes to Langiewicz's camp in the region of Sandomierz, where it was thought the insurgent forces were strong enough to permit an open government to be set up, but it proved that there was no other answer than that the revolutionary leaders should find their way back to Warsaw, which offered better security, but where conditions forced them to maintain their own anonymity.

Ludwik Mierosławski, however, when he accepted the dictatorship, acted in accordance with the original plan. On 17 February he crossed the Prussian frontier and established himself at the village of Krzywosąd, where he was met by his supporter, Daniłowski, with sixty young men who were to serve as the dictator's 'personal bodyguard'. In their passage across Poland they had left so many traces of their journey that the Russians had no difficulty in locating Mierosławski. On 19 February Mierosławski was compelled to withdraw into Prussia, covered by the desperate resistance of his bodyguard. No one had received official news of his appointment as dictator, nor had he made his acceptance known to the Central Committee.[1] Nevertheless rumours of his participation in the rising soon began to circulate and gave the propertied classes concern. After his withdrawal from the Kingdom, he returned to Paris, where he fell ill, but soon he reappeared in Cracow, his beard shaved off and keeping in hiding, to claim his rights as the dictator of the national movement. The Central Committee had in the meantime reconstituted itself in Warsaw under Bobrowski, Aweyde, Maykowski and Agaton Giller, who had now overcome his objections to serving the insurrection. The Committee received news of Mierosławski's plans only on 27 February, when Daniłowski arrived as Mierosławski's plenipotentiary, announcing the dictator's intention of entering the Kingdom from Cracow. The situation had, however, changed. The decision to nominate Mierosławski had been taken when it was thought that the revolutionary government could establish itself in the open, but now that it had returned to Warsaw and decided to remain a secret organization there was no longer any need for a well-known figure to lend it prestige. Daniłowski was informed that the dictatorship would be kept open until 8 March and that, if Mierosławski had not appeared in the Kingdom by that date, it would lapse. Daniłowski retorted that the committee could not deprive Mierosławski of his rights and that it existed itself only by his sanction, a constitutional nicety. Mierosławski thus remained a factor in the situation, a thorn in the side of the Reds and the bogyman of the Whites.

The Whites were unable to adopt any positive attitude towards the insurrection. The first public reaction was the brochure of Count Edward Łubieński, *L'Armistice entre les Russes et les Polonais*, published in Leipzig and dated 2 February 1863. This was nothing less than a declaration that the crisis was dangerous in view of the fact that the east was menaced by a

---

[1] His 'Address' of 16 February 1863, printed as No. 2 of *Dokumenta urzędowe do dziejów organizacyi jeneralnej powstania narodowego w latach 1863 i 1864* (Paris, 1864), was a piece of window dressing, which was unknown at the time.

great social revolution. The time, he wrote, had come to close the ranks of the propertied classes in Poland and in Russia against the ferment among the peasantry. His proposal was that a Bonapartist constitution should be adopted, with a system of universal franchise, but leaving effective power in the hands of the property owners. The former eastern provinces might conveniently be united with the Kingdom and the alliance of the Polish nobles and Tsarism firmly cemented. He had small regard for the national claims of the non-Polish peoples of the east, or for the Jews, to whom he did not wish to grant civil rights on the grounds that they would corrupt the peasants with vodka and the *szlachta* by the usury.[1] Except in as far as Łubieński looked forward to a plebiscitarian constitution in which the votes of the peasants swamped the votes of the Reds, the motives of his suggestions were the same as those of Wielopolski, whose conscription of the radicals he defended. This was no doubt a programme which might have attracted more support, if the Alvensleben convention of 8 February and the prospect of diplomatic intervention had not suggested other courses to the White Directory and its sympathizers. When the rebellion broke out the Hotel Lambert in Paris received many gloomy complaints from Poland.[2] Correspondents described the uprising as madness and the Central Committee in Warsaw as consisting of madmen. One letter of 10 February reveals the state of mind of the Whites:

From news given to me by Mr. K. [Kronenberg] the most important concerns the Directory and the present position of the moderate party. Of the details of lesser weight I will give you a personal account. Here I can only mention the most important matter, that the Directory has decided to use all the influence at its disposal to restrict the movement, for the consequences of which the country today pays with great losses, and will adhere to this position for the future, for the struggle has absolutely no chance of success before it.

[1] *L'Armistice entre les Russes et les Polonais proposé par le comte Edouard Łubieński* (Leipzig, 1863), pp. 4-6, 15, 20.

[2] For a work critical of the part played by the Czartoryski faction see I. Koberdowa, *Polityka Czartoryszczyzny w okresie powstania styczniowego* (Warsaw, 1957). It would seem, however, that Władysław Czartoryski merely represented abroad ultra-conservative views which existed within Poland.

Augmenting the existing insurgent bands can only cause a greater disaster. . . .[1]

There can be no doubt that the Polish Whites had no intention of supporting the insurrection and were prepared at the outset to await its inevitable extinction. When Czartoryski telegraphed to Cracow on 16 February that the situation had changed, new visions of international intervention opened up before the eyes of the Polish conservatives. Stanisław Koźmian replied to his father in Paris in code jargon:

Créanciers [i.e. the Russians] prévoyants secours capitalistes [from the western powers] accélèrent énergiquement liquidation. Dépêchez vous de conclure l'affaire. Hausse pas probable retard de liquidation tout au plus.[2]

In spite of the doubts which were entertained in Cracow it was possible to hope that all was not lost. Unofficial advice in Paris seemed to point to probable French assistance. Walewski was reported to have said: 'Faites durer et faites élargir les limites de l'insurrection territorialement, car cela peut influer sur les limites dans lesquelles la reconnaissance des droits nationaux sera exigée et comprise.'[3] Poles, deprived of real political experience by the fact of partition and subject to strong emotional appeals, were by nature inclined to grasp at the straws held out in Paris, however dubious their origin. The idea gained currency in conservative circles that perhaps after all a diplomatic solution might be possible, reinforcing the natural inclination of the Whites to take positive action in order to wrest control from the Reds.

The landed proprietors of the Kingdom realized that they were in danger of being swept along into co-operation with the revolt, to avoid which no less than 3,000 of them had taken refuge in Warsaw. It might have been of assistance to them if they could have secured the dismissal of Wielopolski and the substitution of a more popular Pole as head of the administration, but the Russian government could hardly dismiss the

---

[1] *Muzeum X. Czartoryskich, 5687*, G . . . to Władysław Czartoryski, Dresden, 10 February 1863.
[2] *Muzeum X. Czartoryskich, 5701* (*Télégrammes*), 18 January 1863.
[3] S. Koźmian, *Rzecz o roku 1863* (Cracow, 1894–6), I, 41–2.

man whom they had held up as the symbol of their willingness to grant concessions. The gentry therefore fell back on the sterile solution of 'recognizing the insurrection as a national one, but taking no part in it'. The insurgent government, however, behaved as the supreme national authority. Bobrowski, as Chief of the Town, on 4 February ordered the landed proprietors to return to their estates where they could be controlled by the insurgents.[1] On 5 March the National Committee claimed that the Directory had submitted to its authority.[2] Pressed by the Reds and spurned by the Russians the White Directory saw a way out in the new conditions created by the Alvensleben convention. If the Whites could assume leadership of the insurrection, they could prove its respectability, which would make intervention easier, and at the same time induce the leaders of the guerrilla bands to apply the revolutionary decrees of 22 January with less enthusiasm.

Similar ideas were entertained in Cracow, where a large number of landed gentry had also taken refuge. The Galician Whites knew that their own Reds were weak, but they dreaded the possibility that the insurrection might extend itself to Austrian Poland. Similar anxieties were felt by prominent leaders in Poznania. Rumours were circulating that Mierosławski, held in exaggerated awe by Polish conservatives, was preparing to call a *levée-en-masse* and let loose the peasants on the manors.[3] Leopold Kronenberg, the effective leader of the Directory in Warsaw, Chrzanowski and his influential friends on the editorial board of *Czas*, the Cracow conservative newspaper, and the leading Galician Whites therefore began to hatch a plot. It was at first suggested that the Whites should set up their own National Government in Cracow, but this was open to the objection that they would appear to be dividing the national energies in a moment of crisis. An alternative seemed to be the nomination as dictator of Marian Langiewicz, who was keeping the field in the Sandomierz area with some four battalions of infantry, which he supplied from Cracow. He had

[1] T. Filipowicz, *Confidential Correspondence*, pp. 37-8.
[2] A. Giller, *Polska w walce*, I, 104.
[3] A. Zdanowicz, *Dziesięc dni dyktatury* (Gorlice. 1901), p. 12; H. Sutherland Edwards, *The Private History of a Polish Insurrection* (London. 1865), II. 11.

shown a determination not to permit excesses and had issued on 9 February a stern warning to the peasants that a jacquerie would be met with severe reprisals. The situation among the peasants in the southern districts of the Kingdom was uneasy. On 16 February a miserably led expedition from Cracow to the town of Miechów had encountered the opposition of the peasants, who, hostile to the Poles in 1831 and in 1846, took the opportunity to attack the insurgents as they fled before the Russians.[1] In the circumstances Langiewicz seemed an ideal choice. The sole difficulty was that the Central Committee in Warsaw had announced that it alone represented the Polish nation and its approval of Langiewicz would have to be obtained, but difficulties of this kind were never insuperable in Poland. A certain Count Adam Grabowski, a man of seedy reputation, whose fast living and bankruptcy had forced him to leave Poznania, had obtained a commission from the Central Committee to convey 1,000 roubles to the *émigré* officer, Józef Wysocki, who had come forward to Galicia to assist the national cause and perhaps organize an expedition into the Kingdom. It happened that the Central Committee had provided Grabowski with credentials, which the Whites in Cracow proposed to use in order to represent him as a plenipotentiary of the Committee, charged with the responsibility of making far-reaching decisions on its behalf. Grabowski was persuaded to go to Langiewicz's camp and induce him in the name of the Central Committee to accept the office of Dictator, with a guarantee of support from a national administration in Cracow.

The position of Langiewicz was by no means as rosy as the Whites had supposed. He had 3,000 men under his command, but all of them were badly armed. Faction was rife in the camp, in which there were some supporters of Mierosławski, while a subordinate commander, Jezierański, was nursing a personal dislike of Langiewicz, which did not improve discipline. The situation was not eased by the delegation from Cracow on 9 March. Some doubt was expressed whether Grabowski in fact was empowered to conclude the transaction appointing Langiewicz dictator. Jerziorański took the opportunity to suggest that

---

[1] W. Tokarz, *Kraków w początkach powstania styczniowego i wyprawa na Miechów* (Cracow, 1914), II, 153–5, 211–13.

Langiewicz must resign his military command on appointment. Langiewicz clearly had doubts, but at length he agreed to assume the office of Dictator. He declared his formal adherence to the programme of 22 January, but dissolved all other organizations in Poland, appointing new commissioners to act on his behalf. His manifesto of 10 March was greeted with enthusiasm by the moderates everywhere who saw in this step the regularization of the insurrection.[1] The Whites congratulated themselves on what seemed to them an astute move. On 10 March all the Polish members of the Council of State resigned, ostensibly as a protest against the Grand Duke's order of 6 March for the establishment of peasant guards to attend to local security.[2] It was in fact a gesture of solidarity with the national movement led by Langiewicz, in accordance with whose orders the White Directory was dissolved on 12 March. On the same day Archbishop Feliński lent his moral support by tendering his resignation from the Council of State, addressing a letter to the Tsar indicating the impossibility of his co-operation under the existing political conditions.[3] Leopold Kronenberg, the architect of White policy, expressed his satisfaction with the way in which things had turned out, though he would have liked a more specific promise to the peasants:

With regard to the proclamation [i.e. of Langiewicz] I should have liked something about the peasants, that our future properly constituted government will settle their problems.[4]

It appeared that a new solution of the peasant question would be found in the future, but of more immediate concern was the appointment of a representative of Langiewicz in Warsaw to supersede the National Central Committee as the principal authority in the city. If White control could have been established in Warsaw the entire insurrection would have come under moderate influence.

The National Central Committee, however, was not without some initiative. Giller characteristically was prepared to acknowledge the authority of Langiewicz and seek a compromise with

---

[1] T. Filipowicz, *Confidential Correspondence*, p. 291. [2] *Ibid.*, p. 180.
[3] *Wydawnictwo materyałów*, I, 44–5, for the text of his letter of 15 March 1863.
[4] *Listy Leopolda Kronenberga do Mieczysława Waligorskiego z 1863 roku*, edited by S. Kieniewicz (Wrocław, 1955), pp. 18–19.

P

the Whites,[1] but the rest of the Committee resented the scandalous manner in which the Whites had tricked them. The favourable reception of Langiewicz's dictatorship by the middle classes, however, might have meant that the Committee would seem to represent a factional interest if it repudiated Langiewicz. The ingenious device was adopted of announcing recognition of Langiewicz as dictator in those territories which were under his direct control, but that the administration of those parts of Poland which remained under Russian occupation rested as before with the Central Committee.[2] Thus for the moment the Committee preserved its authority in Warsaw and two of its members, Giller and Janowski, were sent to Cracow to disentangle the muddle which had been created.

The action of the Whites, however, revealed one miscalculation which ought from the start to have been obvious; the dictatorship of Langiewicz could last only as long as he himself kept the field or maintained his own position as an independent centre of authority. No thought seems to have been entertained that even with the best of luck an insurgent force, badly armed and composed of untrained volunteers, could scarcely hold its own in open battle against regular troops. Langiewicz managed to escape defeat at Chrobierz on 17 March and at Grochowiski on 18 March, but he expended all his ammunition and was left with no alternative but to attempt evasion of the Russian forces. A plan was made to divide the band into four groups, while Langiewicz himself withdrew into Cracow to seek his fortune again in the Lublin area, but the insurgent rank and file did not relish dispersal and demanded that all should seek the security of the Austrian frontier. There was already a strong suspicion in the camp that Langiewicz's elevation to the dignity of Dictator had been achieved by none too scrupulous methods. Some of the Mierosławski party were for the repudiation of Langiewicz's authority, because Mierosławski on 11 March from his hiding-place in Cracow had drawn up a manifesto of protest against Langiewicz's action.[3] It could have been only a question of time before discipline

[1] J. K. Janowski, *Pamiętniki*, i, 231.
[2] T. Filipowicz, *Confidential Correspondence*, pp. 290–1.
[3] *Dokumenta Urzędowe*, No. 3.

broke altogether and Langiewicz's control of his men dissolved. Langiewicz therefore decided to leave the camp himself without their knowledge, but with a formal declaration of the purity of his motives.[1] He no sooner crossed the Austrian frontier on 21 March than he was arrested by the police. Though he expected a quick release, he was in fact kept in prison and played no further part in the rising. In this way the White intrigue achieved its end for no more than ten days.

The first thought of some leading Whites was to call off all further efforts to support the insurrection. Alexander Kurtz, a leading White, wrote from Warsaw to the Hotel Lambert in Paris, bitterly condemning the insurgent leaders whom he represented as socialists living in opulence on forced contributions:

Pour quiconque réfléchit, il n'est malheureusement non plus douteux que nous serons bientôt ruinés aussi moralement que matériellement et que la Pologne deviendra un foyer d'anarchie européenne.[2]

Leopold Kronenberg, however, was soon busy looking for new expedients. In a letter of 21 March he suggested to his agent in Cracow, Waligorski, that fresh trickery might be possible:

You can print a proclamation of the Dictator antedated as being issued from the Kingdom, in which Langiewicz authorized Wysocki or some committee to act in an emergency instead of the dictator or in his name.[3]

The Chief of the Town, Stefan Bobrowski, was too quick for the Whites and for Mierosławski. On 21 March he issued on his own authority a declaration that with the fall of Langiewicz all power reverted to the National Central Committee as the only legally constituted government of Poland.[4] This announcement was followed on 27 March with a second declaration that the device of a dictatorship would not henceforth be employed and that if the dictatorship were assumed by any other person his action would be judged to be high treason.[5] The announcement which spoke of 'the return of authority into the hands of the

---

[1] T. Filipowicz, *Confidential Correspondence*, p. 294.
[2] *Muzeum X. Czartoryskich, 5739*, pp. 371–4, letter of 4 April.
[3] *Listy Kronenberga*, pp. 48–9.   [4] A. Giller, *Historja*, I, 316.
[5] T. Filipowicz, *Confidential Correspondence*, p. 364.

men who had called the insurrection', contained a clear implication that the dictatorship of Langiewicz was the result of
intrigue. When Bobrowski arrived in Cracow he made no
secret of the fact that he regarded the Cracow Whites as guilty
of dishonesty. The upshot of the affair was that a 'court of
honour' was assembled to consider the rights and wrongs of the
case. Giller was prepared to accept the explanations offered by
the disreputable Grabowski who had been the tool of the Whites,
but Bobrowski, persisting in his accusations, found himself
challenged to a duel, which for the moment he declined to
accept. The Whites were now sufficiently enamoured of the
diplomatic possibilities to be willing to repeat their attack upon
the Reds. The dictatorship had been outlawed, but this did
not frustrate the ingenuity of Kronenberg. The new course which
recommended itself to the Whites was that a formal submission
should be made to the National Central Committee and that
the Reds as a gesture of confidence should admit a person of the
suppressed White Directory to their counsels. Kronenberg calculated that he could trust in Giller, in whom he had more than
once expressed confidence during the Cracow discussions.[1] It
was possible that, if Kronenberg's creature, Karol Ruprecht,
could be introduced into the Central Committee, he and Giller
might form a coalition against the genuinely left-wing element
in the Red organization. The proposal of a White submission to
the Central Committee succeeded with surprising ease, even
to the admission of Ruprecht to membership of it. Stefan Bobrowski, the Chief of the Town, was virtually assassinated. He
was evidently persuaded that he must take up the challenge
issued by Grabowski in Cracow, though he was short-sighted
and quite incapable of fighting a duel on even terms with the
marksman, Grabowski. The person who persuaded him was
almost certainly Giller,[2] assisted possibly by Aweyde. On 12
April Bobrowski died at Grabowski's hand in a duel at Rawicz.[3]
The other representative of the extreme left wing, Jan Maykow-

---

[1] *Listy Kronenberga*, pp. 36–7, 40–1.

[2] Cf. J. K. Janowski, *Pamiętniki*, I, 344–5, who wrote: 'Giller did not like and
did not wish to talk about this affair and when he was asked about it he used to dismiss it with generalities, or used to start talking about another matter.'

[3] Stefan Bobrowski was brother of Ewelina Korzeniowska, wife of Apollon Korzeniowski and mother of Joseph Conrad.

ski, was far less resolute than Bobrowski. He was persuaded that he was in danger of immediate arrest and appointed to the post of Commissar in Austrian Poland for his own safety. In this way the moderates, Giller, Aweyde and Ruprecht, took control of the newly constituted Temporary Government of Poland, a Red-White coalition, achieved at far less cost than the complicated intrigue which led to the appointment of Langiewicz.

Leopold Kronenberg was never to claim any detailed knowledge of the Temporary Government's affairs, but his satisfaction was nevertheless clear. On 10 April he wrote to Waligorski, saying that 'although the new members of the government do not entirely answer my expectations, I hope that the business will prosper'.[1] Four days later, he reported that:

Although not all members have been appointed according to our ideas, namely, that no landed proprietor is included among them, yet, as I told you sometime ago, it [i.e. the government] is close in its outlook to the members of [our] organization. If anything is done, which is not completely satisfactory, it is because it wishes to act along the line of its previous manifestoes and consequently everything is announced in haste without its seeking different opinions or thinking out principles, as for example in the peasant question.[2]

The supposition now was that the decrees of 22 January should remain in force, but that in practice no real effort should be made to enforce them. When the Central Committee announced its new policy on 16 April, it protested that it was an all-party organization:

The Central Committee as the Temporary National Government, being the expression not of a single party, but of the needs and efforts of the whole nation, will make without prejudice to political and social questions the recovery of independence its only task and issues a summons for action, self-sacrifice, combat, for unity, of which the nation has given so many fine and imposing demonstrations, and over which the National Government will watch, possessing sufficient energy and strength to preserve it from any kind of disruption.[3]

These sentiments were echoed in the underground newspaper, *Prawda*, which pleaded for a non-party approach to the problems of the national cause and declared that there was no

[1] *Listy Kronenberga*, pp. 86–7. [2] *Ibid.*, pp. 100–1. [3] A. Giller, *Historja*, I, 319.

longer any need for the separate existence of Whites and Reds.[1] National unity was indeed required, but insistence upon it meant in the circumstances of Polish politics that some vital principle must be discarded. Omission of mention of the peasant question showed that the Red-White coalition intended to execute a retreat from the position adopted when the revolt opened, that the peasants should be granted their freeholds without the obligation of making redemption payments. The calculation was that, if the diplomatic intervention on behalf of Poland succeeded, this awkward question could be settled in a different form from that originally proposed on 22 January. Yet even this compromise did not meet with the approval of all members of the right. Paweł Popiel wrote to the Czartoryski faction from Cracow, urging the need for pressure upon the National Central Committee for restraint; for him Prince Sapieha in Lvov represented the ideal, keeping out the influence of the insurgent authorities in Warsaw.[2] He urged Czartoryski to rally the landlords of the Kingdom against the Temporary National Government and bring it to heel by refusing it money.

Popiel's fears were for the moment groundless. The insurrection had obtained its original energy from Dąbrowski, Padlewski and Bobrowski, men from the former eastern provinces of pre-1772 Poland, men born in the *szlachta* tradition. Now the insurrection passed into the hands of Giller, Ruprecht and Aweyde, assured of the financial support of the capitalist, Kronenberg. The triumvirate and its leading supporter bore names which were not Polish in origin. They represented the point of view of the lower middle class of the towns, radical in as far as they could visualize the opportunities which an independent Polish state might bring, but with little instinctive comprehension of the peasants' needs. Giller was little more than a hack journalist, whose contribution to victory was the newsletter, *News from the Field of Battle*, filled with highly coloured and generally inaccurate information of clashes between the Russian forces and the Polish partisans. Ruprecht watched over

[1] *Prawda*, No. 1 (19 April 1863), No. 3 (7 May 1863).

[2] *Muzeum X. Czartoryskich, 5683*, f. 295, P. Popiel to W. Kalinka (Stockholm for transmission to Paris, 11 April 1863.

internal policy and collected funds, aided by the ubiquitous Kronenberg, who never took any responsibility which might compromise him in the eyes of the Russian government if the rising should fail. The Temporary Government now became a passive instrument, issuing communiqués, writing to diplomatic agents abroad and succeeding in remaining hidden from the Russian police. The population of Warsaw exhibited an immense loyalty to the secret government, in part out of a feeling of patriotism, in part because the insurgent chief of the town was prepared to enforce absolute obedience, if necessary, by assassination.

In the countryside the war continued to be waged by the commanders of the Polish bands, but without clear purpose. On 28 March the civil and military functions of the revolutionary commanders were separated, with the consequence that the left-wing enthusiasts actually engaged in the fighting were in theory not empowered to enforce the programme of 22 January with regard to the peasants, but individual leaders might adopt varying attitudes. The landlords found themselves in a position of great difficulty. The aristocracy could escape abroad, but the medium gentry could hardly afford to neglect their estates. On the one hand they must hide the insurgents in their manors, lest they incur the penalties of revolutionary justice. On the other hand they laid themselves open to the reprisals of the Russian soldiery. On the whole the landlords out of self-respect chose the patriotic course of siding with the insurrection. Their position is perhaps best illustrated by the excuse offered to a Russian general by a member of the gentry accused of aiding the insurgents:

If the insurgents come to my place and ask for horses, carts and corn, I must give them what they want, or they will hang me. If, on the other hand, I let them have anything more than I am actually forced to give, you will hang me. However, if *they* hang me my son will never find a wife in Poland, nor my daughter a husband, and fifty years after my death people will turn their backs upon my grandchildren. If *you* hang me, monuments will be erected to my memory. On the whole, then, as a mere matter of prudence I cannot refuse to assist the insurgents.[1]

[1] H. Sutherland Edwards, *The Private History of a Polish Insurrection*, II, 20.

From the insurgent leaders' point of view there was every reason
to show restraint in dealing with the landlords. The manors
provided food and shelter and therefore served as a base of
operations which must be preserved. There were isolated instances of insurgents being betrayed by landlords, but the
majority acted as allies of the insurrection. The Temporary
Government's policy of avoiding too rigid an interpretation of
the decree granting freeholds could be accepted. Not all insurgents took their role seriously. For many the rebellion merely
demanded that they should show a token activity in order in
after-years to declare with pride that they had done their duty.
A marked feature of the rebellion was the large number of photo-
graphs which the insurgents managed to have taken of themselves. The heroic and romantic, but often ludicrous, postures
adopted in them were sheltered from the inclemency of the
weather by the warmth and comfort of the photographers'
studios. For others the insurrection was a serious business, which
had little connection with a desire to leave a record in the family
album. Those leaders whose opinions veered towards the Whites'
ideas saw themselves as having the duty to maintain discipline
against the elements which threatened the efficiency of the
national struggle. For them the peasants who helped the Russian government with information were treated as the enemies
of Poland. Other leaders, for whom the revolt had the object
of converting the peasants to the national cause, tended to take
a more lenient view of the peasants' non-co-operation, or even
hostility, because the illiterate countryman could not easily
appreciate that the insurrection was being carried out to provide him with a better life. For centuries the immediate oppress-
or had been the landlord who now supported the insurgents.
The normal insurgent practice was to call together the villagers
and explain to them the aims and purposes of the manifestoes of
22 January. The peasants did not always show belief in their
declarations, but almost without exception in the summer of
1863 they assumed that the payment of rents was to cease. The
grant of freeholds was achieved *de facto*, but uncertainty prevailed. It would appear that the peasants were not entirely
convinced that their obligations to the manor would not be
reimposed if the insurrection succeeded.

A fight was thus undertaken for the peasants' loyalties. Local Russian commanders played upon their uncertainty and pointed to the more solid advantages which they might obtain from support of the official government. It was therefore not surprising that insurgent bands were sometimes betrayed. Some insurgent leaders had recourse to terror. Langiewicz hanged peasants. Oxiński in the Kalisz area discovered that peasant soldiers had been released on furlough from the Russian army in order to stiffen resistance to the revolt in their native villages, a practice which had earlier been adopted by the Austrians in Galicia. Oxiński's answer was to make a search of the villages affected and to hang the released soldiers out of hand; in six days he carried out seventeen executions.[1] Dionyzy Czachowski, a good disciplinarian and one of the 'most successful insurgent leaders, seems at times to have behaved like a homicidal maniac, hanging peasants and shooting prisoners in a most arbitrary manner.[2] When he went to execute the sentence of the Temporary Government, which had ordered the peasants of Wólka Klucka, who had attacked manors, to be put to the sword, some 2,000 peasants took refuge in the woods, but Czachowski organized a search and hanged eleven persons. In very few cases did insurgent leaders mete out similar justice to the landlords. It will never be known exactly how many executions were carried out, because Russian propagandists naturally exaggerated their numbers, while the Poles sought to minimize them. Assistance was subsequently given to 634 families which had suffered from insurgent terror.[3] This figure included all classes of the community including Jews and Germans and perhaps only 200–300 were actually Polish peasants.[4] However much insurgent terror may be reduced, its proportions were large enough to contrast sadly with the idealism contained in the manifestoes of 22

[1] J. Oxiński, 'Wspomnienia z powstania', *Rocznik Oddziału Łódzkiego Towarzystwa Historycznego*, III (1939), pp. 204–7.

[2] Cf. A. Drążkiewicz, *Wspomnienia Czachowczyka z 1863 r.* (Lvov, 1890), pp. 187, 223–4.

[3] J. Grabiec-Dąbrowski, *Rok 1863* (Poznań, 1913), p. 408.

[4] S. Kieniewicz, *Sprawa włościańska w powstaniu styczniowym*, p. 324. I have investigated the gubernial archives at Lublin (*R.G.L.*, *1638, 1639, 1640, 1641, 1642, 1643, 1644 and 1645*) and discovered about 100 persons done to death by the insurgents. Acts of violence by Russian soldiers were insignificant, though Russian sources, even if they draw upon the reports of Poles, may be unreliable.

January. Summary executions bore too close a resemblance to the old arbitrary actions of the manor. They filled the Russian officers with a feeling of disgust.[1] In St. Petersburg Lord Napier reported to Russell in terms of intense dislike of the Polish atrocities.

Not all peasants turned a deaf ear to the pleas of the insurgents for aid. In the area of Lublin and Płock the insurgents found that they could rely upon the larger peasant farmers. Certain elements among the landless rural labourers in Poznania were disposed to join the rising and many crossed into the Kingdom. In the southern areas of the Kingdom, where conditions were similar to those in the western districts of Galicia, the peasants had a long tradition of hostility to the landlords. Their holdings were small and many barely scratched a living from the indifferent soil to which the landlords had relegated them. Peasant response to the rising was therefore only partial, but there was hope that a *levée-en-masse* might bring more peasants into the open as active participants in the struggle. There were many good arguments against a *levée* and the chief among them was the fact that a mass rising before harvest would bring famine in its train. Nevertheless, the idea was canvassed, but it was quashed by the order of 29 April from the Temporary Government, which demanded that 'each district should be organized on military lines, but there should be called to revolt only such persons as provide firearms or sidearms'.[2] Advice had come from Prince Władysław Czartoryski in Paris that the insurgents should be prevented from throwing their full resources into the struggle; for the moment token resistance would suffice to keep the Polish question before the public eye.[3] On 4 May the Temporary Government issued the clear and definite order that the Polish forces should employ only guerrilla tactics.[4]

During the summer of 1863 the Polish insurgents kept the field more by avoiding Russian troops than by engaging in substantial actions. It was possible to suppose that the disturbances were only of a desultory character and that it was merely

[1] Cf. *Souvenirs et correspondance du Prince Emile de Sayn-Wittgenstein-Berlebourg* (Paris, 1888), II (1863–78), pp. 57, 94.
[2] A. Giller, *Historja*, II, 400–1.
[3] A. Lewak, *Polska działalność diplomatyczna*, I, 252–3, Czartoryski's letter of 30 March 1863.
[4] A. Giller, *Historja*, I, 320–1.

a question of time before the rising collapsed. At least, Constantine and Wielopolski persisted in this belief and still hoped for the co-operation of a section of the Polish population. General Berg, on the other hand, wanted to apply absolute military coercion, but the Russian government in St. Petersburg could not for the moment get rid of Constantine or Wielopolski. The Polish insurgent authorities continued to hope that diplomatic intervention would yield its fruits. The Russian offer of an amnesty of 12 April gave the Poles the opportunity of submitting within a month, but to emphasize its defiance the Temporary Government on 10 May declared itself the National Government of Poland and reaffirmed the principles of 22 January, asserting that Poland as a state must be restored not only in the Kingdom, but also in Lithuania and Ruthenia.[1] On 13 May the call was issued for the rejection of the amnesty and for the insurgents to carry on the fight.[2]

In Lithuania the rising was sinking into the same inertia as in the Kingdom. The legal position of Russia in Lithuania was different from that in the Kingdom; the treaties of Vienna did not apply to provinces which were legally part of the Russian Empire. From the first, therefore, the Russian administration was less mindful of possible international complications. On 29 January Nazimov declared a state of war in the districts bordering upon the Kingdom and in an appeal for calm called upon the peasantry to maintain order. The Tsar for his part in a rescript of 7 February ordered that insurgents should be tried by court martial and executed at the place of capture. On the same day a conference of the Lithuanian Whites met, with the knowledge of Nazimov, to consider pressure from the side of the Reds and the appeal of the newsletter, *Ruch*, which on 29 January called for a Lithuanian rising. A committee was formed under the chairmanship of Count Starzyński to enter into relations with the White Directory in the Kingdom. Impressed by the possibilities of diplomatic intervention the Lithuanian Whites issued a pamphlet entitled 'The Voice of the Lithuanian as a Confession of His Faith and a Programme of Action', recommending patience. In fact, some insurgent units from the Kingdom had already crossed into Lithuania, while some local Reds

[1] *Wydawnictwo materyałów* I, 55–6.   [2] *Ibid.*, I, 57–8.

had responded to the appeal from Warsaw. In Samogitia a priest of petty *szlachta* origin, Mackiewicz, had long been preparing a rising among the native Lithuanians, whose loyalties were still religious rather than national.[1] He was able to assemble a band of peasants, 250 strong, whom he took into the Krakinów forest, in the middle of Samogitia, to prepare for action. To the south, beyond Samogitia, in the district of Lida, Ludwik Narbutt, a son of the celebrated historian and a man who had served a period of exile as an officer in the Caucasus, gathered together in the forest of Rudnik a band of petty *szlachta*, acquiring so formidable a reputation that a special expedition was sent out from Vilna to destroy him. Action from below, independent of control from Vilna and promulgating the policy of the Warsaw Central Committee, forced the hand of the Lithuanian Whites. In order to control the Lithuanian movement the Whites submitted to the authority of the Temporary Government in Warsaw and from it obtained permission to call themselves 'The Department administering the Provinces of Lithuania', subject to the oversight of Wacław Przybylski, who had returned from Vologda, acting as 'State Secretary for Lithuanian Affairs'. The submission of the Lithuanian Whites was in the nature of a coup, which enabled them to declare the Department the sole authority and to suppress the Red committee of Kalinowski.

The revolt of Lithuania came to a pathetic end. Zygmunt Sierakowski, the army officer, who arrived in Vilna in March 1863, proposed that the Poles should wrest the semi-derelict fortress of Dünaborg from the Russians in order to obtain the arms in its magazine. This would in its turn make possible the capture of Riga and the Lithuanian port of Polanga, into either of which might sail a ship chartered in London, the S.S. *Ward Jackson*, bringing volunteers and arms. Farther east in the *gubernia* of Mogilev an attack was to be launched upon Hory Horki, where the population was to be raised for an incursion into the *gubernii* of Smolensk, Tver and Moscow, and then to Kazan, where the Lithuanian, Hieronim Kieniewicz, had

---

[1] For the backward condition of Samogitia prior to the rising see L. A. Jucewicz, *Wspomnienia Żmudzi* (Vilna, 1842) and T. Tripplin, *Dziennik podróży po Litwie i Żmudzi odbytej w 1856 roku* (Vilna, 1858), volume ii.

undertaken to raise a local insurrection among the dissatisfied intelligentsia and Tartars. Nothing less than the total dissolution of Muscovy was envisaged. It soon turned out that there were other forces to reckon with than the Russian regular army.

The insurgent committee in Vilna discovered that on 26 April 1863 a transport of arms was to leave Dünaborg for Dzisno. Though the rising was not due to begin until 31 April orders were issued to Count Leon Zyberg-Plater, under pain of death if he refused, to seize this supply of weapons. In spite of some hesitation Plater undertook this mission, but when his men began to assemble in the village of Krzesławka, the local peasants, many of them Old Believers descended from Russians who had taken refuge from innovation in seventeenth-century Muscovy, exacted a heavy revenge from the *szlachta* for their harsh treatment of the common people. The Polish attack upon the convoy succeeded, but almost immediately the insurgents were surrounded by the peasants and taken prisoner. A three-day orgy followed, in which thirty-seven properties were looted and fourteen manor houses burned to the ground. The authorities in St. Petersburg were frightened lest the peasants' action excite a jacquerie elsewhere and attacks be made upon Russian landlords. A regiment of uhlans was actually sent to impose order, but reprisals against the peasants were prevented when it was pointed out to the Tsar that repression of peasant loyalists was hardly the best means of securing support against insurgent Poles.

Ludwik Zwierzdowski came out from Moscow to lead the revolt in the *gubernia* of Mogilev, but he was no more successful than Zyberg-Plater. Everywhere the clergy were preaching against the Poles, who they declared aimed to restore labour services. Cadres of old soldiers were sent into the villages to organize local security guards and the townspeople of Mogilev were roused to support the government. On the night of 5/6 May Zwierzdowski launched his attack upon Hory Horki, but the resistance of the local population showed that even a guerrilla campaign could hardly be maintained in an area so far to the east.[1] Zwierzdowski was obliged to disperse his followers and

[1] Cf. S. Kulesha, 'Gori-Goretskaya katastrofa, 22-go i 23-go Aprelya 1863 g.', *Russkaya Starina*, xxxix (1883), pp. 609–24.

himself to escape from Russia through Constantinople and thence to Paris and western Poland. In Samogitia, however, it had been shown in 1831 that the insurgents could count on local support. There Sierakowski was able to form his band and carry out his preparations in broad daylight. Joined by Father Mackiewicz he quickly assembled a formidable force, which rumour enlarged and induced Russian commanders to approach it with care, but its relatively small size soon became known. Sierakowski held to his original plan of moving north towards the Kurland border, but he was caught by the Russian general, Ganetsky, at the township of Birzhe on 6 May. In an unequal fight the insurgents were defeated and Sierakowski captured.[1] With his failure the rising in the Lithuanian sector was virtually at an end.

An echo of the revolt in Lithuania was the affair at Kazan, where Hieronim Kieniewicz had issued on 12 April a manifesto, purporting to be that of the Tsar, granting the peasants complete ownership of their lands with no obligation to make redemption payments, abolishing military service and instructing peasant soldiers to leave their units. This move was calculated to let loose on Russia another Pugachev rebellion, but it would have been a people of a very low level of political consciousness to have been deluded by Kieniewicz's manifesto. Many arrests followed, though it was not until the autumn that Kieniewicz himself was arrested after his return from a visit to Warsaw.[2]

The insurrection in the southern group of provinces, the *gubernii* of Kiev, Podolia and Volhynia, was worse prepared than in Lithuania. The strength of the Reds lay in the towns of Zhytomir, Kamenets and Kiev. In 1862 the Central Committee had charged Stefan Bobrowski to enlist support and a 'Ruthenian Provincial Committee' was set up, but there were strong local doubts concerning the possibility of a rising. In Vol-

---

[1] For details of Sierakowski see J. Laskarys, 'Wyprawa Sierakowskiego na Kurlandyi w 1863 r.', *Pisma Zbiorowe* (Bendlikon, 1865), pp. 36 f.

[2] There is a considerable literature dealing with the Kazan episode, cf. A.Yershov, 'Kazanskii zagovor (Epizod iz polskago vosstaniya 1863 g.)', *Golos Minuvshago*, 6–7 (1913); Z. Odrzywolski, *Powstanie polskie nad Bajkałem i sprawa kazańska* (Lvov, 1878); and L. Bazylow, Helena Brodowska and K. Dunin-Wąsowicz, *Z dziejów współpracy rewolucyjnej Polaków i Rosjan w drugiej połowie XIX wieku* (Wrocław, 1956).

hynia Edmund Różycki was pessimistic, while Zygmunt Miłkowski, officially entrusted with the task of collecting supplies,
had hardly begun his task when the insurrection broke out in
the Kingdom. The Whites in Lvov, led by Prince Adam Sapieha,
Florian Ziemiałkowski, Alexander Dzieduszycki and Franciszek
Smolka, were extremely reluctant to associate themselves with
an incursion from Galicia into the Russian Ukraine. When it
proposed that Józef Wysocki, originally designated commander
on the left bank of the Vistula, was given direction of operations
in the south-east and the task of invading Russia, Dzieduszycki
and Smolka walked out of the Lvov committee rather than be
involved in the affair. A miserably conducted expedition under
a local Red, Czarnecki, had given an impression of Polish weakness while the diplomatic possibilities, opened up by the Alvensleben convention, likewise seemed to point to the need to stage
a demonstration that Poland not only had claims upon the
Ukraine, but had a following to sustain them. At the beginning
of April Wysocki, Miłkowski and Różycki agreed upon a plan
to raise 6,000 Poles in revolt against Russia on 8 May. Wysocki
was to enter Volhynia and Miłkowski to invade Podolia, while
further south an Italian, Menotti, was to make a landing, but
Wysocki could not be ready in time and outside help came to
nothing. In consequence Różycki was left high and dry and
forced to seek refuge in Galicia. A small party of students from
Kiev was overwhelmed by the peasants in the village of Solo-
viovka in the district of Radomysl.[1] Local feeling ran high in
Galicia against persistence in organizing expeditions, but a
telegram from Paris said:

Empereur a dit sang qui coulera marquera frontières de la future
Pologne.[2]

Reluctantly the White leaders agreed to support an incursion
into Russia by Wysocki against the town of Radziwiłłów in
order to show the Polish flag. Although it was well supported
with contributions and by Polish standards excellently armed,
it was only with the greatest difficulty that it could be got to the

[1] See T., 'Solowjówka (Ustęp z powstania na Ukrainie)', *Kalendarz Polski na rok
1866* (Bendlikon, 1866).
[2] W. Przyborowski, *Dzieje 1863 roku*, III, 292.

frontier on account of the hostility of the Ruthenian peasants.[1] The Polish recruits from Galicia were poor material and ran away at the beginning of the action. When Wysocki crossed the frontier on 1/2 July the Russians soon dispersed his men, who gave a demonstration not of Polish strength, but of Polish weakness. A subsequent incursion by Edmund Różycki at the beginning of November never exchanged a shot with the Russians.

In the disturbed situation in the governor-generalcy of Vilna and with the possibility of a French landing during the summer, the Tsar was called upon to make proper provision for the defence of his empire. The anti-Polish party raised its head against all attempts at conciliation. The general defence of Lithuania and the Baltic provinces was entrusted to the celebrated general, Nikolai Muraviev-Karski, while his brother, General Andrei Muraviev-Amurski, was called in for consultation. Muraviev-Karski demanded adequate provision for internal security. The third of the famous brothers, Mikhail Muraviev, was summoned unexpectedly to the palace on 7 May and told that he must take over the duties of the governor-general from the lenient Nazimov.[2] Mikhail Muraviev, who had experience of dealing with Poles in the *gubernia* of Minsk after the war of 1831, bluntly told the Tsar that he had a poor opinion of the methods hitherto adopted by Nazimov and insisted that a policy of russification must be undertaken. In spite of the opposition of the party of conciliation, headed by Valuyev and Dolgorukov, Muraviev got his own way. Gorchakov, fearing that the powers might persist in their diplomatic pressure if the Lithuanian troubles continued, insisted that it was in the international interests of Russia that an early pacification be achieved.[3]

From the beginning of Muraviev's term of office it was made clear that the utmost rigour would be employed.[4] Count Leon

---

[1] Cf. the eyewitness account of H. Sutherland Edwards, *The Private History of a Polish Insurrection*, II, 77–8.

[2] *Pamiętniki hr. Michała Mikołajewicza Murawiewa, 1863–1865* (Cracow, 1896), pp. 27–30.

[3] V. G. Revunenkov, *Pol'skoye Vosstaniye*, pp. 273–4.

[4] For a summary of Muraviev's measures see N. Tsilov, *Sbornik razporyazhenii grafa Mikhaila Nikolayevicha Muravieva po usmirenii polskago myatezha v severno-zapadnikh guberniyakh, 1863 i 1864 g.* (Vilna, 1866).

Zyberg-Plater was hanged. Two priests were hanged in order to show that even the clergy would not be exempt from punishment if they sided with the insurrection. Count Wiktor Starzyński was warned that he must co-operate with the government. Under the rules of 5 June 1863 almost any act which seemed to favour the insurgents rendered a person liable for severe punishment, including the immediate sequestration of his goods and chattels. Women were forbidden under any circumstances to wear mourning, which had been a mark of political dissatisfaction ever since February 1861. Russian officials who appeared too lenient towards the Poles were transferred to other posts outside the Polish areas. Even the inoffensive bishop of Vilna, Krasiński, was exiled to the depths of Russia. For the Poles Muraviev was a man of sinister and evil reputation, lampooned as 'The Hangman'. Having battered the *szlachta* into acceptance of defeat, he demanded of them an admission of defeat in the form of a loyal address to the Tsar as the condition of his calling off the campaign of intimidation. Domeyko, the marshal of the nobility of Vilna, was commissioned to canvass support and obtained 235 signatures in time for the Empress's birthday on 8 August, but on 6 August the Red chief of the town in Vilna, Małachowski, issued a sentence of death upon Domeyko for high treason. Skilled assassins were brought from Warsaw to execute the sentence, but they succeeded only in wounding Domeyko on 11 August. The result was to destroy what little harmony was left between the Whites and the Reds.

Muraviev, however, was not merely a heavy-handed tyrant. The *szlachta* were too weak to present a serious threat, but the peasant problem remained. The discords of landlords and peasants were especially serious in Lithuania. In April 1862 the privy councillor, Soloviev, was sent to investigate the reasons for the slow progress in obtaining agreement to the regulatory charters required by the decree of 2 March 1861. He reported that out of 3,919 charters prepared for confirmation in the governor-generalcy only 217 had been agreed, while out of 913 charters presented, in which the abolition of all obligations and the assignment of land to the peasants were proposed, no less than 722 had required the intervention of the government to

Q

get them composed.[1] Even before the appointment of Muraviev the Russian government had realized that it must make a bid for the loyalties of the peasants. In a ukaz of 1/13 March 1863 it was ordered that all connection between the manor and the village in Lithuania was henceforth to be severed and the peasants to be considered the owners of their lands.[2] In return they were required to convert labour services into rents at the rate of twenty kopeks per rouble less than the rates laid down in the previous tables of conversion. In future all rents were to be paid into local treasuries and thus to be officially supervised. Upon this basis the government of Muraviev could represent itself as the friend of the peasant. On 14 June the peasants were invited to co-operate with the government in the maintenance of order and on 20 July landlords were ordered to remain on their properties, where the peasants could watch them. To make matters worse Muraviev imposed a tax of 10 per cent upon landed estates to finance the emergency measures of the government, with the proviso that it should not fall heavily upon Russians or persons not suspected of sympathy with the Polish revolt. For all the punitive measures adopted by Muraviev the ukaz of 1/13 March 1863 was the cornerstone of his system, a measure which he had not devised himself. The Russian government had gone part of the way at least to accepting the revolutionary agrarian programme as the basis of victory in the political struggle. So successful was this measure in ensuring the loyalties of the peasants in Lithuania that it was extended to the *gubernii* of Kiev, Podolia and Volhynia by the ukaz of 30 July/11 August 1863 and by the ukaz of 2/14 November 1863 to the entire *gubernia* of Mogilev and to those parts of the *gubernia* of Vitebsk unaffected by the decree of 1/13 March.[3] The result of these measures in the areas affected by the Polish rebellion was that the peasants in western Russia retained a relatively higher proportion of the land than was possible for the peasants elsewhere in European Russia. Lands in peasant possession in the former Polish provinces were increased by 2,314,696 diesiatins as a consequence of the revolt.[4]

[1] *Otmena krepostnogo prava*, p. 135.

[2] *Polnoye Sobranie Zakonov* (ii series), xxxviii, No. 39337.

[3] *Ibid.*, xxxviii, Nos. 39928, 40172. The original decree for Lithuania embraced former Polish Livonia, which was part of the *gubernia* of Vitebsk.

[4] P. A. Zayonchkovsky, *Otmena krepostnogo prava v Rossii* (Moscow, 1954), p. 186.

While the Russian government was taking the first steps to outbid the revolutionaries, the National Government in Warsaw persisted in the belief that it had nothing to do except wait for the signatory powers of the Vienna treaties to intervene and save them from Russia. This policy, however, began to excite the suspicions of the left wing. The rising had begun with an appeal for the mass response of the peasantry, but now the insurgents were asked to wage only a guerrilla struggle. The misgivings of the radical left seemed to be confirmed by the diplomatic activity of the Czartoryski group in Paris. The National Government had no agents of its own and was forced to take advantage of what diplomatic contacts offered themselves. Władysław Czartoryski and Władysław Zamoyski both commanded an easy entry into the salons of important persons and could obtain audiences with ministers. Czartoryski was appointed a plenipotentiary on 28 April 1863 and on 15 May given control of all Polish missions abroad. Traditionally the name of Czartoryski stood for the reconstruction of Poland by the intervention of the powers and upon a conservative basis, in distinction from the Polish Democratic Society's policy of a people's war for independence and social justice. Now it appeared to the radical left that the National Government no longer intended to honour the revolutionary decrees of 22 January, but aspired to the social policies of the Whites.

A group of diverse elements on the extreme left began to combine to overthrow the National Government. The supporters of Mierosławski, of whom there were still a few, and the band of Ignacy Chmieleński, the organizer of the attacks upon Constantine and Wielopolski in 1862, turned their attention to the task of winning control over the insurgent organization in Warsaw. Chmieleński's followers opened negotiations with the deputy-chief of the town, Lempke, who commanded the loyalties of the working class in the city, but before the arrangements for a Red counter-coup were complete Chmurzyński, Mierosławski's agent in Warsaw, on 24 May obtained possession of the official seal of the National Government. Without the seal stamped upon a printed order the subordinate insurgent commanders would not implement it. In other words, the authority of the National Government disappeared. In this situation Lempke presented it with an ultimatum to surrender its documents and resign. Giller had already got wind of a design to assassinate him and had taken refuge in a monastery. Ruprecht was absent at the time of the coup and took the first opportunity to go abroad.

With the extreme Reds in control a comic situation ensued. Neither Chmieleński's supporters nor Mierosławski's men trusted one another. None of them had any experience of the higher workings of the National Government and they were obliged to call upon Oscar Aweyde and the secretary, J. K. Janowski, who alone understood the details of the organization. The solution adopted by the Warsaw district leaders was the constitution of a 'Committee of Public Safety' under their own leader, Kwiatkowski, to supervise a new government. For the personnel of the government they chose four lawyers, of whom Franciszek Dobrowolski was to be the effective leader, but assisted by Aweyde and Janowski. Their task was to devise a new and more vigorous policy to give substance to the decrees of 22 January. Superficially the policy proposed by Dobrowolski was to be one of terror. On 2 June two decrees were issued, the one appointing revolutionary tribunals in every district to try offences against the insurrection and the other outlining the procedure they were to adopt.[1] The second was the more alarming for the Whites. All acts likely to weaken the activity of the National Government, hamper the revolutionary movement, and in general to be harmful to the common cause were to be regarded as treason, punishable either by death or exile, or, where it was not possible to execute a death sentence, by outlawry. Every citizen was to have the right to accuse another by means of a formal deposition. If there was any justification for this system, it was that up to this time the insurgents had adopted the practice of hanging out of hand peasants who had transgressed against the revolutionary code, but that this new procedure would at least put an end to the murders which were being committed throughout the country. To the Whites, however, it appeared that the propertied classes would be liable to revolutionary justice.

The Red government in fact lasted only two or three weeks. The moderates were not likely to sit down and give their loyal

[1] A. Giller, *Historja*, II, 401–3.

co-operation to a National Government which sought to put into effect those policies which they had striven to avoid. As ever, Leopold Kronenberg rallied the right wing and called a meeting of his supporters, Kurtz, Władysław Zamoyski, Józef Mianowski, rector of the university school established by Wielopolski, the lawyer, Wincenty Majewski, and above all his brother, Karol Majewski. It was agreed that the insurgent government could not obtain diplomatic recognition if it pursued a policy of terrorism and that therefore a more moderate government must take its place. It was proposed that Karol Majewski should be the instrument of this new policy. Majewski had disappeared from the political scene after his arrest in the summer of 1862 and had been released only in May 1863, but during his detention he had learned about the structure of the insurgent government from a fellow prisoner, Bronisław Szwarce, who had been arrested in December 1862.[1] He had, moreover, the prestige of a long record of conspiratorial work behind him, without in any way being in sympathy with the Polish Reds.

Majewski, however, was at first doubtful of his chances, even though Kronenberg guaranteed him the same financial support which he had given Giller and Ruprecht. Majewski insisted that money by itself was not enough. He must carry out some spectacular feat which would impress the public and swing support to him before he ousted the Reds. This in short was to be the theft of funds and bonds deposited in the treasury offices. His supporter, Alexander Waszkowski, promised to arrange for this robbery and to hand over the funds to Majewski alone. In fact, Waszkowski could lay his hands for the most part only upon bonds with serial numbers which could be cancelled as soon as the theft was discovered, an indication that prestige rather than money was the object of this exploit. Accordingly Waszkowski removed during 6–9 June paper to the nominal value of 3·6 million roubles from the treasury in Warsaw. News of the robbery at once threw the Red government into confusion, because they knew that they had not organized it. Majewski gave them to understand that Waszkowski would surrender the money and bonds only if the National Government transferred its authority to him. After some mutterings

[1] *W 40-tą rocznicę powstania styczniowego*, p. 457.

the Red government meekly capitulated and delivered up to Majewski its seals and documents. Once more the Whites took control of the rising and sat down to await the results of diplomatic intervention.

There was nothing radical in the composition of the new government. Majewski, as the link with Kronenberg, took control of finance and internal affairs. Krzemiński, who counted for nothing, took charge of the press and foreign propaganda. J. K. Janowski as ever retained the secretariat. Aweyde was entrusted with the affairs of Lithuania. The gravest threat to Majewski's authority was the city of Warsaw. Here he divided the military and civil functions of the chief of the town; the Lithuanian Wacław Przybylski became civil chief of the town, but the military functions were given over to Jan Kozieł Poklewski, who was subservient to Majewski. Every effort was made to induce the more resolute Warsaw insurgents to leave the city and take part in the guerrilla warfare in the countryside, where they could do no harm to the insurgent government. To neutralize Mierosławski, who still had a following among sections of the Reds, Majewski appointed him 'General Organizer of the Armed Forces', which was a sop to his vanity, giving him not one tittle of power, but many obligations. Thus secure in power Majewski could inform the nation that complete unity of purpose existed:

There are no political parties today. There are no social discords. Aristocrats and democrats, conservatives and progressives, priests, the bourgeoisie, landlords and peasants, catholics, protestants and Jews, are today merely soldiers in the camp of Poland.[1]

The Red programme was not the only casualty of Majewski's coup. The Marquis Alexander Wielopolski had reached the end of his career. The Russian military would gladly have dismissed him, but Constantine insisted upon retaining him in office in order to maintain the pretence that there were at least some Poles who were faithful to Russia. Rumours of the impending theft of public funds had reached the ears of the police and the government had ordered a check of the treasury strong rooms on 29 May, which revealed that everything was in order. Wielopolski had not lost the opportunity to rub home the lesson that

[1] *Dziennik Narodowy*, No. 7 (21 July 1863).

senior Polish officials could be trusted. When it was discovered that Waszkowski's coup had been carried out with the assistance of two officials, Stanisław Janowski, aged sixty years, and Stanisław Hebda, aged fifty-four years, Wielopolski's arguments were immediately turned against him. The Russians could argue that no Pole was to be trusted. The strain of his exertions had already begun to tell upon Wielopolski. He had suffered a slight stroke, which left some traces of paralysis, and he no longer had the will to persist in the hopeless task of reconciliation. On 7 July he was granted leave of absence pending retirement and departed from Poland for Germany. The insurgent government gave him what amounted to a safe-conduct. In the same railway carriage travelled Wincenty Majewski, the brother of the man who stood at the head of the rebel government.

Wielopolski's departure made little difference to the situation. Collaboration between the Poles and the government of the Grand Duke Constantine had long been impossible on account of the Whites' decision to adhere to the insurrection. It was only to be a short time before the Grand Duke himself was to be removed and all pretence at concessions to the Poles abandoned. The replies of Gorchakov on 13 July to the notes of Austria, France and Britain were more than a declaration of resistance to outside pressure. They meant, if the powers did not choose to offer a stiffer challenge, that the Russian government was free to apply in the Kingdom of Poland the methods which Muraviev had already adopted in Lithuania. The Polish Whites had executed three coups against the Reds, but there was to be no means controlling a Russian administration determined to enforce its will.

CHAPTER IX

The Russian Pacification of the Kingdom of Poland and the End of the Rising

I N the mid-summer of 1863 the Polish insurgents in the Congress Kingdom were beginning to lose heart. Gorchakov's replies to the powers on 13 July revealed that the Russians were not ready to capitulate to diplomatic intervention, while events in Lithuania seemed to show that no aid could be expected from that quarter. Indeed the Russian government now turned itself to the task of applying Muraviev's coercive methods in the Kingdom itself. It would have been difficult not to apply them, because Muraviev had now become the hero of Russian society. Addresses flowed into his headquarters from all over Russia, commending his success in restoring order in Lithuania. The diplomatic situation, moreover, seemed to point to a need for haste. The pressure of the three powers had for the moment been relaxed, but there was no indication that it would not be applied again in the spring. For the time being, however, it appeared that the August notes of the powers contained no immediate threat to follow up the Six Points with concerted military action. At a conference on 28 and 29 August and 2 September at Tsarskoe Selo, attended by the leading ministers and the Grand Duke Constantine, there was a bitter discussion on the first day, in which Constantine for the last time defended the policy of conciliation, but Alexander II was clearly convinced that the methods of Muraviev should be extended to the Kingdom; Muraviev was demanding that the northern districts of the *gubernia* of Augustów should be handed over to his administration in order to prevent incursions into Lithuania, a request which could mean only that the methods adopted by Constantine were ineffective.[1] Alexander II's simple family loyalties forbade him to ask for Constantine's resignation, but Constantine himself devised the face-saving solution that he should be granted sick leave and hand over his functions temporarily to General Berg. The Tsar's view was that 'in the Kingdom we must have recourse to a system of the most severe military dictatorship according to the model which Muraviev follows in Lithuania. I hope that Berg will put this system into operation, taking advantage of poor Kostia's absence.'[2] Poor Constantine's wife put the matter more simply when she left the Kingdom, declaring that 'it was impossible for the Emperor's brother to remain in Warsaw to act the part of an executioner'.[3]

The change in Russian policy coincided with grave discontent among the left-wing insurgents with the tactics adopted by Majewski. The failure of the western powers to back their diplomatic intervention by active measures to secure compliance, which had revealed to the Russian government that it need no longer stay its hand in the Kingdom, equally showed the Polish insurgents that the policy of waiting for the assistance of Britain and France could no longer be justified. Indeed, the insurgent government itself was beginning to crumble. Aweyde had departed to Lithuania to put some semblance of order into the organization in Vilna, only to fall into the hands of the Russian police.[4] On 7 September Krzemiński resigned. Conscious of his growing isolation Majewski tried to get rid of his enemies in Warsaw by proposing that the leader of the revolutionary police, Landowski, should take his men into the provinces to fight as partisans, but the rank and file would hear nothing of

[1] For Muraviev's complaints against the Grand Duke Constantine see *Golos Minuvshago*, 10 (October 1913), pp. 181, 184–5, 186.

[2] V. G. Revunenkov, *Pol'skoye Vosstaniye*, p. 336.

[3] F.O. 65/643, Stanton to Russell, 9 September 1863.

[4] Aweyde was guilty of grave carelessness. He had travelled to Vilna in the guise of an unemployed shop assistant. When he was detained, it was revealed that he had been spending money far too freely for a person in his circumstances. The police consequently checked his story in Warsaw, where it was revealed to be a complete fabrication, cf. *Pokazaniya i zapiski o pol'skom vosstanii 1863 goda Oskara Aveide*, Edited by S. Kieniewicz and I. Miller (Moscow, 1961), pp. 4–5. In consequence Aweyde broke down in April 1864 and betrayed the secrets of the rising in order to save his own skin.

this suggestion. An attempt was made to hold a revolutionary trial of certain extreme left-wing leaders, but this in its turn produced no results. At length it was the appearance of one of the most prominent provincial leaders, Stanisław Frankowski, which decided matters. Majewski agreed to hand over the direction of affairs to Frankowski on condition that there should be no terror and no proscription of the Whites, but it soon appeared that, when Frankowski and with him Ignacy Chmieleński took command on 17 September, there would be no relaxation of measures against the Russian government. The new insurgent leaders acted upon the principle that their lack of success had been due to the half-measures employed hitherto. It was thought that sharper means were required to whip up enthusiasm and it was not long before this policy was put into operation. On 19 September an attack was made upon Count Berg himself as he was passing the Zamoyski palace at the point where the Nowy Świat meets the Krakowskie Przedmieście. A bomb was thrown from the palace, but Berg himself was unhurt and quickly drove off. The Russian soldiery, however, hurled themselves upon the palace and ransacked it from top to bottom.

Berg now had the excuse to answer Red terror with official terror, directed not so much against the actual malefactors as against the solid phalanx of the Warsaw middle class which by its non-co-operation with the official government had throughout provided a cover for the insurgents within the city. In short, Berg set out to destroy the morale of the Warsaw citizens by the methods employed by Muraviev in Lithuania, convinced that the complete subjection of the city would tear the heart out of the insurrection. To prove that the government was in earnest Berg ordered five of the so-called 'National Gendarmes' to be executed publicly on 30 September. On 7 October a workman of the English firm, Evans and Co., was shot in the workshops as an example to his comrades. All witnesses of acts of terror were made responsible if they failed to attempt the apprehension of the offender. Houses in which a terrorist took refuge were sequestrated. If a criminal fled through a shop, the contents were confiscated. Owners of apartment blocks were made responsible for the good behaviour of their tenants. An effort to render subscription to insurgent funds more difficult was made by imposing an 8 per cent tax upon the inhabitants of the city, while arrears of taxes were collected with more than the usual energy. To its horror the population discovered that precisely those measures which the Whites had feared would be undertaken by the extreme wing of the Reds were now employed by the Russian authorities. Depressed by the failure of diplomatic intervention and harried by the government, the middle class began to lose enthusiasm for the rising. On 18 November Stanton wrote that:

all reports tend to confirm the belief that the majority within the country are thoroughly tired of the insurrection and convinced of the futility of its efforts if left unsupported and as I believe would gladly avail themselves of the opportunity of ceasing the struggle that might be offered by an honest avowal of the leaders in Paris that their hopes of active assistance have proved unfounded.[1]

British consular reports always represented so faithfully the views of the Polish Whites that it must be supposed that this despatch was an appeal for international action to secure a relaxation of revolutionary pressure.

Long before Stanton could make this obervation the insurgent organization had fallen into confusion. Chmieleński and Frankowski wished to rid themselves of the Whites still left in the central command, but Dobrowolski, now leading the moderates, wished to purge Chmieleński and Frankowski. In fact, Chmieleński and Frankowski found Warsaw too hot for them and departed. Leaderless the left wing fell into disarray. A semblance of order was restored on 17 October when a certain Romuald Traugutt, an ex-colonel of the Russian army, assumed sole and undivided control. Traugutt was not a Red, but he was an honest man. He aimed in the first place to ensure that the insurgents survived the winter and were able to carry on the revolt in the spring of 1864. It was decided that those insurgents who could cross the East Prussian frontier should lie up for the winter in the farmsteads of the Mazurian population. In the spring of 1864 the rebels were to emerge and lead a *levée-en-masse*. Traugutt was not in sympathy with the Reds, but he recognized that there was now no alternative to the Red policy

[1] F.O. 65/473, Stanton to Russell, 18 November 1863.

of calling upon the people at large to assist in expelling the Russians. He therefore attempted to restore a sense of purpose in the rising by the strict enforcement of the revolutionary decree granting the peasants their freeholds.[1] Traugutt's decree of 27 December declaring this intention supposed that the Tsarist government itself had no initiative.

The decision had already been taken in St. Petersburg to make concessions to the peasants of western Russia. Alexander II had as early as 10 April been advised by William I of Prussia to seek the support of the peasants,[2] but at the time he had seen no further than granting the peasants the right of choosing their own mayors for the rural communes.[3] The separate legal system did offer the possibility of a far more radical solution of the agrarian problem in the Kingdom than was politically desirable in western Russia, where radical measures might seem to offer precedents for similar action in Russia proper. For the elaboration of a more drastic scheme of emancipation in the Kingdom of Poland a reliable Russian official was needed. The name of Nicholas Milyutin must have sprung automatically to mind, for he had already been mentioned in the spring of 1862 as an alternative to Wielopolski. In 1863 the situation had changed and by the autumn there was no longer any inclination to seek the support of the Polish Whites. Milyutin was called to Tsarskoe Selo on 31 August and given instructions to investigate the peasant question in Congress Poland with the object of presenting a plan for the complete liquidation of the peasants' dependence upon the landlords. Alexander II was afterwards to remark that Milyutin did his task well: 'Si j'avais tenu bon et nommé Nicolas Milutine, disait-il parfois, tout cela ne serait pas arrivé.'[4]

Rumours were soon current in Warsaw of impending legislation of a sweeping kind, but Poles at first thought that a

---

[1] 'Dekret o wprowadzeniu w życie uwłaszczenia' (27 December 1863), reproduced in *Wybór tekstów źródłowych z historii Polski w latach 1795–1864* (Warsaw, 1956), No. 252. For a discussion of Traugutt's attitude to the peasant question see E. Halicz, *Kwestia chłopska w Królestwie Polskim w dobie powstania styczniowego* (Warsaw, 1955), pp. 291–305.

[2] *Die auswärtige Politik Preussens, 1858–1871*, III, 456–7.

[3] *Ibid.*, III, 512, Alexander II to William I, 25 April 1863.

[4] A. Leroy-Beaulieu, *Un homme d'état russe*, p. 161.

scheme would be evolved by which the peasants would make redemption payments for their freeholds into a state fund, from which the landlords would be reimbursed.[1] It soon became apparent, however, that these dreams were not to be fulfilled and complaints were made that Milyutin was not consulting persons with local knowledge.[2] The Polish gentry supposed that the Russians would persist in the old policy of seeking an understanding with the propertied classes, but in fact Milyutin and his assistants, Cherkassky and Samarin, conceived their main purpose to be to discover the impression that the insurrection had made upon the minds of the peasants, which in itself represented a revolution in the thinking of Russian officialdom. Facts and figures were already available from the period of Wielopolski's tenure of office and no detailed research into peasant problems was made. Under the guard of a troop of cossacks Milyutin visited the easily accessible villages along the line of the Warsaw–Vienna railway, calling the villagers together to obtain their views and taking the precaution of excluding all manor officials from the discussions, lest the peasants should not feel inclined to speak freely. His investigations revealed that everywhere the peasants expected social justice. In the early stages of the revolt the peasants had generally sought the protection of the government, but as the intentions of the insurgents had become clearer there had been a general weakening of their allegiance to the official authorities. This in part had been brought about by the fear of insurgent reprisals and the lack of resolution shown by officials, but in some measure also it was due to a growing sympathy for the insurgent programme.[3] Different conditions applied in the different parts of the country. In some regions the peasants, even on government estates, did not wish to pay dues established on a temporary basis by Wielopolski in 1861, while in others dues had been paid regularly or had been paid after an interval in which the peasants had refused to fulfil their obligations. In spite of local variations the impression everywhere was the same in one respect, that after the

---

[1] F.O. 65/473, Stanton to Russell, 14 October 1863.

[2] *Ibid.*, Stanton to Russell, 1 December 1863.

[3] N. Milyutin, *Izsledovaniya v Tsarstve Pol'skom*, I, fascicule entitled 'O deistviakh pol'skikh myatezhnikov v otnoshenii k krest'yanam', pp. 12-13.

revolutionary decrees of 22 January 1863 there could be no reversion to Wielopolski's system of emancipation and liquidation. The continued Russian occupation of the Kingdom demanded that every possible concession should be made to the peasants, which would satisfy their basic economic aspirations and once and for all destroy the power of the landlords over them. This was the tone of the appreciation which Milyutin drew up for Alexander II on 2 January 1864.[1]

Milyutin's approach to the agrarian question did not entirely please General Berg, now enjoying the full authority of a viceroy, nor did it offer much comfort to the Polish landlords. Berg, like many senior officers in Russian service, disliked establishing a precedent in the Kingdom which might subsequently be applied elsewhere. Prince Władysław Czartoryski actually advised the landlords to continue in support of the insurrection, declaring that success alone could save them from losing everything.[2] All manner of intrigues were undertaken to prevent a measure of radical reform from being carried through.[3] The discussions in the special committee at St. Petersburg were not influenced substantially by protests from the landlords or Berg. In the main the reforms adopted by the Russian government followed the lines suggested by Milyutin, nothing less than a solution which went beyond what even the Red manifestoes of 22 January had proposed.

The decrees settling the agrarian question were signed on 2 March and issued with some ceremony on 6 March in Warsaw.[4] The general proclamation declared that the reforms were adopted with the object of proving to the peasants that they could expect more generous treatment from Russia than they could hope for from the Poles, hypocritically stating that the insurrection had been undertaken to frustrate the fatherly intentions of the Tsar. In the principal decree it was announced that the lands possessed by the peasants, by any title whatsoever, and with no reservations concerning the size of holdings, on

[1] The text is given in N. Milyutin, *Izsledovaniya*, i.
[2] *Wydawnictwo materyałów*, i, 89, Czartoryski to the National Government, 24 February 1864.
[3] Cf. S. Kieniewicz, *Sprawa włościańska w powstaniu styczniowym*, pp. 374–5.
[4] The texts may be found in *Dziennik Praw Królestwa Polskiego* and in N. Milyutin, *Izsledovaniya*, vol. i, Appendix.

private and state lands, passed into their hands absolutely as freeholds. The Russian government did not follow the example of the Austrian government in leaving open the questions of woods and pastures as a source of discord between the gentry and the peasants, but secured to the peasants their rights to existing privileges, which might be altered only by a voluntary agreement of the two parties concerned. The peasants were likewise not called upon to make redemption payments. The landlords were to be compensated from a state fund guaranteed by the government. The separation of the manor and the village was completed by the abolition of the 1818 system, by which the landlord was *de jure* the mayor of the village commune. Henceforth the landlord was excluded entirely from the affairs of the village by a new arrangement under which the demesne lands constituted a commune entirely separate from the peasant lands. Thus for the first time the peasants stood in a direct relationship to the Russian functionary. This reorganization, which freed the peasantry from the manor, was completed by a gesture towards the landless labourers. The insurgents had offered to the landless peasants, who took up arms on behalf of their country, small holdings of three morgs in extent from the government estates. The Russian executive committee charged with the supervision of the reforms of 2 March 1864 adopted the policy of distributing this class of land to the rural proletariat. Altogether about 130,000 holdings were ultimately created for the landless peasants, the last possible source of strength for the Polish insurgents.[1]

The total result of the Russian reforms was that nearly 700,000 families obtained their freeholds on terms which were certainly more generous than those which the Austrian and Prussian governments accorded their Polish peasants and which were easier to enforce than the complicated regulations which passed for agrarian legislation in the Russian Empire in 1861. The Polish insurrections of 1846 and 1863 failed. 1848 was a year of disillusionment, but the efforts of the Polish revolutionary movement had not been entirely to no purpose. Where the insurrection was strongest, the solution of the agrarian question was the most radical. Without armed struggle the Russian govern-

[1] W. Grabski, *Materiały w sprawie włościańskiej* (Warsaw, 1907), p. 12.

ment would almost certainly have surrendered the peasants to Wielopolski. In 1864 the peasants emerged as a completely independent force. With the emancipation of the peasantry the educated classes and the mass of the people could for the first time merge to form one political community with an identical national consciousness. In the course of time peasant political parties were to arise as convinced as other Polish political parties of the need for national independence.

Emancipation was not, however, to bring prosperity to the village. A less obvious result of reform was that the social structure of the village changed with the exclusion of the landlord. In the days when the lord drew upon the labour services of the village for the cultivation of the demesne, he considered his own requirements for the type of labour he needed. Ploughing services were provided by full-peasants and half-peasants and manual labour by the cottagers. Thus was determined the distribution of thirty-morg and fifteen-morg holdings and the number of allotments upon an estate, but with emancipation the power of deciding the size of holdings passed into the control of the peasants. Land was a condition of peasant marriage and peasants found themselves under pressure from their children to subdivide their lands. The result was that the birth rate rose sharply where subdivision took place, creating a demand for further subdivision. The creation of a peasant class with minute holdings in one way produced poverty and discontent in the countryside, but in another provided the labour force for the expansion of industry in the towns. In fact, it was in the Congress Kingdom that Polish industrial development was most marked in the nineteenth century. Emancipation was not a solution in itself, but merely a step towards a new phase in the economic life of the Polish community.[1]

The long-term problems of emancipation were not those which confronted the insurgents who kept the field in 1864. Enthusiasm cooled in Galicia with the announcement of a state of siege in January, in spite of a pious exhortation

---

[1] For repercussions of peasant emancipation in Galicia see W. Styś, *Rozdrabnianie gruntów chłopskich w b. zaborze austriackim od roku 1787–1931* (Lvov, 1934); *Drogi postępu wsi* (Wrocław, 1952); and *Współzależność rozwoju rodziny chłopskiej i jej gospodarstwa* (Wrocław, 1959).

that the war must be carried on.[1] There was little desire to continue the struggle in Poznanian circles. Within the Kingdom the Russian reforms of 2 March had destroyed the programme of 22 January 1863. The peasants had other things to think of than rising in revolt against authorities who offered them more than the insurgents. The sole task of the Russian government was to deal with the remnants of revolt. On 11 April the dictator, Traugutt, was arrested by the police in Warsaw. On 19 April the last important insurgent leader to operate in the countryside, Bosak-Hauke, a revolutionary aristocrat who scarcely spoke Polish at all, was compelled to take refuge in Galicia. Paralyzed at the centre and without men under arms in the countryside the insurrection petered out. The Russian government issued on 4 August an account of the insurgent government's activity and the changes in its personnel up to 10 October, when Traugutt had taken command.[2] On the following day Traugutt was publicly executed before the Citadel to show that insurgent government ceased to exist. In fact, a token resistance was maintained by one Bogdan Brzeziński into whose hand the seal of the National Government had fallen, but he found no support among the Polish public. The last insurgent leader to persist in the fiction that Poland was still at war with Russia, Alexander Waszkowski, was captured in December 1864 and hanged in the following January. The follower of Mierosławski, Daniłowski, returned to Warsaw from Paris to revive the insurrection, but was himself soon arrested and sent into exile. The Kingdom was too weary of partisan warfare to continue hostilities when there was no longer any hope of intervention from outside and no means of raising mass support within Poland. The time had come not for action, but for a reappraisal of the Polish question.

The almost immediate result was for the extreme right wing of the Whites to raise their heads and declare, as they had done in 1846 and 1848, that there was nothing to be gained from resistance. The argument was again advanced that the best way to serve Poland was to promote her economic and social reconstruction. Paweł Popiel, a right-wing landlord, was the first to come out into the open with a campaign for the acceptance of

---

[1] Cf. *Zadanie organizacyi narodowej w sprawie polskiej* (Leipzig, 1864), pp. 29–31.
[2] *Dziennik Warszawski*, No. 177, 23 July/4 August 1864, p. 1604.

R

foreign domination. When Prince Adam Sapieha issued an appeal after his nomination as plenipotentiary of the National Government in France, Popiel composed an anonymous pamphlet condemning further revolutionary activity.[1] It was now regretted that advantage had not been taken of Wielopolski's efforts to secure some form of self-government within the Kingdom. Instead, it was argued, revolution had brought about a collapse of all hopes. There was no discipline and the peasants had turned against the *szlachta*. Popiel's programme was that the Poles should accept collaboration with Russia in the Kingdom and the western *gubernii* of the Empire, as collaboration with the partitioning power was accepted in Galicia and Poznania:

> The formula of duty, by which today every Pole ought to be bound, is as follows: No conspiracy, no secret organization, no assistance under any form or name whatsoever to be given for unrevealed purposes.[2]

Popiel criticized the younger generation which had been converted to revolution, the clergy whom he considered to have been left for thirty years without discipline, the junior officials who had taken part in conspiratorial activity, and, above all, the *szlachta* who had capitulated before the revolutionary movement. Popiel presented Poland's greatest misfortune as her moral decay, but his immediate aim was to secure some modification of the emancipation laws in the Kingdom:

> Thus it is necessary, above all, to restore law and order in the country so that legislation, of whatever kind it may be, shall be put into operation in the least harmful way possible.[3]

Similarly the editorial board of the Cracow newspaper, *Czas*, appearing in the first quarter of 1864 as *Chwila* on account of a temporary suspension by the Austrian authorities, pleaded for co-operation. It had at first made the conventional complaint that the Polish *szlachta* had wished to grant the peasants emancipation with land, but had only been frustrated by Russia. This was a sterile argument to adopt and *Czas* soon changed its tune to a recommendation that the landlords of the Kingdom should

---

[1] *Kilka słów z powodu odezwy X. Adama Sapiehy* (Leipzig, 1864).
[2] *Ibid.*, p. 7.   [3] *Ibid.*, p. 6.

accept the Russian decrees in order to bring an end to confusion, which could only be harmful to themselves and encourage 'cosmopolitanism and communism' among the peasants.[1] A certain Artur Kolonna demanded to know why the violence of the Russians during the insurrection should constitute an obstacle to a Russo-Polish understanding:

If the Galician massacre did not restrain the Poles from seeking relief from Austria, why should the Muscovite cruelties stand in the way of a compromise with Russia?[2]

He attacked likewise the ideological objections which were commonly put forward:

Poles clamouring for the frontiers of 1771 are like a man who, having lost a great fortune through the cunning of others and his own negligence, prefers to die of hunger in a lazar-house rather than have a respectable, though perhaps modest income.[3]

Count Ludwik Dębicki in an anonymous pamphlet with the gloomy title of *Poland in the Moment of Calamity* pleaded for peace and argued that 'from the fall of Langiewicz the insurrection, which appeared already to have collapsed, prolongs itself only by means of narcotics'.[4]

There were many reasons which could be advanced for calling off the armed struggle, but the ideals of Popiel and his friends in Cracow and Galicia were indeed narrow. In 1865 Popiel returned to the political scene with his *Letter to Prince Jerzy Lubomirski*, in which he revealed his desire for support of Belcredi's ultra-conservative ministry in Vienna. For Popiel there were two enemies, the bureaucracy and the revolutionary movement. To counteract their influence there must be some restoration of the nobility's influence:

The towns and the middle classes are blown up with the spirit of revolution grafted on to a conception of patriotism. The peasants have been stirred to violent lusts and, because they have no national traditions, have become the pliant tool, not of the dynastic interest, but of the interest and dislikes of the bureaucratic caste. The whole

---

[1] *Chwila*, No. 61 (15 March 1864) and No. 74 (31 March 1864); *Czas*, No. 45 (26 May 1864); No. 3 (3 April 1864); and No. 6 (8 April 1864).
[2] *Polska w 1865 roku* (Leipzig, 1865), p. 17.   [3] *Ibid.*, p. 22.
[4] *Polska w chwili pogromu* (Leipzig, 1865), p. 27.

country has been impoverished, because we larger property owners still do not know how to work and because the peasant class, having got everything for nothing, does not need to work.[1]

The assumption that all virtues were embodied in the aristocracy roused the scholar, Józef Szujski, to launch an attack upon the outmoded attitudes of the upper classes, but he was not willing to go as far as uttering praise of the insurrectionary movement.[2] The revolt of 1863 merely confirmed the Galicians in their dislike of armed action. It was this factor which gave the Cracow conservatives an unwarranted degree of initiative and permitted them to lead Galicia along the line of collaboration with Austria. 1866 saw the defeat of Austria in her war with Prussia and 1867 the extension of the hand of friendship to the Magyars. In September 1866 Count Agenor Gołuchowski was appointed Galician viceroy for the second time and the Polish conservatives secured the submission of an address to the Emperor by the local diet in December 1866, expressing Polish willingness to remain within the Austrian state. The phrase used—'From the depths of our hearts we affirm that we stand and wish to stand with Your Imperial Majesty'—must have stuck in the throats of those Galicians who retained left-wing leanings.[3] It certainly did not move Francis Joseph who was under no compulsion to satisfy the Poles when he had bought off the Magyars. Refusal to grant the Galicians autonomy led Florian Ziemiałkowski and his followers to begin a campaign to force the Emperor to change his mind, but never at any moment was it intended to revive the revolutionary movement. When the National Democratic Society was founded in Lvov in February 1868 with a programme of preparing for independence, its president, Smołka, could conceive only of a federal Austrian Empire with five dominant nationalities, the Germans, Magyars, Czechs, Poles and Croats. Disappointments in the parliamentary struggle gave rise to bitter feeling, which compelled Ziemiałkowski and Gołuchowski to resign their seats at Lvov. To com-

---

[1] P. Popiel, 'List do księcia Jerzego Lubomirskiego', in *Pisma* (Cracow, 1893), I, 68.

[2] J. Szujski, *O broszurze p. Pawła Pobiela pod tytułem: List do księcia Jerzego Lubomirskiego* (8 October 1865); for Popiel's reply see *Pisma*, I, 77 f.

[3] For the text see M. Bobrzyński, W. L. Jaworski and J. Milewski, *Z dziejów odrodzenia politycznego Galicyi* (Warsaw, 1905), pp. 120–2.

bat this feeling of annoyance a group of Cracow intellectuals, led by Count Stanisław Tarnowski, Koźmian, two members of the Wodzicki family and Józef Szujski, began, in the periodical *Przegląd Polski*, to attack the entire revolutionary tradition in Poland, declaring that the besetting sin of the old Poland had been the *Liberum Veto* and that the vice of the present was the *Liberum Conspiro*, by which any Pole could in the name of his fatherland consider himself at liberty to enter into revolutionary activity and thus bring ruin and disaster to his country, when in fact the country needed economic and social reconstruction. This theory, which has coloured the interpretation of Polish history both in Poland and abroad, was intended to provide a moral basis for keeping the attention of Galicians to their petty provincial affairs. In 1873 the Poles in Galicia were able to achieve virtual autonomy within Austria. The province came under Polish administration. A Polish school board, district councils dominated by Poles and the local diet set about the task of polonizing the province, giving to the administration in Vienna unconditional support in the Reichsrath. Many Poles managed to convince themselves and foreigners that a renaissance occurred in Galicia. There are doubtless old men in southern Poland who still declare that life was good under Austria, but this merely means that they could travel freely in an international community, holiday in Dalmatia, drink Hungarian wine and attend concerts in Vienna. The truth is that Galicia remained one of the most backward provinces of the Habsburg Empire. Economically stagnant, dominated by conservatism, oppressing the peasants and denying the Ruthenians their rights, Galicia was to be the living picture of the Poland which Wielopolski might have created in the Kingdom.[1]

If the Russians had invited co-operation in the Kingdom they would have found Poles willing enough to follow the example of the Galicians. A direct answer to the question what answer should be adopted towards Tsarism appeared in 1865 under the title of *Our policy towards Russia, what ought it to be?*[2] The correct

---

[1] For details of Galicia see the introduction to *Galicja w dobie autonomicznej (1850–1914)*, edited by S. Kieniewicz (Wrocław, 1952); K. Wyka, *Teka Stańczyka na tle historii Galicji w l. 1849–69* (Wrocław, 1951).

[2] *Nasza polityka wobec Rosyi, jaką być powinna?* (Leipzig, 1865).

conclusion was drawn that the Russian people had remained faithful to their government and that it was hopeless to carry on the struggle, but this seemed to point to the need for a new policy, for there were in fact two main streams of thought in Russia, the reactionary represented by German officialdom, and the progressive from which Herzen and others had been drawn. Outright opposition to the Russian government could mean only further russification of the former eastern provinces and prevent their developing along their own lines, which might not necessarily be Polish. The task before the Poles was the cessation of conspiratorial activity and the diversion of energies to economic and social reconstruction, the policy of 'organic work':

If we shall take up 'organic work' only for a while and consider it as a preparation for insurrection, the authorities will be compelled to hamper us in that work. . . . To save our most treasured possession, nationality and family happiness, we must resign all intention of rebuilding an independent Polish state, because this intention is not only the reason for our misfortunes, but also is now absolutely and utterly unobtainable. But whether it shall be obtainable in the future, that is, as far as the question goes—What ought to be our policy towards Russia today?—, a matter of complete indifference.[1]

The Poles under Russia could choose no other path than that 'which is trodden by the Poznanians in their relations with Prussia and the Galicians with regard to Austria'. This writer did not overlook the fact that association with Russia offered certain advantages which could not be obtained in the German states. The Poles could become the technocracy of the vast Russian Empire, which as Slavs they could easily penetrate. In the early 1870's this conception of placing Poland in the main current of Russian economic development was endowed with a theory by the Warsaw Positivists under the leadership of Alexander Świętochowski, who launched an attack upon the traditional social values of the Polish *szlachta* and exalted the middle-class entrepreneur and technician. The Kingdom of Poland began to change very quickly in the 1870's and 1880's under the impact of industrialization. The landed gentry, weakened by the reforms of 1864 followed by the agrarian crisis

[1] *Ibid.*, p. 24–5.

of the 1870's, began to yield their social predominance to the business man and the industrialist. Acceptance of foreign domination resulted in the Kingdom's taking a share in general Russian progress, in sharp contrast with Galicia where economic and social stagnation were the fruits of Polish renunciation of revolt, but capital investment in Congress Poland was controlled by the foreigner. Those Poles who favoured 'organic work' doubtless had the consolation that their patriotism lined their pockets well, but their successes were on too small a scale materially to affect Poland's political position. Poland enjoyed only a colonial status within the Russian system.

Not all Poles were prepared even in the straitened circumstances of defeat to accept co-operation as an ideal, for it was nothing less than the indefinite postponement of independence. The author of the pamphlet, *To all Poles*, condemned defeatist programmes and declared that 'organic work' could be only a tactical deviation:

Let the voice of the unbeliever who says that the insurrection is finished be silent for ever, because in Poland the insurrection will never end until the moment of victory.[1]

When the clerical party tried to show that armed rebellion was not encouraged by the Catholic church,[2] there were still to be found defenders of the revolutionary ideals.[3] There was likewise little disposition to accept with equanimity the role which the *szlachta* had played in the revolt. Wiktor Wiszniewski was at pains to expose the Galician gentry, who had made a great commotion, but in fact done very little to assist the revolt in the Kingdom and waited patiently for the Austrian government to declare a state of siege.[4] There were those, like Władysław Koziebrodzki, who declared that it had been folly to expect the peasants to respond immediately to the revolutionary decrees of 22 January 1863, but argued that as the rising had progressed

---

[1] *Do wszystkich Polaków* (Leipzig, 1865), p. 23.

[2] Cf. *Z powodu allokucyji Piusa IX mianej na tajnym konsystorzu 29 października 1866 r.* (Poznań, 1867).

[3] Cf. D. Zan (W. L. Chotomski), *Autorowi broszury pod tytułem 'Z powodu allokucyi Piusa IX mianej na tajnym konsystorzu 29 października 1866 r.', Kilka uwag* (Poznań, 1867).

[4] W. Wiszniewski, *Galicja, czyli rok 1863 i 1864* (Leipzig, 1865), pp. 41, 68.

the people had shown more and more willingness to lend assistance to the insurgents.[1] Mateusz Gralewski realized that a new era had come and that new concepts must be applied. Whether the *szlachta* liked it or not, the peasant had become a citizen and must be treated as one. The old notion of the peasant being raised to the status of being an equal with the landlord no longer had any practical validity. The peasants were now an independent force:

> With regard to the last insurrection they remained only passive factors in the state organism, but henceforth after the act restoring them to their property rights they emerge from their misery and more and more, heart and soul, are looking to their own interests and the interests of the nation.[2]

It followed that the peasant peoples of Lithuania and Ruthenia could not be treated in the old manner, but must be regarded as having distinct aspirations of their own. Gralewski saw in conception of national equality the basis of an alliance between the peoples stretching from the gulf of Finland to the river Volga. Jarosław Dąbrowski, who managed to escape from prison and to become the general of the Paris Commune, seems to have held somewhat similar views concerning the attitude to be adopted towards the former eastern provinces.[3] There were left-wing thinkers who considered that the position of the Poles had been strengthened in western Russia, because the settlement of the agrarian question removed the main cause of dissension between the Polish *szlachta* and the peasants; the struggle in the east was to be between the state and the peasants.[4]

The revolutionary thinking of the past, however, had to be laid aside. The insurrectionary programme, based upon agrarian concepts, had no meaning. There was neither the will to take the field again nor yet a policy to present to the people other than the vague postulates of Polish nationalism. The

---

[1] J. Bolesta (W. Koziebrodzki), *Być albo nie być* (Bendlikon, 1865), pp. 33, 36–7.

[2] M. Gralewski, *Myśli o naszych działaniach w kraju i za granicą* (Leipzig, 1865), p. 11.

[3] Cf. M. Złotorzycka, 'Jarosław Dąbrowski o sprawie ruskiej', *Niepodległość*, IX (1934), pp. 455–63.

[4] Gozdawa, *Ruś przed i po powstaniu zbrojnem 1863 r.* (Bendlikon, 1865), pp. 22, 27–8, 32.

Polish Left was compelled to wait for new social conditions to crease the bases for a fresh trial of strength with the partitioning powers. For the immediate future the Left was submerged in the general conviction that Triloyalism was the only solution. Conservatism seemed to be the heir of the great revolutionary movement, but the struggles of the Polish Left had already shaped the future. *Szlachta*, peasants, middle class and industrial workers were now all in theory equal before the law, but all were subject to foreign rule. The victory of 1864 was in the long run empty of advantage for the Russian government. It destroyed the one justification which might have been advanced, that the Russian bureaucracy protected the Polish peasants from the manor. In future the peasants would seek relief from the pressure of Russian officialdom. The Russians remained in the Kingdom of Poland by no right except that of conquest. The literature of the great revolutionary struggle of 1832–64 was predominantly anti-Russian in tone and this was the intellectual and political heritage which descended to the common people of Poland when literacy began to extend itself to the countryside and to the masses of the towns.

The inevitable consequence was that the only means by which a Russian government could transform a Pole into a loyal citizen was to convert him into a Russian. From 1864 the process of russification began. The pretence was scarcely maintained that the Kingdom of Poland was to have a separate existence. The Polish secretariat of state in St. Petersburg was abolished and its business transferred to the Tsar's personal chancery. All decisions upon policies to be adopted in Poland were taken in a 'Committee for the Affairs of the Kingdom of Poland', which was personally dependent upon the Tsar. Within the Kingdom the effective government was the Executive Committee over which General Berg presided. The real ruler, however, was Nicholas Milyutin, through whose hands all orders passed, whether in Warsaw or in St. Petersburg. Until a stroke brought his active career to an end in December 1866 Milyutin and his assistants, Cherkassky and Samarin, transformed the internal administration of the Kingdom. By the 1870's very little was left of the system of 1815. The Polish council of state was abolished on 22 March 1867 and the administrative council on 15 June 1867.[1] All the public departments of the administration were brought into line with the system prevailing in the Russian Empire. Even the bulletin of the laws, the *Dziennik Praw*, lost its existence in 1871 and was replaced by the *Sbornik Zakonov*. In 1866 new administrative divisions were created; the Kingdom was divided into ten *gubernii*, in order that in smaller units a closer watch might be kept on the Poles. The gendarmerie was much enlarged to give the local governors a better control over the countryside.[2] Education likewise received attention. Wielopolski's reforms of 1862 were to be maintained, but they were to serve Russian purposes. Peasant education was to be encouraged and developed, while the intelligentsia was to be induced to turn its attention to practical matters and not to revolution. In his rescript of 11 September 1864 Alexander II gave the following direction:

3. In the organization of academic foundations, namely in medium and higher establishments, more especially from the point of view of instruction, the chief task of the government must be the extension of healthy views among the students and the encouragement in them of a liking for solid work and basic academic training. Not permitting itself or anyone else to turn the spread of learning into an instrument for the attainment of political ends, the education authority must maintain a single-minded devotion to the interest of education, in order to improve continually public instruction in the Kingdom and raise the standard of learning.[3]

The Russian government clearly had the same conception of what was good for Poles as the Cracow conservatives. Instructions were given, moreover, to purge teachers who were not politically reliable. There was little emphasis upon Polish culture and history in the secondary schools. Small time was given to the Polish language, while the history and geography of Russia and Poland was to be taught in Russian. The salary scales were weighted in favour of non-Polish subjects; teachers of the Russian language and geography were to receive a stipend of 1,500 roubles, of French and German 1,200 and of Polish 1,000 in secondary schools. The intention was clearly to attract teachers from Russia and at the same time to debase the status of

---

[1] *Dziennik Praw*, LXVII, 34–7, 88–9.   [2] *Ibid.*, LXVI, 114–93, 194–203.
[3] *Ibid.*, LXII, 328–31.

Polish teachers. On the other hand, there was much to be said for an education syllabus which drew Polish attention away from belles-lettres. There was never a shortage of poets in Poland, but there were always too few technicians. Probably more annoyance was caused by the administration's interference with the affairs of the church. In November 1864 religious houses which contained less than eight ecclesiastics were closed, together with those which had been proved to have aided the insurgents.[1] Some effort was made to assist the Uniate church, but this was half-hearted. In 1866, on the other hand, the Jews were given the right to serve in the public administration, provided that they had a qualification from a Russian university, or an equivalent Polish certificate from the Central School established in Warsaw by Wielopolski. In general, it may be said that the Russian government adopted the pretence that there was nothing especially Polish about the Kingdom of Poland and that it was merely a mixed nationality area appended to the Russian Empire.

It was true that Poles could make for themselves a career in Russia and could be russified, but the Kingdom of Poland remained Polish. A tradition had been established in Warsaw in 1831 and again in 1863–4. When the Russian Empire itself collapsed in 1917 the January insurrection of 1863 was still a living memory. The tragedy was that so many Poles, thinking only of their own traditions, dreamed in the new conditions of Europe that they could re-establish Poland once again in the frontiers of 1771, the frontiers of the old agrarian state, which had been the ideal in 1863. It was hard indeed to surrender areas which had provided a disproportionate number of national heroes and men of letters. Emotional nationalism triumphed over political reality, but political realities are appreciated only by peoples which have a normal political existence. This Russia, in common with Austria and Prussia, had denied the Polish nation. In 1917 the Russian and the Polish nations reacted differently according to their own political traditions. That despair and submission, counselled by the Polish conservatives, had not destroyed Polish morale was in no small measure due to the revolt of 1863.

[1] *Ibid.*, LXII, 406–19.

Select Bibliography

THE history of Poland before and during the insurrection of 1863 is the subject of a vast literature. In this bibliography I have limited myself to major works only and to a selection of memoir and pamphlet material illustrative of political problems. The standard bibliographical work is K. Estreicher, *Bibliografia Polska*, Cracow, 1870–80, with supplements published in 1873, 1881 and 1882, and its successor *Bibliografia Polska xix stulecia, 1881–1900*, Cracow, 1906–16. Reference should be made also to J. Gąsiorowski, *Bibliografia druków dotyczących Powstania Styczniowego, 1863–5*, Warsaw, 1923, a bibliography of printed works concerning the January Insurrection of 1863–5, though obviously fresh sources have come to light since its publication. A critical analysis of the more important works dealing with the rising is provided by S. Kieniewicz, 'Historiografia polska wobec powstania styczniowego', *Przegląd Historyczny*, XLIV (1–2) (1953) (Polish historiography and the January Insurrection).

I. SOURCES

The losses sustained by Polish archives during the last war were very severe. In consequence the major sources are already in print, but they may still be supplemented from manuscript material. I have cited the British consuls, reports from Warsaw during the crisis years from 1857 to 1865; these reports must be accepted with caution, because they owe much to the pen of William Arthur White, later British ambassador in Constantinople, who was a protégé of the Czartoryski family and the Zamoyskis and tended to report the situation in the light of the interests of the Polish upper classes. The Russell papers, housed in the Public Record Office, are essential to an understanding of the diplomacy of 1863. British ambassadorial despatches from St. Petersburg are sympathetic to the interests of Wielopolski and the Russian aristocracy. There are some unprinted sources in Polish archives; valuable material may be found in the Museum of Czartoryski Princes in Cracow and in the State Archives preserved in the Wawel Palace. It is obvious that there must be in the Soviet Union excellent sources for the history of the Polish insurrectionary movement, but they remain inaccessible. In the meantime reliance must be placed upon the principal printed sources listed below.

Affaires de Pologne—Exposé de la situation suivi de documents et de pièces justificatives.
   Paris, 1863. Contains some documents of interest; published by the
   Czartoryski agency in Paris.

Aweyde, O., *Pokazaniya i zapiski o pol'skom vosstanii 1863 goda Oskara Aveide*, edited by S. Kieniewicz and I. Miller, Moscow, 1961. (Evidence and Memoirs of Oscar Aweyde concerning the Polish rising of 1863.) A very important source for the history of the insurgent movement; the *Zapiski* were originally printed for Russian official use.

Bermansky, K. L., '"Konstitutsionnye" proyekty Tsarstvovaniya Aleksandra II', *Vyestnik Prava*, xxxv (9) (November 1905), pp. 223–91. ('Constitutional' projects of the reign of Alexander II.) Gives the text of the plan of Valuyev; the existence of a plan for a constitution in 1863 reveals how nervous the Russian government was.

Constantine Nikolayevich, Grand Duke, 'Iz dnevnika V. K. Konstantina Nikolayevicha' (18 April–31 December 1862), *Krasny Arkhiv*, x (1925), pp. 217–60. (From the diary of the Grand Duke Constantine Nikolayevich.) An important source for Russian policy.

Correspondence relating to the Affairs of Poland (July 1862–March 1863), *Accounts & Papers* (1863), LXXV, p. 19. In the same volume may be found, *Correspondence relating to the Insurrection in Poland (December 1862–April 1863)*, p. 25; *Further Correspondence (April, May 1863)* (Part II), p. 203; *Correspondence respecting the Insurrection in Poland (June 1863)* (Part III), p. 279; *Correspondence respecting the Insurrection in Poland (July 1863)* (Part IV), p. 285; *Further Papers respecting the Affairs of Poland (July 1863)*, p. 297. The modicum of information the British government saw fit to release in 1863.

Documents sur les affaires de Pologne. Paris, 1863. The French Yellow Book.

Dziennik Praw Królestwa Polskiego, 1815–1871. (Bulletin of the Laws of the Kingdom of Poland.)

Filipowicz, T., *Confidential Correspondence of the British Government respecting the insurrection in Poland, 1863*. A facsimile of a British confidential print which found its way into Polish hands and was published in 1914.

Giller, A., *Historja powstania narodu polskiego w 1861–1864 r.* 4 vois. Paris, 1867–71. (The history of the Polish Nation's uprising 1861–4.) Contains documents and Giller's comments upon memoirs and pamphlet material. Important, but should be accepted with caution in view of the equivocal part played by Giller in the rising of 1863.

Kalendarz wydawany przez Obserwatoryum astronomiczne warszawskie. Published annually between 1857 and 1861. (Calendar issued by the Warsaw Observatory.) Contains important statistics from official sources: these are reproduced in the calendars for 1859 and 1860 by L. Wolski.

Kartsov, P. P., 'Varshava v 1860 i 1861 gg.', *Russkaya Starina*, xxxvi (1882), pp. 534–84. Warsaw in 1860 and 1861. Texts of telegrams between Prince Mikhail Gorchakov and Alexander II.

Langiewicz, M., *Pisma wojskowe Dyktatora Marjana Langiewicza (Listy o powstaniu 1863 r. Fragmenty organizacyjne)*, ed. B. Merwin. Warsaw, 1920. (Military writings of the Dictator Marian Langiewicz.)

— *Relacje o kampanji własnej w r. 1863*, ed. B. Merwin. Lvov, 1905. (An account of his campaign in 1863.)

Lisicki, H., *Aleksander Wielopolski, 1803–1877*. 4 vols. Cracow, 1878–9. A biography of Wielopolski, of which vol. II is devoted to documents. A French version of the text without documents is *Le Marquis Wielopolski, sa vie et sons temps.*

Listy Leopolda Kronenberga do Mieczysława Waligorskiego z 1863 roku, ed. S. Kieniewicz. Wrocław, 1955. (Letters of Kronenberg to Waligorski.) A very important discovery by S. Kieniewicz of coded letters passing between Warsaw and Cracow in 1863; reveals Kronenberg's counter-revolutionary activity.

Mierosławski, L., *Dokumenty urzędowe do dziejów organizacyi jeneralnej powstania narodowego w latach 1863 i 1864*. Paris, 1864. (Official documents on the General Organizer's department of the National Insurrection, 1863–4.)

Milyutin, N. A., *Izsledovaniya v Tsarstve Pol'skom po vysochaishemu poveleniyu proizvedenniye pod rukovodstvom stats-sekretarya Milyutina*. 6 vols. St. Petersburg, 1864–5. (Investigations in the Kingdom of Poland . . . carried out under the direction of State Secretary Milyutin.) An essential collection of documents and statistical tables concerning the peasant question.

Morokhovets, E. A., *Krest'yanskoye dvizheniye 1827–1869 gg*. Moscow, 1931. (The peasant movement, 1827–69.)

— *Krest'yanskoye dvizheniye v 1861 godu posle otmeny krepostnogo prava*. Moscow, 1949. (The peasant movement in 1861 after the abolition of serfdom.) Valuable illustrations of discontents in Lithuania.

Pavlishchev, N. V., *Sedmitsy Pol'skago myatezha 1861–4*. 2 vols. St. Petersburg, 1887. (Reports on the Polish Revolt, 1861–4.) Reports sent to Alexander II, November 1861 to May 1864.

'Perepiska Imperatora Aleksandra II-go s velikim knyazem Konstantinom Nikolayevichem z vremya prebyvaniya ego v dolzhnosti namyestnika Tsarstva Pol'skogo v 1862–1863 gg.', *Dyela i Dni*, I–III (1920–2), ed. A. I. Lebedev. (Correspondence of the Emperor Alexander II and the Grand Duke Constantine Nikolayevich in his capacity as viceroy in the Kingdom of Poland, 1862–3.) Very important.

'Pisma O. Bismarka A. M. Gorchakovu', *Krasny Arkhiv*, LXI (1933), pp. 3–25. (Letters of Bismarck to A. M. Gorchakov.) Throws some light on Bismarck's opposition to reform in Poland.

Polnoye sobraniye zakonov Rossiskoy Imperii. (2nd series, 1825–81.) St. Petersburg, 1830–84. (The complete collection of the Laws of the Russian Empire.) Contains the statutes for Lithuania and the Ukraine.

Pravila dlya sostavleniya likvidatsionnykh proyektov na goroda i myestechki. Russian and Polish, Warsaw, 1866. (Rules for the reorganization of towns and hamlets.)

Proces Romualda Traugutta i członków rządu narodowego—Akta audytoriatu polowego z lat 1863–1864. 2 parts, ed. E. Halicz. Warsaw, 1960. (The trial of Romuald Traugutt and members of the National Government—Documents of the military court of 1863–4.)

Rozkaz dzienny Naczelnika Miasta (Order of the Day of the Chief of the Town.) These orders were issued as handbills. I have seen the originals of Nos. 3–6, 8–12, 14–25, 28–32 (February 1863–September 1864). Some of these orders are not numbered serially, cf. 6 September 1863, 21 October 1863, two orders of 26 October 1863, 3 January 1864, 22 February (?) 1864, 20 May 1864 and 1 February 1865. Some orders are reproduced in T. Filipowicz, *Confidential Correspondence of the British Government respecting the insurrection in Poland,* 1863.

Sbornik pravitel'stvennykh rasporyazhenii po Uchreditel'nomu Komitetu v Tsarstve Pol'skom. 6 vols. Warsaw, 1867–70. A collection of the orders issued by the Executive Committee for the reorganization of the Kingdom of Poland.

Sbornik tsirkulyarov Voyenno-Politseiskago upravleniya v Tsarstve Pol'skom. Warsaw, 1867. (A collection of the Circulars of the Military Police in the Kingdom of Poland.)

Shatilov, N. I., 'Pisma M. N. Muravieva k A. A. Zelenomu', *Golos Minuvshago,* 9–10 (September–October 1913). (Letters of M. N. Muraviev to A. A. Zelenoy.) Throws some light on the discussions in Russian official circles with regard to the suppression of the Polish rising.

Shilder, M. D., 'Sostoyaniye Tsarstva Pol'skago v 1861 i 1862 gg.', *Russkaya Starina,* c. (1899), pp. 115–34. (The situation of the Kingdom of Poland in 1861 and 1862.) Reports of Prince Mikhail Gorchakov to St. Petersburg.

Shilder, N. K., 'Pisma General Getsevicha k **** v 1861 g.', *Russkaya Starina,* c (1899), pp. 135–50. (Letters of General Getsevich to **** in 1861.) Important for the attitude of the Russian military.

Tsilov, N., *Sbornik razporyazhenii grafa Mikhaila Nikolayevicha Muravieva po usmireniyu pol'skago myatezha v severno-zapadnykh guberniyakh 1863 i 1864 g.* Vilna, 1866. (A collection of the orders of Count M. N. Muraviev for the suppression of the Polish rising in the north-western provinces, 1863–4.)

Ustimovich, M. P., *Zagovory i pokusheniye na zhizn'* . . . *grafa Berga.* Warsaw, 1870. (The conspiracies and the attempt on the life of Count Berg.) The first attempt to analyse the composition of Polish conspiratorial groups.

Valk, S. N., *Otmena krepostnogo prava—Doklady ministrov vnutrennikh dyel o provyednii krest'yanskoy reformy 1861–1862.* Moscow, 1950. (The abolition of serfdom—The reports of the Ministers of Internal Affairs on the execution of peasant reform, 1861–2.) Useful for the Polish areas of western Russia.

Wybór tekstów źródłowych z historii Polski w latach 1795–1864, ed. S. Kieniewicz, T. Mencel and W. Rostocki. Warsaw, 1956. (A selection of sources for the History of Poland, 1795–1864.) A popular selection, but contains some rarities.

Wydawnictwo materyałów do historii powstania 1863–1864 r. 5 vols. Lvov, 1888–1894. (Documents on the History of the Insurrection of 1863–4.) Contains the principal documents of the insurrection together with important memoirs.

Zbiór powstanowień Komitetu Urządzającego w Królestwie Polskiem. Warsaw, 1864–5. A collection of orders of the Executive Committee in the Kingdom of Poland.

Zeznania śledcze o powstaniu styczniowym, ed. S. Kieniewicz. Wrocław, 1956. Statements under examination concerning the January Insurrection. The depositions of Z. Jaczewski, K. Majewski, O. Awejde and W. Daniłowski.

Żmichowska, Narcyza, *Listy,* ed. S. Pigoń. 2 vols. Warsaw, 1957–60. A new edition of Żmichowska's correspondence; interesting for the point of view of the Jurgens group.

II. POLITICAL PAMPHLETS AND TRACTS

Akt z roku 1834 przeciw Adamowi Czartoryskiemu, wyobrazicielowi systemu polskiej aristokracyi. Poitiers, 1839. (The act of 1834 against Adam Czartoryski, the personification of the system of the Polish aristocracy.) The initial rejection of a diplomatic solution of the Polish question.

Bolesta, J. (W. Koziebrodzki), *Być albo nie być.* Bendlikon, 1863. (To be or not to be.) Realization that the people had emerged as a political force in Poland.

de Breza, E., *De la Russomanie dans le grand duché de Posen.* Berlin, 1846. A plea for collaboration with Prussia.

Centralny Komitet Polski w Warszawie i Wydawcy 'Kolokola' w Londynie. London, 1862. (The Polish Central Committee in Warsaw and the Publishers of 'Kolokol' in London.) A Russian version was published at the same time; an account of an agreement between the Polish Left and Herzen with regard to the agrarian and national questions.

Dębicki, L., *Polska w chwili pogromu.* Leipzig, 1865. (Poland in the moment of calamity.) A condemnation of the insurrection.

Do wszystkich Polaków. Leipzig, 1865. (To all Poles.) An effort to combat defeatism.

Garbiński, W., *Listy o wlasciwym u nas stanowisku w kwestji włościańskiej.* Warsaw, 1858. (Letters on the proper position in the peasant question.)

Gozdawa, *Ruś przed i po powstaniu zbrojnem 1863 r.* Bendlikon, 1863. (Ruthenia before and after the rising of 1863.) Thought reform strengthened the Polish position in the Ukraine.

Gralewski, M., *Opowiadanie o pańszczyźnie* (offprint from *Czytelnia Niedzielna*). Warsaw, 1862. (A description of labour services.) An appeal for solidarity of peasants and gentry.

— *Myśli o naszych działaniach w kraju i zagranicą.* Leipzig, 1865. (Thoughts on our activity at home and abroad.) A reassessment of the peasant question; more favourable to the peasants than in his pamphlet of 1862.

Kolonna, Artur, *Polska w 1865 roku.* Leipzig, 1865. (Poland in 1865.) A plea for co-operation of Poles and Russians.

Lelewel, J., *Lotniki—piśmiennictwa tułaczki polskiej*. Brussels, 1859. (Pamphlets—writings of the Polish emigration.) Important for their influence upon the *émigré* mind.

Łubieński, E., *L'Armistice entre les Russes et les Polonais proposé par le comte Edouard Łubieński, le 2 février 1863*. Leipzig, 1863. A plea for the collaboration of the Russian and Polish propertied classes against revolution.

Lubliner, O. L., *De la condition politique et civile des Juifs dans le royaume de Pologne*. Brussels, 1860.

Malinowski, T., *Kilka rad ku oswobodzeniu Polski*. Paris, 1843. (Some words of advice for the liberation of Poland.) Advised caution with regard to Poznań before 1846.

Mazurkiewicz, W., *Emigracya polska w 1863 roku (Szkola genueńska—Zjednoczenie)*. Paris, 1862. (The Polish Emigration in 1862: The school at Genoa —reconciliation.) Illustrative of the opposition to Mierosławski in *émigré* groups.

Mikoszewski, K., *Słowo polskiego duchowieństwa do polskiego obywatelstwa*. Poznań, 1861. (A word from the Polish clergy to the Polish gentry.) An appeal for a more liberal attitude towards the peasants.

Milewski, O. K., *Uwagi nad kwestyą włościańską na Litwie*. Paris, 1858. (Observations on the peasant question in Lithuania.)

Miniszewski, J. A. (pseudonym J. Cześnikiewicz), *Ruch polski z 1861 roku*. 2nd ed. Leipzig, 1863. An apologist for Wielopolski, who was murdered by left-wing assassins.

Moller, E., *Situation de la Pologne au 1-er janvier 1865*. Paris, 1865. A Russian propagandist work, but of solid quality; contains documents.

Nasza polityka wobec Rosyi, jaką być powinna? Leipzig, 1865. (What ought our policy towards Russia to be?) A plea for conciliation.

O wyswobodzeniu włościan na Litwie. Berlin–Poznań, 1863. (On the liberation of the peasants in Lithuania.)

Popiel, P., *Kilka słów z powodu odezwy X. Adama Sapiehy*. Leipzig, 1864. (A few words on account of the address of Prince Adam Sapieha.) (Available also in his *Pisma*, Cracow, 1893, vol. I.)

— 'List do księcia Jerzego Lubomirskiego', in *Pisma*, vol. I. (A letter to Prince Jerzy Lubomirski.)
Two pamphlets urging collaboration with Austria in order to defeat the revolution forces in Polish society.

Potocki, T. (pseudonym A. Krzyżtopor), *O urządzeniu stosunków rolniczych w Polsce*. 2nd ed. Poznań, 1859. (On the regulation of agrarian conditions in Poland.) The point of view of a man who thought that agrarian reform could prevent insurrection and revolution.

— *Poranki karlsbadzkie*. 1958. (Mornings in Karlsbad.) A discussion of the social question.

Roczniki gospodarstwa krajowego. Warsaw, 1st series, vols. 1–21 (1854–61), 2nd series, vols. 1–10 (1862–4). (Yearbooks of domestic agriculture.) A

S

publication of the Polish Whites, containing important articles on the agrarian question.

Ruprecht, K., *Zadanie obecnej chwili*. Paris, 1862. (The task of the present moment.)

— *Kwestya socyalna wobec narodowej sprawy*. Paris, 1862. (The social question and the national cause.) Two attempts to induce the Polish educated classes to concentrate upon material reconstruction rather than insurrection.

Stawiski, E., *Poszukiwania do historii rolnictwa krajowego*. Warsaw, 1857. (Researches on the history of Polish agriculture.) The point of view of a prominent White.

Szczepański, A., *W tył! (Na Śląsku, 18 June 1863)*. (Backwards! Silesia, 1863.) A left-wing attack upon the Polish Whites and an appeal for reversion to the programme of 22 January 1863.

Tak lub nie, czyli królestwo kongresowe wobec nowo-prowadzonych reform. Paris, 1861. (Yes or no—or the Congress Kingdom and the newly introduced Reforms.) A plea for co-operation with Russia.

Towarzystwo Demokratyczne Polskie—Dokumenty i Pisma, ed. B. Baczko, Warsaw, 1954. (The Polish Democratic Society—Documents and Writings.) A useful collection of documents concerning the most important Polish *émigré* society.

Wielopolski, A., *Lettre d'un gentilhomme polonais sur les massacres de Gallicie adressée au Prince de Metternich*. Paris, 1846. A plea for collaboration with Russia.

Wielopolski, Z. *Lettre adressée à M. le comte Stanislas Tarnowski par Sigismond Wielopolski*. Cracow, 1880. A defence of Alexander Wielopolski by his son, who argued that Wielopolski's intervention in Polish politics in 1861 prevented social chaos.

Zadanie organizacji narodowej w sprawie polskiej. Leipzig, 1864. (The task of the National Organization in the Polish cause.) A plea for renewed struggle.

Zan, D. (W. L. Chotomski), *Autorowi broszury pod tytułem 'Z powodu allokucyi Piusa IX mianej na tajnym konsystorzu 29 Października 1866 r.', Kilka uwag*. Poznań, 1867. (Some observations for the author of the pamphlet entitled 'On account of the allocation of Pius IX . . .') An attack upon the clerical party's rejection of insurrection.

Z powodu allokucyji Piusa IX mianej na tajnym konsystorzu 29 października 1866 r. Poznań, 1867. (On account of the allocation of Pius IX delivered in the secret consistory of 29 October 1866.) An effort to show that the pope did not approve of insurrections.

III. NEWSPAPERS AND NEWS-SHEETS

The official newspaper, *Dziennik Powszechny*, founded by Wielopolski (from 1 July 1864 *Dziennik Warszawski*) represents the point of view of the Russian authorities. The Cracow newspaper *Czas* (appearing as *Chwila* in the first

quarter of 1864 on account of *Czas*'s suspension) adopts the political attitudes of the Polish Whites. The insurgent press consisted mainly of handbills,
which even in Poland are difficult to find today. The two most important
publications are *Strażnica* of which I have seen Year I (1861), 1–2, 4–7,
10–15; Year II (1862), 1–2, 4–5, 9, 11–12, 14–20; Year III (1863), 2–5; and
Ruch of which I have seen Nos. 1–17, July 1862–June 1863. *Prawda* appeared
between April and July 1863 (Nos. 1–12), but was suppressed by the Majewski insurgent government for interference in foreign affairs. I have seen
Sternik, No. 4 (1 February 1862); *Ojczyzna*, No. 1 (15 October 1863); *Słowo*,
No. 1 (8 January 1863); *Dziennik Narodowy*, Nos. 1–12, May–August 1863.
Wiadomości z placu boju, issued by Agaton Giller, scarcely merits attention,
being accounts of engagements between the Russian forces and the insurgents, which Giller interpreted in a light favourable to the Poles.

IV. MEMOIRS AND EYEWITNESS ACCOUNTS

Arsenyev, I. A., 'Varshava v 1861 godu', *Istorichesky Vyestnik*, xxvi (1886),
pp. 513–61. Illustrative of Russian distrust of the Poles, especially of Polish
officials and the Warsaw working class.

Biłgorajski, F., *Pamiętniki o sprawie chłopskiej w 1863 roku*, ed. by S. Szczotka,
Wrocław, 1956. (Memoirs on the peasant question in 1863.)

Czartoryski, W. *Pamiętnik*, Warsaw, 1961. (A memoir.) Published after this
work had gone to press.

Daniłowski, W., *Notatki do pamiętników*, ed. J. Czubek. Cracow, 1908.
(Notes for my memoirs.) The recollections of a somewhat muddle-headed
admirer of Mierosławski, but important for the genesis of the insurrection
in 1863.

Day, W. A., *The Russian Government of Poland, with a narrative of the Polish
insurrection of 1863*. London, 1867. Visited Poland in 1863, 1864 and
1865 and interviewed all the leading Russian officials as well as Polish
leaders; reasonably objective, but has small sympathy for the Polish left
wing.

Drążkiewicz, A., *Wspomnienie czachowszczyka z 1863*. Lvov, 1890. (Recollections of a follower of Czachowski.) Useful sidelights on a guerrilla band.

Edwards, H. S., *The Polish Captivity—An Account of the Present Position of the
Poles in Austria, Prussia and Russia*, 2 vols. London, 1863.

— *A Private History of a Polish Insurrection*, 2 vols. London, 1865. Sutherland
Edwards was *The Times* correspondent in Poland in 1863, but he wrote
most of his reports from Galicia.

Feliński, Z. S. *Pamiętniki*. 2 parts, 2nd ed. Lvov, 1911. Memoirs of the Archbishop of Warsaw.

Gieysztor, J., *Pamiętniki Jakóba Gieysztora z lat 1857–65*, ed. T. Korzon. 2
vols. Vilna, 1913. Important memoirs of a leading Lithuanian conspirator.

Giller, A., *Polska w walce—Zbiór wspomnień i pamiętników*. 2 vols. Paris,
1868–75. An important collection of insurgent memoirs.

— *Manifestacye Warszawy 1861 r.*, ed. by J. Sokulski. Stanisławów, 1908. (Demonstrations in Warsaw, 1861.)

Goremykin, N. D., 'Varshava v 1861 godu', *Istorichesky Vyestnik*, LXXV (1899), pp. 440–56. (Warsaw in 1861.) Critical of Polish officials and of the conciliatory attitude adopted by Prince Mikhail Gorchakov.

Guttry, A., *Pamiętniki.* 2 vols. Poznań, 1891. Memoirs of a leading Poznanian White.

Janowski, J. K., *Pamiętniki o powstaniu styczniowym.* 3 vols. Lvov, 1923, Warsaw, 1925–31. Memoirs of the secretary to the insurgent government in 1863; important, but written long after the actual events.

Jeziorański, A., *Pamiętniki jenerała Antoniego Jeziorańskiego—powstanie 1863.* 2 parts, Lvov, 1880. Memoirs of Langiewicz's rival.

Kraushar, A., *Publicystyka Tajna Warszawska w dwuleciu przed powstaniem styczniowym i w roku 1863.* Warsaw, 1919. (The secret Warsaw press in the two years before the January rising and the year 1863.)

— *Kartki z pamiętniki Alkara.* 2 vols. Cracow, 1910–13. Kraushar was actively engaged in the production of insurgent newssheets in Warsaw during 1863.

Laskarys, J., 'Wyprawa Sierakowskiego na Kurlandję w 1863 r.', in *Pisma Zbiorowe.* Bendlikon, 1865. (Sierakowski's expedition to Courland.)

Łukaszewski, J., *Zabór pruski w czasie powstania styczniowego 1863–1864.* Jassy, 1870. Considers the attitude of the Poznanian Whites towards the rising to have been lukewarm.

Mierosławski, L., *Pamiętnik Mierosławskiego 1861–1863*, ed. J. Frejlich. Warsaw, 1924. Mierosławski's memoirs.

Muraviev, M. N., 'Graf Mikhail Nikolayevich Muraviev—Zapiski ego o myatezhe v severno-zapadnoy Rossii v 1863–5 gg.', *Russkaya Starina*, XXXVI (1882), pp. 387–432, 623–44; XXXVII (1883), pp. 166, 291–304, 615–30; XXXVIII (1883), pp. 193–206, 459–63. (Memoirs of Muraviev on the revolt in north-western Russia in 1863–5.) Available in a Polish version, *Pamiętniki hr. Michała Mikołajewicza Muravieva 1863–1865.* Cracow, 1896.

Oliphant, L., *Episodes in a Life of Adventure.* London, 1887. Contains an account of a visit to an insurgent unit.

Oxiński, J., 'Józefa Oxińskiego wspomnienia z powstania polskiego 1863/64 roku', *Rocznik Oddziału Łódzkiego Polskiego Towarzystwa Historycznego*, III (1939), pp. 157 f. The memoirs of one of the most successful guerrilla leaders.

Podvysotsky, A., *Zapiski ochevidtsa o sobytiyakh v Varshave v 1861 i 1862 godakh.* St. Petersburg, 1869. (Notes of an eyewitness on events in Warsaw, 1861–1862.) Contains some important documents.

Sawicki-Stella, J., *Galicja w powstaniu styczniowem.* 2nd ed. Lvov, 1913. (Galicia during the January Insurrection.)

T. (J. Tretiak ?), 'Sołowjówka (Ustęp z powstania na Ukrainie)', *Kalendarz Polski na rok 1866*. Bendlikon, 1866. An account of the abortive effort of the Kiev students to raise the standard of revolt in the Ukraine.

W czterdziestą rocznicę powstania styczniowego. Lvov, 1903. (On the fortieth anniversary of the January Insurrection.) An important collection of memoirs.

Wilska, Stefania, *Pamiętnik o Ignacym Chmieleńskim*, ed. S. Kieniewicz. Wrocław, 1952. Personal recollections about a member of the Polish ultra-left.

Wiszniewski, W., *Galicya czyli rok 1863 i 1864*. Leipzig, 1864.

Wittgenstein, Prince E., *Souvenirs et correspondance du prince Emile de Sayn-Wittgenstein-Berlebourg*. 2 vols. Paris, 1888. Recollections of a conventionally minded officer serving in the Russian forces.

Zamoyski, A., *Moje przeprawy—pamiętnik Andrzeja hr. Zamoyskiego o czasach powstania listopadowego (1830–1)*, ed. A. Kraushar. 2nd ed. Cracow, 1911. (My experiences.) The text of the memoir deals with events in 1830–1, but Kraushar published extracts from Andrzej Zamoyski's papers in the introduction which shed much light upon his political attitudes.

Zamoyski, W., *Jeneral Zamoyski, 1803–1868*. 6 vols. Poznań, 1910–30. The letters of Władysław Zamoyski; vol. VI covers the period from 1853 to 1868; interesting for the views and ideas of a man who was never far from the centre of Polish affairs.

V. Secondary Works

Balaban, M., 'Zydzi w powstaniu 1863 r.', *Przegląd Historyczny*, XXXIV (1937–8). (Jews in the rising of 1863.)

Bazylow, L., Brodowska, Helena and Dunin-Wąsowicz, K., *Z dziejów współpracy rewolucyjnej Polaków i Rosjan w drugiej połowie xix wieku*. Wrocław, 1956. (On the history of revolutionary co-operation between Poles and Russians in the nineteenth century.) Contains essays on Zygmunt Padlewski, the Kazan conspiracy and Konstanty Kalinowski.

Berg, N. V., *Zapiski o polskikh zagovorakh i vosstaniyakh*. 4 vols. Poznań, 1883–5. (Notes on the Polish conspiracies and insurrections.) An essential work, available in Polish translations.

Charles-Roux, F., *Alexandre II, Gortchakoff et Napoleon III*. Paris, 1913.

Dranitsyn, S. N., *Pol'skoye vosstaniye 1863 i ego klassovaya sushchnost'*. Leningrad, 1937. (The Polish rising of 1863 and its class content.)

Dubiecki, M., *Romuald Traugutt i jego dyktatura podczas powstania styczniowego, 1863–1864*. 5th ed. Poznań, 1924. (Romuald Traugutt and his dictatorship during the Insurrection of 1863–4.)

Feldman, J., *Bismark a Polska*. New edition, Warsaw, 1947.

— *Mocarstwa wobec powstania styczniowego*. Cracow, 1929. (The powers and the January Insurrection.)

Fedorov, A. F., *Russkaya armiya v 50-kh–70-kh gg. xix v.* Leningrad, 1959. (The Russian army from the 1850's to the 1870's.) Emphasizes Russian military weakness.

Friese, C., *Russland und Preussen vom Krimkrieg bis zum polnischen Aufstand.* Berlin, 1931.

Gąsiorowska, Natalia, 'Mieszczaństwo w powstaniu styczniowym', *Przegląd Historyczny*, xxxiv (1937–8). (The bourgeoisie in the January Insurrection.)

(Rawita-) Gawroński, F., *Rok 1863 na Rusi.* 2 vols. Lvov, 1902–3. (The year 1863 in Ruthenia.)

—— *Stefan Bobrowski i Dyktatura Langiewicza.* Warsaw, 1914. Recognizes that Bobrowski's death amounted to murder, but suggests the presence of suicidal tendencies.

Gentsen, F. H., 'Zabór pruski w dobie powstania styczniowego', *Kwartalnik .Historyczny*, lxii (1955).

Gesket, S., *Voyennye dyeistviya v Tsarstve Pol'skom v 1863 godu.* Warsaw, 1894. (Military action in the Kingdom of Poland, 1863.) Covers only January, February and part of March 1863.

Giller, A., *Karol Ruprecht—Szkic biograficzny.* Lvov, 1875. A biography of Ruprecht.

—— *Dzieje delegacji warszawskiej* (see *Wydawnictwo materyałów do historyi pow stania 1863–1864*, vol. 1).

Grabiec (-Dąbrowski), J., *Powstanie styczniowe 1863–1864.* Warsaw, n.d. (The January Insurrection.)

—— *Ostatni szlachcic—Aleksander Wielopolski Margrabia Myszkowski na tle dziejów.* 2 vols. Warsaw, Cracow, 1924. (The last nobleman—Alexander Wielopolski . . . in his historical setting.)

—— *Rok 1863.* Poznań, 1922. (The year 1863.)

Grabski, W., *Historya Towarzystwa Rolniczego.* 2 vols. Warsaw, 1904. (The history of the Agricultural Society.)

Grynwaser, H., *Kwestia agrarna i ruch włościan w Królestwie Polskim w pierwszej połowie xix wieku*, republished in *Pisma*, ii, Wrocław, 1951. (The agrarian question and the peasant movement in the Kingdom of Poland in the first half of the nineteenth century.)

—— *Sprawa włościańska w Królestwie Polskim w latach 1861–62*, republished in *Pisma*, iii, Wrocław, 1951. (The Peasant Question in the Kingdom of Poland, 1861–2.) The modern study of Polish agrarian history in the Kingdom of Poland begins with Grynwaser.

Halicz, E., *Kwestia chłopska w Królestwie Polskim w dobie powstania styczniowego.* Warsaw, 1955. (The peasant question in the Kingdom of Poland during the January Insurrection.) A careful study of much unprinted material.

Handelsman, M., *Adam Czartoryski.* 3 vols. Warsaw, 1948–50.

Harley, J. H. 'Britain and the Polish Insurrection of 1863', *Résumés de communications presentées au Congrès International des sciences historiques*. Warsaw, 1933.

Jabłoński, H., *Aleksander Waszkowski, ostatni naczelnik miasta Warszawy w powstaniu 1863–4*. Warsaw, 1937. (Alexander Waszkowski, the last Chief of the Town in Warsaw in the Insurrection of 1863–4.)

Kieniewicz, S., *Adam Sapieha, 1828–1903*. Lvov, 1939. A biography of an important Galician leader.

— *Ruch chłopski w Galicji w 1846 roku*. Wrocław, 1951. (The peasant movement in Galicia in 1846.)

— *Konspiracje galicyjskie (1831–1845)*. Warsaw, 1950. (Galician Conspiracies, 1831–45.)

— *Między ugodą a rewolucją—Andrzej Zamoyski w latach 1861–1862*. Warsaw, 1962. (Between reconciliation and revolution—Andrzej Zamoyski in 1861–2.) Published after this book was written.

— *Społeczeństwo polskie w powstaniu poznańskim 1848 r*. Warsaw, 1935. (Poznanian society in the rising of 1848.) (Available in a new edition, 1960.)

— *Sprawa włościańska w powstaniu styczniowym*. Wrocław, 1953. (The peasant question in the January Insurrection.)

— *Warszawa w powstaniu styczniowym*. Warsaw, 1954. (Warsaw in the January Insurrection.)

Stefan Kieniewicz is the most prolific of Polish historians of this period; his work deserves the closest attention.

Koberdowa, Irena, *Polityka Czartoryszczyny w okresie powstania styczniowego*. Warsaw, 1957. (The policy of the Czartoryskis in the period of the January Insurrection.) Highly critical of the Czartoryskis.

— *Wielki Książę Konstanty w Warszawie 1862–1863*. Warsaw, 1962. (The Grand Duke Constantine in Warsaw, 1862–3.) Published after this book was written.

Korolyuk, V. D. and Miller, I. S., *Vosstaniye 1863 g. i russkopol'skiye revolyutsionnye svyazi 60-kh godov*. Moscow, 1960. (The Insurrection of 1863 and Russo-Polish revolutionary connections in the 1860's.)

Kotarski, S., *Opatów w latach 1861–1864*. Opatów, 1935. (Opatów in the years 1861–4.) Some interesting details of peasant attitudes to the rising of 1863.

Kowalski, J., *Rewolucyjna demokracja rosyjska a powstanie styczniowe*. Warsaw, 1955. (Russian revolutionary democracy and the January Insurrection.)

Koźmian, S., *Rzecz o roku 1863*. 3 vols. Cracow, 1894–6. (An essay on the year 1863.) Concerned mainly with the reactions of Cracow conservatives.

Kukiel, M., *Czartoryski and European Unity, 1770–1861*. Princeton, 1955. A useful work covering the many aspects of Czartoryski's activity.

Leroy-Beaulieu, A., *Un homme d'état russe d'après sa correspondance inédite*. Paris, 1884. A biography of Nicholas Milyutin.

Leshchenko, N. N., *Krest'yanskoye dvizheniye na Ukraine v svyazi s provedeniyem reformy 1861 goda*. Kiev, 1959. (The peasant movement in the Ukraine in connection with the execution of reform in 1861.)

Leslie, R. F., *Polish Politics and the Revolution of November 1830*. London, 1956.

Limanowski, B., *Historia ruchu narodowego 1863 i 1864*. 2 vols. Lvov, 1882. (A history of the national movement, 1863–4.) A pioneer study.

Łoziński, B., *Agenor hr. w pierwszym okresie rządów swoich*. Lvov, 1901. (Count Gołuchowski in his first period of office.)

Lyaskovsky, A. I., *Litva i Byelorussiya v vozstanii 1863 g*. Berlin, 1939. (Lithuania and White Russia in the rising of 1863.)

Minkowska, Anna, *Organizacja spiskowa 1848 r. w Królestwie Polskim*. Warsaw, 1923. (Conspiratorial organization in the Kingdom of Poland in 1848.)

Naidenov, M., *Klassovaya borba v poreformennoy derevne, 1861–1863 gg*. Moscow, 1955. (The class struggle in the countryside after reform, 1861–3.)

Nechkina, M. V. (ed.), *Revolyutsionnaya situatsiya v Rossii v 1859–1861*. Moscow, 1960. (The Revolutionary situation in Russia, 1859–61).

Niemojowski, J., 'Leon Frankowski, komisarz cywilny i organizator wojskowy województwa lubelskiego w latach 1862–1863', *Sprawozdania Towarzystwa Naukowego Warszawskiego*, xxx (1937). (Leon Frankowski, civil commissar and military organizer of the Lublin province, 1862–3.)

Oncken, H., *Die Rheinpolitik Kaiser Napoleons III von 1863 bis 1870 and der Ursprung des Krieges von 1870/1870*. 3 vols. Stuttgart, 1926.

Oppman, E., 'Rewolucyjna organizacja miasta stołecznego Warszawy w powstaniu styczniowym', *Przegląd Historyczny*, xxxiv (1937–8). (The revolutionary organization of the capital city of Warsaw in the January Insurrection.)

Przyborowski, W., *Historia dwóch lat, 1861–2*. 5 vols. Cracow, 1892–6.

— *Historia sześciu miesięcy*. Warsaw, 1904.

— *Dzieje 1863 roku*. 5 vols. Cracow, 1897–1919.

— *Ostanie chwile powstania styczniowego*. 5 vols. Poznań, 1887–8.
Some criticism may be made of Przyborowski's point of view, but his writings remain the most complete history of the January Insurrection and its antecedents.

Przybyszewski, E., 'Jarosław Dąbrowski i jego rola w organizacji narowodej 1861–1863', *Sprawozdania z posiedzeń Towarzystwa Naukowego Warszawskiego* (Wydział I), xx (1927). (Jarosław Dąbrowski and his role in the national organization, 1861–3.)

Revunenkov, V. G., *Pol'skoye vosstaniye 1863 g. i evropeyskaya diplomatiya*. Leningrad, 1957. (The Polish insurrection of 1863 and European diplomacy.) Cites some material inaccessible to non-Soviet historians.

Rudzka, Walentyna, *Karol Majewski w latach 1859–1864*. Warsaw, 1937. A biography of the moderate left-wing leader who headed the National Government in June 1863.

Sabowski, W., *Józef Hauke Bosak*. Cracow, 1871. A slight biography of an energetic guerrilla leader.

Skałkowski, A. M., *Aleksander Wielopolski w świetle archiwów rodzinnych*. 3 vols. Poznań, 1947. (Alexander Wielopolski in the light of the family papers).

Spasovich, V. D., *Zhizn' i politika Markiza Vyelepol'skago*. St. Petersburg, 1882. An apology for Wielopolski.

Strumiński, J., 'Rady miejskie i powiatowe w Królestwie Polskim (1861–1863)', *Czasopismo prawno-historyczne*, IV (1952). (Town and district councils in the Kingdom of Poland, 1861–3.)

Szczechura, T., 'Ukaz o okupie pańszczyzny z dnia 16 maja 1861 r.', *Przegląd Historyczny*, XL (1949). (The decree converting labour services of 16 May 1861.)

Szymański, Z. *Jarosław Dąbrowski*. Warsaw, 1947. A popular biography.

Tokarz, W., *Kraków w początkach powstania styczniowego i wyprawa na Miechów*. 2 vols. Cracow, 1914. (Cracow at the beginning of the January Insurrection and the expedition to Miechów.)

Ulashchik, N. N., 'Krepostnaya derevniya Litvi i Zapadnoy Byelorussii nakanune reformi 1861 goda', *Voprosy Istorii*, 1948 (XII). (The serf village in Lithuania and White Russia at the beginning of reform in 1861.)

— 'Iz reskripta 20 Noyabrya 1857 g.', *Istoricheskiye Zapiski*, XXVIII (1949). (On the Rescript of 20 November 1857.)

— 'Pogotovka krest'yanskoy reformy 1861 g. v Litve i Zapadnoy Byelorussii', *ibid*, XXXIII (1950). (The preparation of the peasant reform of 1861 in Lithuania and White Russia.)
Important series of articles.

Wereszycki, H., *Austria a powstanie styczniowe*. Lvov, 1930. (Austria and the January Rising.)

— *Anglia a Polska w latach 1860–65*. Lvov, 1934. (England and Poland, 1860–1865.)
Basic works for the understanding of the diplomatic problem.

Widmann, K., *Franciszek Smolka, jego życie i zawód publiczny od 1810 do 1849*. Lvov, 1886. A biography of Smolka in his early days.

Wrona, S., 'Chłopi w powstaniu styczniowym', *Przegląd Historyczny*, XXXIV (1937–8). (Peasants in the January Insurrection.)

Wrotnowski, A., *Porozbiorowe aspiracje polityczne narodu polskiego*. Lvov, 1882. (The political aspirations of the Polish nation after the partitions.) An apology for the Whites by a writer closely connected with the events of 1861–3.

W stulecie Wiosny Ludów 1848–1849, ed. Natalia Gąsiorowska. 5 vols. Warsaw, 1948–53. A collective work dealing with the revolutions of 1848.

Wyka, K., *Teka Stańczyka na tle historii Galicji w l. 1849–69*. Wrocław, 1951. ('Teka Stańczyka' against the background of Galicia history, 1849–69.)

An investigation of the reasons why the Galician Poles adopted a policy of co-operation with Austria.

Zayonchovsky, P. A., *Otmena krepostnogo prava v Rossii*. New ed. Moscow, 1960. (The abolition of serfdom in Russia.)

— *Provyedeniye v zhizn' krest'yanskoy reformy 1861 g.* Moscow, 1958. (The execution of peasant reform in 1861.)

— *Voyennye reformy 1860–1870 godov v Rossii*. Moscow, 1952. (The military reforms of the 1860's and 1870's in Russia.)

Złotorzycka, M., 'Jarosław Dąbrowski o sprawie ruskiej', *Niepodległość*, IX (1934). (Dąbrowski and the Ruthenian Question.)

— 'Bronisław Szwarce o sytuacji okręgu białostockiego 1861 r.', *Przegląd Historyczny*, XLV (1954). (Szwarce on the situation in the district of Białystok in 1861.)

INDEX